OUT IN THE MIDDAY SUN

Elspeth Huxley was born in 1906 and spent most of her childhood in Kenya. She was educated at the European School in Nairobi and at Reading University, where she took a diploma in agriculture, and at Cornell University, USA. In 1929 she joined the Empire Marketing Board as a press officer. She married Gervas Huxley in 1931 and travelled widely with him in America, Africa and elsewhere. She was on the BBC General Advisory Council from 1952 to 1959, when she joined the Monckton Advisory Commission on Central Africa. She wrote novels, detective fiction, biography and travel titles, and her books include *The Flame Trees of Thika* (1959), *The Mottled Lizard* (1962), *The Challenge of Africa* (1971), *Livingstone and His African Journeys* (1974), *Florence Nightingale* (1975), *Scott of the Antarctic* (1977), *Nellie: Letters from Africa* (1980), *Whipsnade: Captive Breeding for Survival* (1981), *The Prince Buys the Manor* (1982) *and Last Days in Eden* (1985, with Hugo van Lawick). She died in 1997.

OUT IN THE MIDDAY SUN

My Kenya

ELSPETH HUXLEY

PIMLICO

Published by Pimlico 2000

2 4 6 8 10 9 7 5 3 1

First published in Great Britain by
Chatto & Windus Ltd 1985
Pimlico edition 2000

Pimlico
Random House, 20 Vauxhall Bridge Road,
London SW1V 2SA

Random House Australia (Pty) Limited
20 Alfred Street, Milsons Point, Sydney,
New South Wales 2061, Australia

Random House New Zealand Limited
18 Poland Road, Glenfield,
Auckland 10, New Zealand

Random House (Pty) Limited
Endulini, 5A Jubilee Road, Parktown 2193, South Africa

The Random House Group Limited Reg. No. 954009
www.randomhouse.co.uk

A CIP catalogue record for this book
is available from the British Library

ISBN 0-7126-6437-8

Papers used by Random House are natural,
recyclable products made from wood grown in sustainable forests.
The manufacturing processes conform to the environmental
regulations of the country of origin.

Printed and bound in Great Britain by
Mackays of Chatham PLC

Contents

Illustrations vii

Map of Kenya viii

Foreword ix

1 Hat Overboard 1

2 Nuggets and Covered Wagons 18

3 Nellie's Friends 27

4 Adolescent Nairobi 45

5 Cockie, Blix and the Prince of Wales 59

6 Umbrellas, Tea-birds and the Nandi Bear 72

7 Livestock Barons of the Rift Valley 92

8 A Man of Big Ideas 110

9 Under the Mountain 119

10 The Powys Saga 133

11 Safari with Sharpie 148

12 Tales of the Northern Frontier 162

13 Among the Kikuyu 182

14 Lamu to London 204

15 Fifty Years On 224

Notes and Sources 250

Glossary 257

Index 258

Illustrations

1 Statue of the 3rd Baron Delamere by Kathleen Hilton-Young.
2 Denys Finch Hatton and Glady Lady Delamere, 1928.
3 Group at Wanjohi, 1924: Hon. Josslyn Hay, Major Roberts, Jos Grant, Lady Idina Hay, Cockie Birkbeck, Princess Philippe de Bourbon, Nellie Grant.
4 Locust swarm, 1933.
5 On safari in 1930: Cockie von Blixen, HRH Edward Prince of Wales, and Captain Alan Lascelles.
6 Galbraith Cole at Kekopev, Gilgil, 1916.
7 Lady Eleanor Balfour and Galbraith Cole, 1917.
8 Llewelyn Powys at Kekopey.
9 Will Powys at Kekopey, 1920.
10 The original Treetops at Nyeri.
11 Denys Finch Hatton, Jack Pixley, Tich Miles and Lady Colvile at Ngara Road House, 1914.
12 Foot safari on the upper slopes of Mount Kenya, 1936.
13 H. B. Sharpe with elephants at Wamba, 1936.

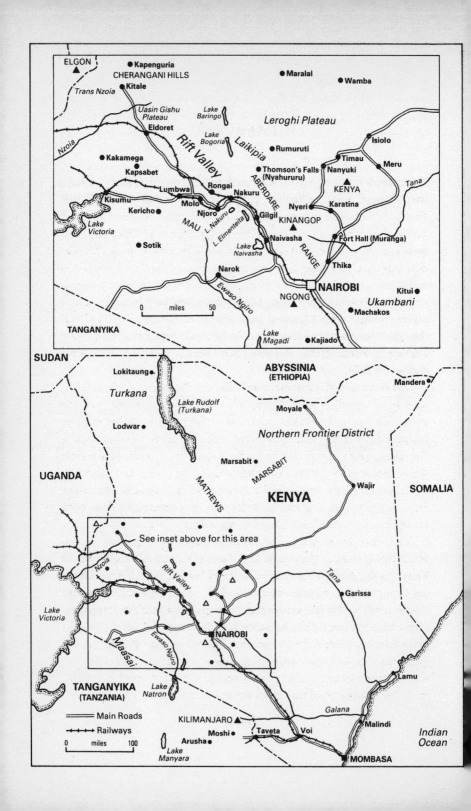

Foreword

If you live long enough you find, much to your surprise, that you have lived through a part of history; people and events that you recall as if they had lived and happened yesterday vanish into a seamless past and turn into legends. To anyone aged thirty, what happened fifty years ago seems as remote and peculiar as, say, the Crimean War or the War Between the States appeared to people of my generation. I think this is especially so in the case of British colonial history in Africa, which ended over twenty years ago. Elderly colonials have become period pieces in their own lifetimes; and now that they are obsolete and therefore harmless, a certain indulgence has crept into the general attitude towards them, softening the disdain in which they were previously held.

This book is not, most emphatically not, an attempt at a political history, or any other kind of proper history. Nor does it take a stance on the wrongs and rights of colonialism. For good or ill, colonialism happened, as it has throughout the centuries from the time of the Assyrians, and I expect before, to the time of the USSR. I have little doubt that it will continue to happen, since the strong and confident will always wish to spread their doctrines and customs, and often their rule, to the less strong and confident, thereby enhancing their own strength and (as they hope) security, regardless of ethics.

All I have attempted to do in these pages is to put on record memories of some of the people and places of eastern Africa, mainly of Kenya, in the period between the First and Second World Wars. I have not brought down a guillotine fore and aft, so the time-scale now and then extends backwards into earlier years and forwards into later ones. I have been greatly helped by many friends, some of them children or other relatives of the earlier members of the white tribe of Kenya, some of them tough old survivors pushing ninety, or even past that tidemark, who have lent me letters and diaries, and gone to much trouble to recall their own memories of fifty years ago and more. A list of names at this point would, I think, be rather tedious, so I have acknowledged their help in notes to each chapter at the end of the book. I hope they will forgive this form of thanksgiving which cannot, however offered, be adequate; I am deeply grateful to them all.

After Kenya's independence in 1963 some of the place-names were changed, African ones replacing those bestowed by British geographers and agents. In the main I have continued to employ the old colonial names, because they were in use at the time of which I have been writing, but I have indicated the modern ones.

The Rhodes House Library in Oxford, which has assembled, and continues to assemble, a splendid collection of colonial records, was, as always, most helpful, and my thanks are due to the Librarian, Mr Alan Bell, and his staff; also to Mrs Olive Gorton of Cirencester, who with great patience and, I must assume, at times second sight, has managed to decipher both my handwriting and my two-fingered stabs at a typewriter well on its way to becoming an interesting and, I hope, in due course, a valuable antique.

CHAPTER I

Hat Overboard

An old diary is as good a starting point as any. I have never kept proper diaries, only little pocket ones recording the barest details; somehow or other, that for 1933 survives. It was in January 1933 that I set out to return to Africa after an absence of eight years.

January 19. Left Victoria on P and O Express at 1.50 p.m. Seen off by Frank MacD, Jim and Polly, Michael and Ottilie, Aunt Vera, Basil Marriot, Eaton, Wilkie. Very cold, snow on ground.

'Seen off' – every voyage started with a party then. Station platforms and quaysides were crowded with well-wishers come to say God-speed. Laughter, speculation, promises, awkwardness as time stretched out and one had said all there was to say. Once aboard, there would be flowers, telegrams, an attentive steward disposing of suitcases, the smell peculiar to ships compounded of – what? Paint, ropes, sea-water, some kind of disinfectant? An exciting smell anyway, and an exciting bustle. Departure was a ceremony investing the traveller with a little brief authority, a fleeting importance.

'I'll write from Port Said.'

'Something light for the voyage. A new Ellery Queen.'

'Press photographers. Who d'you think's on board?'

'Some actress . . . '

Puffing grandly, the engine moved, the platform became a mosaic of waving hands, faces blurred and vanished. Once out of the station, sleet rattled on the window-panes. We were bound first for Marseilles.

A year and one month since we married, and now we must part, Gervas for Ceylon and I for Kenya. The Depression was upon us, gaunt faces under shabby caps stared from street corners, the economic blood-stream of the Western world was clogged. One day Gervas said: 'Our horse has been shot under us.' The organisation that employed us both was to be abolished – axed, we called it, the Geddes axe.

We had no resources, but Gervas had a friend called John Still, an

1

unusual man, a poet, who had spent his life, save for an interlude as prisoner-of-war in Turkey, in the jungles and mountains of Ceylon. He had written evocatively about them in a book called *The Jungle Tide*. The Depression had not spared Ceylon and, in particular, the tea plantations. Chests of unsaleable tea were piled up in warehouses and were even, we heard, being thrown into the sea.

A bold counter-stroke was planned. The world had too much tea. If people could be persuaded to drink more of it, even a few cups each per year, the surplus would melt away. A body was formed to carry out this plan (or try to anyway) and someone was needed to direct it, starting from scratch.

One cold November day I met Gervas at Paddington station en route for Oxford, where his father lived. It was dark and drizzly, soot-laden steam swirled around us, locomotives panted, whistles blew, lights were halo'd in smoke, it was like being at the bottom of a grimy sea. Over a cup of tea in the buffet he said: 'Shall I accept?' It would mean, for him, continuous travel for at least three years, and his modest salary would not provide tickets for me. Our perch must be abandoned – a little rented flat, sparsely furnished, in a turret, one room (three in all) on each floor. (On top was the sitting room whose ceiling had been painted midnight blue with silver stars.) The question was rhetorical. Three months later we were on our way.

Gervas had indeed been fortunate, and my luck was in too. Rather more than a year before, the pioneer of white settlement in Kenya, Lord Delamere (third Baron), had died. His life in Africa had spanned, or very nearly spanned, Kenya's colonial period up to date; he had entered into every controversy and been involved in almost every development. To write his life would be to write Kenya's history over the past thirty years, a fascinating but exacting task for which I had no qualifications beyond some experience in journalism and a little knowledge of the country. Nevertheless I wrote to Delamere's widow Glady and she, to my surprise and delight, authorised me to write the biography.

There remained the obstacle of money. Clearly I had to get to Kenya where most of the material lay. Here I was fortunate again: a publisher expressed interest and offered an advance of two hundred pounds. To sign the contract, I was led through silent panelled anterooms, half expecting to see clerks perched on high stools clasping quill pens and bent over ledgers; then up a wide staircase and into the presence of a tall, stooping figure who rose courteously from a commodious armchair, extended an arm and touched my hand – the merest touch, putting me in mind of a limp fish. This was Harold Macmillan.

So here we were, bound for Marseilles and the parting of our ways.

January 20. Lunch on board ss Maloja. Went to Hotel Beauvais, dinner at the Frégate, very good meal. Gervas went on board 10 p.m.

Alone, I returned to the hotel. My ship, the ss *Malda*, was due next morning but failed to arrive. Marseilles in January was bleak, lonely and cold. I wrote letters. Next morning the *Malda* put in; amid a rattle of winches and shouts of seamen I climbed a gangway slippery with salt spray, and we steamed into a wintry Mediterranean sea.

January 23. Sick. Cold. Passed Corsica. Dr Burkitt on board.

Dr Burkitt I knew. He was one of Kenya's characters and a great doctor in his way, but his way was rough and ready and I was thankful that I had never been his patient. Had I been suffering from malaria, I would have been made to sit naked in a tub in the draughtiest place available, such as a veranda, and sponged continuously with cold water – teeth chattering, blue with cold – until either I expired or my temperature sank to normal. This was Dr Burkitt's famous cold-water cure, based on the theory that the parasites which cause malaria and other fevers thrive only at high body temperatures, and perish at normal ones, so that if you can only get the temperature down, you overcome the disease. Apparently the theory worked, and Dr Burkitt cured many sufferers; if he also killed some, they would probably have died anyway. The theory was extended to horses, and became the standard treatment for the disease known as horse-sickness for which no other cure or antidote was known. Many is the hour I had spent sponging down shivering and miserable ponies tethered to a tree while buckets of water were brought in relays. Dread and affection competed equally for ascendancy in the minds of the doctor's patients.

Dr Roland Burkitt had arrived from Ireland in 1911 to start the first private practice in Nairobi.[1] He was a surgeon, not a physician, but in Africa medicine couldn't be shut into compartments. Many Burkitt stories were in circulation, such as that describing how he had driven a hundred miles or so to a sick woman – he would drive any distance, anywhere, by day or night, in an old rattle-trap of a car, to answer a call – and had stripped her naked, bundled her into the back of his jalopy and driven furiously over bumps, potholes, rocks and rivers to the hospital, stopping at intervals to take her temperature. As they proceeded, the woman's temperature fell and Dr Burkitt removed first his jacket, then his shirt and finally his trousers to clothe his patient. When they arrived at the hospital, Dr Burkitt was naked and the woman fully clad.

That, at any rate, was the story. Another related how a patient, loaded into the doctor's car while in a coma, came round to find that he was sharing the back seat with a dead antelope. The doctor always carried a rifle in his car and would now and then alight to shoot something for the pot when on his errands of mercy. Snakes were a favourite in his diet. Another of his favourite cures was bleeding.

Chief among his enemies were the ultra-violet rays of the tropical sun, which he considered lethal. Sun helmets of cork or pith, double terais (two thicknesses of felt with red flannel in between) and spine-pads, also lined with red material and covering the back, were to him essential armour against these ever-threatening rays. Nearly all the Europeans in East Africa at this time held the same views and took the same precautions. I had started the voyage with a handsome new double terai, but it blew off in the Red Sea. 'Hat overboard' was not a cry to galvanise the ship's crew into rescue operations, and the hat bobbed away out of sight.

Next day we anchored off Port Sudan, where passengers disembarked to stretch legs and ride upon camels. Not, perhaps, the most alluring of prospects but I did not want to be left out. Dr Burkitt was horrified. In his powerful brogue he forecast the direst disasters should I venture hatless ashore – dementia praecox, cardiac failure, renal occlusion, possibly even flat feet. Actinic rays softened the brain, rotted the guts and sapped the moral fibre. Having lived since an early age in Africa, and being young, I thought I knew best and went ashore at Port Sudan and had my camel ride. I suffered no ill effects and did not hesitate to rub this in to Dr Burkitt. He bore no malice, merely remarking: 'If God had intended you for a salamander he'd have given you a tail.' I never wore a sunhat in Africa again.

Like all ships plying between British and East African ports, the *Malda* carried a number of colonial officials proceeding on, or returning from, their home leave, which lasted for six months as a rule; and in a very short time they sorted themselves into groups depending on their branch of the service. At the top came the Brahmins, men of the administration – provincial and district commissioners, district officers and officials of the secretariat. Next came men of the various technical services – medical, agricultural, veterinary, educational, police and so on; finally, at the bottom of the heap, employees of the Public Works department and the Railway. Like dairy cows who, on entering their milking parlours, find their way without hesitation to their correct positions, each official knew his place. Wives followed suit. It was interesting to see a pecking order so quickly established and so faithfully observed.

Young cadets going out for their first tour of duty were kept at a distance by the Brahmins, but rewarded now and then, like a dog with a chocolate drop, by a ritual 'good-morning'. For their part they were on the lookout for girls to stroll with on the boat deck and admire sunsets that inflamed sea and sky with passionate colours; or, when darkness fell, to lean over the rail and watch pale green phosphorescence shining and writhing as the ship's bow sliced into the waves; or to search the sky for a first glimpse of the Southern Cross.

Tables in the dining saloon were status thermometers. The grandest passengers – a colonial governor perhaps, a visiting politician or extra-rich Americans going out for a safari – sat at the Captain's table. Next in prestige came the table presided over by the First Officer, then the Chief Engineer's, the doctor's, the purser's and so on down the scale. You always changed for dinner. Very early in the voyage a sports organiser emerged, no one knew quite how, from the ranks of the passengers, and thereafter competitions raged almost without an interval – deck quoits, shuffleboard, deck tennis. Territories in the shape of deck chairs were staked out early on and faithfully respected. At eleven in the morning stewards came round with hot soup west of Suez, cold drinks east of the Canal, when the ship's officers changed from blue uniforms into white ones.

You took in coal at Port Said and at Aden, and the voyage lasted nineteen days. Then came into view the low green island of Mombasa with its coconut palms and customs sheds, its white lime-washed houses and red-tiled roofs and lush vegetation. The *Malda* steamed slowly between island and mainland into Kilindini harbour, by then equipped with deep-water berths so that you could walk down a gangway on to the island instead of, as in the past, being ferried from ship to shore on tenders.

Mombasa's history is long and bloody; the dogs of war have made a killing here, many killings. Now that they were kenneled for the time being the island, lying like a viridian tongue between two mainland lips half-closed over a mouthful of sparkling blue creeks and inlets, presented a gentle aspect to the world. The island of war (its old name) had become an island of colour; bougainvilleas were everywhere, cherry-red, brilliant orange, royal purple, smothering the houses; flamboyants, hibiscus, datura, oleander, frangipani, many other flowering shrubs dazzled the eye: wonderful names, wonderful colours. Dark-foliaged mango trees encircled by a dark band of shade arose from the greenery, queer-shaped baobabs with grey glistening boles and outstretched branches stood starkly upright, coconut palms fringed the mainland like sentinels guarding the outskirts of the continent.

The temptation to indulge in lotus-eating is always strong on Mombasa island and all along this coast, which used to be known by the mellifluous name of Azania: white beaches, coral reefs, warmth and somnolence, singing cicadas and brilliant-plumaged birds inhabiting aromatic bush, the rustle of palm-fronds, melodious Swahili words falling softly on the ear. But the impulse had to be resisted; the up-country train left at half-past four. There was time, however, for a visit to the Old Town on the other side of the island, and the old harbour with its immemorial dhows. The time was right for such a visit for the harbour was crowded with dhows from Oman and Dubai, from Jeddah and the coast of Malabar, coming in on the north-east monsoon, the *kaskazi*, as they had been doing for centuries, almost unchanged. And Dr Burkitt was the ideal companion, for he had a house on the mainland and knew Mombasa well. I never visited his house but was told that, like everything else about Dr Burkitt, it was unusual. The walls of both ground floor and upper storey were built only half-way up, leaving a four-foot gap between wall and roof, and wire netting was substituted for glass; agreeable when zephyr-like breezes whispered in from the sea, less so when torrential rain and force-nine gales soaked and flooded everything and everyone inside.

We proceeded, as everyone did, to the big, hot customs shed where dhow captains spread their intricately patterned carpets for sale. Many are the homes of retired East Africans enriched by the glowing colours of a rug bought for a few pounds in that sweltering shed.

Then there were Zanzibar chests, thickly studded with brass nails and also much-sought-after when the dhows came in. Few of them actually came from Zanzibar; most were made in the Gulf ports or in India with the European market in mind. But now and again you could find one that had been used for its proper purpose, to stow the clothing and possessions of the sailors. My father had managed to find one such and had bought it for me as a wedding present. It was a Lamu chest, smaller and simpler than the Zanzibar ones and more roughly carpentered. Sometimes I wish that it could tell of its experiences, of the creaking dhows in which it had traversed the Indian ocean, of the ports at which its crew had whiled away the furnace days, drinking endless cups of sweet thick coffee poured from those tall, thin, swan-necked pitchers of the Arab world, while waiting for the monsoon to blow their vessel back to Lamu.

In the old harbour the dhows lay almost hull to hull, their sails furled, their waists populated by sailors in round white caps and brightly printed kekois, cooking on charcoal braziers, chewing betel nut or mira'a, sleeping, gossiping, stowing or unloading cargo. I would not have cared to be one of their women who, when they travel, were packed into a sort of cage made of coconut matting, windowless and airless, swathed in black robes with only slits for eyes, horribly seasick and never allowed to emerge for fresh air and exercise.

The mottled walls of Fort Jesus slope almost to the sea's brink, leaving just enough room for a narrow beach on which men were at work mending the big lateen sails, now made of canvas, formerly of coir matting. There are many kinds of dhow and they have fascinating names: Booms, Sambuks, Ghanjabs, Kotias, Badans, Zarooks, M'tepes, each built in a different sea-port and to a different design.

Their cargoes are innocent now – salt fish, dates, henna, copper wire, mangrove poles, cooking pots, ghee – but less than a century ago, could one have stood on the ramparts of Fort Jesus, one would have seen slaves whipped on board, to be packed in layers, one atop the other so there would have been no room to move. How many perished! And these were the survivors of those who had trudged, yoked and fettered, from the far interior. This was an Arab trade, and it was put an end to by the Royal Navy.

Every guide book to Mombasa tells the story of Fort Jesus, built by the Portuguese at the end of the sixteenth century, Kenya's most solid (though by no means oldest) monument to its past. It is a gruesome story of sieges, captures, recaptures, massacres and murders that punctuated three centuries of struggle between Arab and Portuguese for possession of Mombasa and the coast of Azania. One episode in particular, I have often thought, could be made into a powerful drama for stage and screen. It is a tale of revenge.

Yusuf, the Hamlet of the piece, was the son and heir of Hasan, the sheikh of Malindi, who was loyal to the Portuguese overlords. When Yusuf was a boy of seven the Portuguese Captain of Port Jesus, an over-bearing and belligerent man, quarrelled with Malindi's ruler and bribed African tribesmen from the mainland with two thousand pieces of cloth to murder Hasan. He then sent Hasan's severed head to Goa, the seat of Portuguese government, followed by the boy Yusuf, to be brought up as a Christian by Augustinian monks, indoctrinated with Portuguese culture, and groomed to become the sheikh of Mombasa. Translated into Dom Geronimo Chingulia, he was married to a Portuguese girl of good family and, as a grown man, sent back to Mombasa to take over his heritage.

The plan went awry. Back in Africa, the pull of Islam began to loosen the hold of Christianity, and his Arab blood to draw Yusuf back to his own people. It was said that he paid secret midnight visits to his father's grave and prayed there in the Muslim fashion, and that a Portuguese spy shadowed him and reported his behaviour to the Captain.

On 15 August 1631 the Feast of the Assumption was due to be celebrated in the chapel of the Fort. Thither Yusuf made his way with a band of followers. As the Captain greeted him, he stabbed the man to

death and then, in the chapel, similarly despatched the Captain's wife
and daughter together with the officiating priest. A holocaust followed. All the garrison in the Fort were massacred, followed by nearly
all the Portuguese in the town. The women were offered a chance of life
– of a sort, in Muslim harems – if they abjured their faith. They refused,
and were hurled into a boat and drowned in the harbour.

Predictably, Yusuf did not enjoy a prosperous reign and die in his
bed. After beating off an attempt to recapture the Fort by a fleet from
Goa, he laid Mombasa waste and sailed away to the Red Sea. When the
Portuguese re-occupied the island two years later they found it almost
deserted. Yusuf was killed by pirates. History does not relate what
happened to his unfortunate wife.

Thus ended a bungled Portuguese attempt to create a 'good native'
imbued with the culture of the colonial power, loyal to its authority
and trained to govern in its name. After several dreadful sieges and
massacres, Portuguese rule in Mombasa ceased on 26 November 1729,
when Fort Jesus was abandoned and the few half-starved survivors
struggled down to Mozambique in two dhows.[2]

So, after an interlude of three centuries, the Arabs were back to hoist
their plain red flag over Fort Jesus. It was flying there in 1933, for
Mombasa, together with all this East African coastline, still belonged,
in theory, to the Sultan of Zanzibar, the ruler of this residual Arab
empire. The British leased a ten-mile-wide strip for an annual rent that
had started at £17,000 but had gradually risen, in the face of stiff
opposition by the tenant, over the years. This was a British Protectorate, not a colony. Perhaps the distinction was a hair-splitting one, but
Arab law continued to be practised and the Muslim faith and various
Arab customs to be observed. This was one of those untidy form of
modus vivendi that look hypocritical but work pretty well. The
Sultan's representative in Mombasa, the chief Liwali Sir Ali bin Salim,
was much respected by Europeans, generous in charitable causes and
even welcomed in the Mombasa club which, following the general
pattern of the day, admitted only European members with an
occasional exception, like Sir Ali and the Aga Khan.

The true bringers of peace to this Isle of War were no conquering
heroes or bold adventurers but a middle-aged, middle-class consul in
Zanzibar, who persuaded the Sultan to accept a Protectorate, and a

Glaswegian ship-owner, founder of the British India Steam Navigation Company, whose statue, bespattered by bird droppings and looking as if an umbrella should have been included, stands in the commercial centre of the town. It was Sir William Mackinnon who, after years of patient prodding, persuaded a most reluctant government to grant, in 1888, a royal charter to his Imperial British East Africa Company: a charter but no cash, which was subscribed (£250,000) by a number of hopeful philanthropists wishing to open up trade in the interior.[3] Their hopes were not fulfilled; the British Government stepped in to bale out the company; soon after came engineers and surveyors to build the Uganda Railway and, incidentally, to found the club near the foot of the grim fort, with a fine view over the harbour. (And delicious fresh sea-food and an agreeable swimming pool.)

The missionaries were here before the consuls and the engineers: amazing men and women (they brought their wives, and nearly always buried their children) who faced terrible privations and imminent death in a hostile Muslim land whose ruling class they offended deeply by taking in and caring for freed and escaped slaves.

In due course an Anglican cathedral, substantial if not exactly beautiful, arose on Mombasa Island not far from fort and club, also a Roman Catholic one not much farther away. It was still a common practice for a young man making his career in Kenya to seek his bride during his long leave, get engaged, go ahead to build or otherwise acquire a dwelling, and then to send for his fiancée. He would be at the quayside to meet her, and very often she would go direct from ship to cathedral, pausing en route at the home of some unknown but hospitable lady to change into bridal attire. How bleak it must have been for a young girl to plight her troth to a man she might not have seen for a year or more, so far from her family, given in marriage by a total stranger. Did these girls feel elated, or afraid? A bit of both, I daresay.[4]

My parents had hoped to meet me at Mombasa but they were over four hundred miles away up-country and could not afford the fare. The Depression had its strangle-hold on Kenya as on everywhere else, and the farmers' plight was almost desperate. A whole bag of maize fetched only as much as would buy one gallon of petrol, if that, and some farmers hitched oxen to their cars to be towed in to their local town for essential shopping, all on credit, and for interviews with their bank managers, all in vain. To make matters worse the most devastating locust invasion in living memory had struck eastern Africa at the end of the 1920s. Swarms blackened the sky, descended on crops and pastures and left behind barren stalks and earth stripped of all vegetation; branches of trees broke beneath their weight and they had even halted trains by smothering the track so that the wheels lost their grip. They left behind a generation of hoppers which advanced in droves greedy to devour anything the swarms had spared and to invade new territories, where they turned into adult locusts and started the whole process over again. In 1931, nearly half the maize crop grown on European farms was destroyed. By the time of my arrival the worst was over, but the threat was still very much alive and would continue for some years.

What had been the Uganda Railway when I first knew it had become the Kenya and Uganda Railways and Harbours and was very much smartened up. Powerful Garrett engines had replaced the old ones that had run on eucalyptus logs, spat sparks which started grass fires and paused for long drinks at almost every station. The old trains had no corridors, so you were isolated in your compartment except when you got out at stations to stretch your legs, and to have dinner at Voi and breakfast at Makindu. You ate in grubby, unadorned dak bungalows lit by safari lanterns; the food was pretty dreadful and the drinks tepid, but you could make new acquaintances or greet old ones and, at Voi, you might very likely hear lions grunting in the bush around. When you got back to your compartment your bedding would have been spread on the hard seats and you would batten down for the night.

Each compartment had its small washroom, equipped with a built-in bottle-opener which Julian Huxley, in a book about his African travels,[5] adduced as proof of what terrible topers Kenya settlers were. This was thought to be unfair, because you could get no drinking water on the train and so carried bottles of mineral water and needed an opener when you came to brush your teeth. But now there was a corridor, a dining car and five-course meals. There were still three classes: first for senior civil servants (who travelled free), the richer Europeans and a sprinkling of wealthy Indians; second for all the other Europeans and Indians; third for Africans, who crowded into trucks equipped with benches, taking their food and a great many small children and babies. There was nothing official about this grading system; if any African had been rich enough he could have travelled first class if he wanted to; at the time, none was, or did. I travelled second and paid, I noted in my diary, sixty shillings – quite a lot in those days. Third class, I think, cost eight shillings.

Dust was the bane of the journey, a fine red dust that drifted into the compartments no matter how hard you tried to exclude it; and in the heat of the Taru desert to keep the windows tightly shut would have been to consign yourself to an oven. The dust got into everything, your nose, your eyes, your clothing, and when passengers arrived at Nairobi their faces were brick-red and hair and clothes stiff with the red powder.

But when you set the dust and dirt against the sight that greeted you when you looked out at dawn, they weighed as little as a pin against a pyramid. It was one of the great sights of the world. Even without the animals it would have been spectacular, with the thin pure light of sunrise, the colour of a fine Moselle, flooding over this enormous savannah and picking out every tree, every fold in the surface of the plain; far beyond, the white dome of Kilimanjaro seemed to hover in the western sky. But it was the animals that brought life and wonder to the scene. Thousands, tens of thousands of them could be seen from the carriage window, from pygmy mongooses peering out of their burrows to – if you were lucky – mighty elephants in family parties, from dappled, mild-eyed giraffes like tall-masted ships of the veld to graceful little shiny 'tommies' or zebras shimmering in the sunlight: lumbering kongonis, heavy-dewlapped elands, a rhino perhaps, standing foresquare with horn uplifted, silver-backed jackals trotting home to their dens after a night's foraging.

The animals could not, I suppose, be said to be living at peace with one another, because predators were constantly hunting their prey, but only when they were hungry; species did not do battle against species, or herds vie with each other for power and glory; no animal oppressed or tortured another; they shared the pastures, the bush, the shade and foliage of trees, the salt-licks and the drinking places without dispute or rancour. They did not, as Walt Whitman put it, whine about their condition, weep for their sins, or agonise over their duty to God:

. . . not one is demented with the mania of owning things,
Not one kneels to another, nor to his kind that lived thousands
    of years ago,
Not one is respectable or unhappy over the whole earth.

Even man, the arch-killer, fitted into this harmonious-seeming state
of affairs. To the left of the railway line, as far as the eye could see and
farther, lay the Maasai reserve; and the Maasai, by and large, left the
animals alone. They killed lions to protect their livestock, and young
boys might hunt birds with bows and arrows, but otherwise they did
not molest the wild creatures. Being nomadic, they had no crops and
gardens to protect. Wild animals could come and go as they wished on
their seasonal migrations. One of the early pioneers in Kenya, a tough
weather-beaten Scot who made a living by trading in cattle, and had
penetrated with a few porters far into the then little-known Maasai
reserve, told me that when he pitched his camp, somewhere down
beyond the Mara river, the hartebeests and Thomson's gazelles, the
wildebeests and jackals, would come right up to the tent to sniff
unfamiliar odours out of curiosity and quite without fear. He said that
he had felt some embarrassment, if not reluctance, to raise his rifle
against the unsuspecting beasts. 'You didn't shoot them, surely?' I said.
He shrugged his shoulders. 'The porters had to eat.'

At the time of which I write, these great animal herds had not yet
been seriously depleted in the game reserves, although outside them
they were already being harried and in places 'shot out', not by
sportsmen, whose bags were strictly limited by licence, but by
farmers, black and white. National parks were not to come into
existence until 1948, but early in the Colony's history shooting had
been prohibited in game reserves. Poaching was still on an insignificant scale. So the animals, for the time being, had little to worry
about provided they did not stray out of the protected areas. While
they were extraordinarily quick to learn where they were safe from
shooting, the deep urges of migration sometimes betrayed them.
These inbuilt compulsions to trek away in search of fresh feeding and
breeding grounds overrode the lessons of experience, and exposed
them to fatal dangers when they crossed the unfenced boundaries of
the game reserves.

In the eight years that had elapsed since I looked out of the window of the train at this variety of creatures grazing and browsing and frisking their tails, a great change had taken place in my own attitude, and that of many others, towards them. In my childhood, I had enjoyed stalking and shooting the creatures of the veld and bush. I had owned and cherished a rifle; learned from my African companions the elements of tracking; collected and cured the heads, taken measurements of horns, read with enjoyment books by professional hunters, and shared the prevailing belief that shooting wild animals was an exciting test of skill sometimes spiced with danger, to be enjoyed by all who loved the countryside and hoped to learn its lore by trudging on foot through bush and forest with every sense alert.

Even before I left Kenya at the age of eighteen, the fact that the end of a successful hunt was the destruction of a beautiful animal had begun to nibble at the roots of my enjoyment. The pleasures of the hunt were undeniable: those early mornings when shafts of sunlight gilded tree-trunks and sparkled on dew-beaded grasses and on a mantle of silver cobwebs; the bell-like call of birds; the monkey-shaken treetops, the air's purity, the thrilling glimpse of an animal frozen into immobility before bounding silently away. But that these sensual pleasures should lead to pain and death on a bright morning had begun to seem a sacrilege. Not only that, it had begun to seem unnecessary. Animal photography was nothing new, but before the development of telephoto lenses it was crude, and the best photographs were taken at night, by flashlight, which was difficult, expensive to arrange and attended by more failures than successes.

Now that was changing. People were beginning to realise that you could get as much enjoyment, if not more, from safari life and the pursuit of wild animals by shooting them with a camera instead of with a gun. My little pocket brownie had done excellent work on horses, dogs and people, but herds of zebra or kongoni had appeared merely as blurred dots. Now I had brought with me a second-hand Leica, compact and precise, and this was to be my constant companion.

I would like to write that I never slew an animal after my return, but this would not be true. One of eastern Africa's devastating droughts was going on. Crops were wilting, and the wild creatures, made bold by dwindling supplies of food and water, were invading farmlands in a desperate attempt to survive. A number of reedbuck suddenly appeared in my parents' field of maize and started to demolish it. They came at night, and shouts and sticks and flashlights had failed to drive them away. Neither of my parents had wielded a rifle for years, so I volunteered to do so. I shot three of the reedbuck without difficulty – hunger had blunted their wariness – and did not enjoy it; but it was a case of 'us or them' and not a case of sport. There is the inescapable dilemma, the root cause of the animals' doom everywhere – us or them. In the end, a not so very distant end, 'us' must win.

But in the meanwhile the animals on the left-hand side of the railway line were safe in their reserve. On the right-hand side they were unprotected and therefore scarcer, because the land had been fenced into European-owned ranches and, beyond, lay the hills of Ukambani which were closely cultivated by the Kamba tribe; and the Kamba, unlike the Maasai, were hunters and meat-eaters.

The arrival of the Mombasa train was still an event in Nairobi, and most of the population, black, white and brown, seemed to have gathered on the platform to greet relatives and friends. Glady Delamere had come to meet me. This was naturally an anxious moment, but Glady was good at putting people of all sorts at their ease. She had a striking appearance – chalk-white skin, jet-black wiry hair, dark-brown eyes – and gave out a sense of vitality, and of tenseness like a coiled spring. A throaty chuckle and a sense of gaiety softened what would otherwise have been a rather formidable presence. She was welcoming, unpompous and possessed a great store of energy which, at this time, had insufficient outlet; later, when she was elected Mayor of Nairobi, it found that outlet and she proved to be a hard-working and efficient Mayor. Tania Blixen wrote of her that she was like 'a painted wooden doll'.[6] She struck me as the reverse of doll-like, being so animated and unpredictable. People reacted positively to Glady; either they liked her or they did not. 'I remember her', her youngest daughter was to write years later, 'as somebody who lit up a room as she walked in, smelling exotically of Chanel No 5, usually with a gardenia pinned to her dress and often smoking a Turkish cigarette'.[7] Naturally I stood in awe of her – she was thirty-five, twice married, sophisticated and self-assured – but she did her best to dispel this feeling, and swept me off to a hairdresser to have the journey's dust removed, and then to Torr's hotel.

Torr's was Nairobi's grandest building, new since I was last there; a red-brick, four-storeyed edifice on the corner of Sixth Avenue and Hardinge Street (now Kenyatta and Kimathi) and was said, I am not sure by whom, to resemble Stockholm's Town Hall. It had become the rendezvous for Nairobi's café society and for safari parties and others who gathered there for eleven o'clock coffee, pre-lunch drinks and, in the evening, epicurean meals produced by a Swiss chef, and dancing to a fashionable band.

At Torr's I was introduced to Ewart Grogan, its creator and proprietor, who was discoursing to a circle of admirers, mostly female, at his favourite table in a sort of palm court. He was a handsome Irishman, then in his sixtieth year, tall and upright with remarkable blue and penetrating eyes, dark arched eyebrows, greying hair and an inexhaustible flow of talk. Words poured from his lips like wine at some Bacchic orgy, intoxicating at the time but, when the orgy was over, you wondered what he had actually said. The usual starting point was some idiotic blunder on the part of the government or the crass ineptitude of bureaucracy in general. He was an expert, in his own way, on economics and finance and also, one gathered, on seduction, taking little or no trouble to conceal his infidelities (in more than one instance blessed with issue) from a long-suffering wife whom everyone liked and respected.

Grogs, as he was generally known, had wit, intelligence and eloquence as well as a measure of flamboyance, but there was something about him I personally found unattractive, perhaps a certain cruelty in his humour and outlook, a streak (as it were) of the battering-ram. Without question he was courageous; several of his exploits had become legendary, notably his famous walk from the Cape to Cairo to win the hand of his bride by proving to her father that, although without financial assets, he had resources of another kind.[8] This was in 1899, when central Africa was no place to approach with a butterfly-net. Actually the walk was not from the Cape to Cairo, although that was the title he gave his book, but from the northern tip of Lake Nyassa (now Malawi) to Sobat on the upper Nile, but it was gruelling enough, taking him among ferocious cannibals and almost ruining his health.

He had got his girl and, in 1903, arrived in the East Africa Protectorate,[9] just two years after the Uganda Railway had reached its terminus on Lake Victoria. In East Africa he was to make his somewhat chequered career. There was nothing he liked better than to find a vulnerable spot in the government's hide and, like a hornet, puncture it with his sting. A flaw he discovered in the mining laws prompted him to peg claims all round Nairobi and threaten to dig up Government Road, a threat only averted by the hasty summoning of the Legislative Council which passed an amendment within twenty-four hours. Ewart Grogan was a charmer, a cynic, a swashbuckler, a buccaneer born out of time; generous with money, bold in his commercial ventures; when it came to fortune-seeking his scruples weighed, I should guess, about as much as a grain of sand. He had known Delamere well for thirty years and they had shared a number of tempestuous political experiences. He promised to tell me all he knew – or at any rate some of it – about D (as he was always called) and the pioneering days, and in due course he did, but I learnt more about his own exploits and opinions than about D's achievements.

Glady took me to her home at Loresho, a coffee farm about six miles outside Nairobi where she lived with her three children by her previous marriage to Sir Charles Markham.

But pleasant as Loresho was, I could pause there only for a night. Two hundred pounds being insufficient to cover expenses, I had been fortunate enough to secure a commission from *The Times* to write two articles about the goldfields that had recently been discovered in Kenya and Tanganyika, and in particular about those centred on Kakamega, not far from Lake Victoria. A controversy had sprung up, as controversies always seemed to do in Kenya, about the future of this goldfield. So before starting on the biography I had arranged to go to Kakamega to gather first-hand impressions of what was going on.

CHAPTER 2

Nuggets and Covered Wagons

The gold rush of 1931/33 in western Kenya and northern Tanganyika is a forgotten episode in East African history, but at the time it was a matter of the utmost excitement and promise. In the midst of all the gloom engendered by the slump plus drought and locusts, a gleam of light had suddenly appeared. The first discoveries were on an insignificant scale, but they gathered momentum and soon there was talk of another Rand. Farmers raised their last few shillings and departed for the goldfields with a car-load of shovels and kerais – shallow tin basins used for carrying earth etc – basic camping equipment, one or two African assistants and a whole lot of hope. By the time of my arrival at Kakamega, about forty miles from Lake Victoria, upwards of a thousand European would-be miners were encamped there eagerly panning riverbeds and sinking shafts. Most of the gold was alluvial and in the form of tiny particles, but a nugget weighing four to five ounces had been found and everyone was hoping for a major strike.

The district headquarters, or boma, stood in a grove of blue-gum trees which everywhere marked the passage of British district administration, much as mango trees marked the passage of the Arabs. A Union Jack flew outside the office of the District Commissioner, a grey-haired, elderly man called Colonel Anderson, with one leg stiffened by a war wound. He was coping in a most unruffled manner with the unexpected situations that had sprung at him, situations for which no previous experience can have prepared him. The population of his district, I noted, was 385,680, divided into seventeen sub-tribes of a major tribal group called the Abaluyhia who occupied all this region east of the Lake and the Uganda border, known as North Kavirondo.

Like so many things in Kenya, the gold rush had got entangled in politics. This goldfield lay not in a wilderness like the Klondyke, or on the highveld like the Witwatersrand, but in a thickly populated native reserve. The question of land ownership has always been a complex, persistent and explosive political issue, and in 1930, only one year before gold was found, in an effort to stabilise the situation, a Native Lands Trust Ordinance had passed into law. This had defined the various reserves, one for each tribe or sub-tribe, which were to be 'set aside for the benefit of the native tribes of the Colony forever'. You could not be more definite than that. Each tribe was to have its own territory and no one else, whether an African of a different tribe or a European or an Asian, was to have any legal rights therein. So much for the use of the word 'forever' in any human affair, as silly as 'lasting peace'; thirty years on and all this legislation would be swept away; and lasting peace must await the millennium.

Now the question of mining leases had arisen. To sink a mine and to provide sites for machinery and accommodation for miners must mean making use of African land, even if only temporarily. Mining leases must therefore be negotiated. It must then appear to those individuals who, in one way or another, had rights over land, that a mining lease gave those rights away. Three years is indeed a cynical interpretation of 'forever'.

But then – to bottle up, also forever, an important goldfield, if such it should prove to be, in the depths of a depression when the country, a poor one at the best of times, was virtually broke, hardly seemed sensible. It could be argued that a goldfield, by providing revenue that could be spent on education, health, communications, all the things so urgently in need of money, would indeed 'benefit the native tribes of the Colony' as the ordinance had laid down. So it was a dilemma. Much discussion was taking place in Parliament at Westminster, and in the press both in Britain and in Kenya, but no one knew just how to resolve it. Meanwhile, leases for one year only were being granted under strict terms to the mining companies who were beginning to set up shop, and no prospector could come in without a permit.

The result was probably the most gentlemanly gold-rush ever known. Not here swaggering figures in ten-gallon hats and a brace of revolvers flinging down bags of gold-dust on the counters of saloons; not here the drunken quarrels and the bold sharpshooters we had all been accustomed to by the movies. The District Commissioner had powers to keep out, even to throw out, any (in his opinion) undesirable character, and a single white policeman with a handful of African askaris had no difficulty in keeping the peace. Most of the prospectors had settled down, often with their wives, either in tents or in simple dwellings called bandas which could be built at a cost of about fifteen shillings from poles and grass cut from the bush. In the evenings the music of gramophone records and bids at the bridge table were more likely to emanate from tents and bandas than drunken altercating and poker calls.

The local tribesmen sold the gold-seekers milk, eggs (tiny ones from tiny hens) at fifty to the shilling, and plenty of fresh vegetables for a few cents. Kisumu, the railway's original terminus, was only forty miles distant. Kakamega itself was green and pleasant, the gardens full of colour, and drought almost unknown, for it rained nearly every afternoon.

What I remember principally were the fireflies. At night, the ridges and valleys round about sparkled with millions of these insects, flashing their signals till the countless stars overhead were matched, it seemed, by another canopy of stars below, as if they had fallen to earth and yet stayed in the sky. Part of a mating ritual, I was told, but this did not seem to explain it. Thousands, tens of thousands of species of insect find their mates without releasing into the darkness, each one, a pin-point of brilliance.

I stayed in comfort at a mining camp belonging to a syndicate headed by a rich American called de Ganahl, which had a concession on a small river called the Wachecehe near the place where the original find had been made, and I met the original finder. He, also, was an American, by name L. A. Johnson, who had settled in Kenya, if settle is the word, in 1910, after a spell on the Klondyke and adventures in the Spanish–American war. In Kenya he had tried flax and gone bust when the flax boom collapsed in 1921; then he had switched to maize and gone bust again when maize prices collapsed in 1930. That had sent him off prospecting in northern Tanganyika, where he had trudged on foot for thousands of miles and found nothing.

Late in 1930 he formed a syndicate in Eldoret, with four shares of £25 each, to finance a final try. The expedition, consisting of himself, his wife Fanny, two other Europeans and five Africans, set forth from

Eldoret in two very ancient Fords and what was left of the £100 after buying petrol and one sack of flour, one of dried beans, one of potatoes and several sacks of posho (maize meal). Once again, they had no luck. When the money ran out they headed for home, making their final camp in the Kakamega district near the Yala river. Next day they panned a tributary of the Yala and found gold. Back in Eldoret they quickly registered another syndicate, borrowed money for petrol and returned to peg out claims along the Yala river. That was the goldfield's beginning. By now the first stage was almost over, and the next stage had arrived when companies with capital were moving in with machinery and mining engineers to sink shafts and exploit the reefs from which the alluvial gold had come.

L. A. Johnson I remember as a tall, bony man with a jutting chin and an ill-fitting set of teeth, who looked every inch the tough prospector, and was as uncommunicative as a mule. 'A grunt or two', wrote one of his neighbours, 'a great hoik and hefty spit and the word "Jesus" was L. A.'s usual comment on most subjects.'[1] When the difficulties of receiving news of world events in the outback – this was before the days of wireless – were under discussion, someone asked 'What do you do when the weekly *East African Standard* doesn't arrive?' Mr Johnson's reply was simply 'use grass'. He, at least, did well out of the goldfields, and when he went to the United States for a visit, Fanny wore a necklace of nuggets.

After a night in de Ganahl's camp, I was introduced, next morning, to the technique of panning, to be rewarded by two very small nuggets, little more than grains, but still, gold. So I could capture a little of the excitement: next time they might be nuggets weighing half a pound. (Even then, not a great fortune; the price was £4 an ounce.) Then I was lowered down the shaft the engineers were in process of sinking to a depth of over a hundred feet. The reef was yielding gold in payable quantities and everyone was optimistic, the new Johannesburg was on its way. But that reef petered out. Others were found, more machinery imported and, in 1938, gold was Kenya's second largest export, next to coffee. After that, output declined, syndicates folded and only a little residual mining went on, mostly over the border in Tanganyika. I am sorry to say that I persuaded Gervas to buy £50 worth of shares in a syndicate that couldn't fail called Paka Neusi, which means black cat.

(Moonshine Mining Co. was another of the syndicates.) Alas, our cat wasn't lucky and we never had a dividend, not even a cent.

Perhaps, in the long run, the failure of the goldfield was fortunate for Kenya. Gold would have enriched the country, and it could have done with some enrichment. But the growth at Kakamega of a new Johannesburg would have entangled the country in endless disputes about African rights, land tenure and leases, and destroyed the peace of this generous and smiling countryside. There are no fireflies in Johannesburg.

I came back from Kakamega by way of Eldoret, then a little farmers' township with a single dusty main street flanked by squat tin-roofed shops and Indian dukas (small shops), and by battered looking box-body cars angle-parked under rows of blue-gum trees. It was the embryonic capital of the Uasin Gishu plateau. Here you heard more Dutch spoken than English – we called it Dutch but it was really Afrikaans.

On this plateau, Afrikaner farmers outnumbered the British, and they had been the pioneers. I had been fascinated by the plateau's story every since I first heard Cecil Hoey, one of the early settlers who reached East Africa about the same time as Delamere, give his account of how, when he was sitting one day on top of a rock called Sergoit watching three lions at play, he saw on the horizon a long white streak which at first he thought was smoke. Then it became too definite a shape for smoke and it looked more like a river, though he knew this could not be. Gradually it grew closer, and he was able to make out through his binoculars a long line of ox-drawn wagons, their covered tops showing as a dusty white. This was the trek of the Boers to the Uasin Gishu in 1908.

They had not trekked up Africa all the way from the Transvaal – tsetse fly prevented that. They had loaded their wagons, horses, tools, provisions, seeds and ploughs and all their other possessions on to a chartered ship in Delagoa Bay and unloaded them at Mombasa. The railway had laid on five special trains which took them to Nakuru where they camped, and began their preparations for the trek ahead.

Some years later I heard another version of the story from an elderly Dutchman who had taken part in the trek. He had been a boy of fifteen or so. By then in his seventies, he was still alert and active, lean and tough as leather, his brown face wrinkled, his hands calloused from a lifetime of handling reins, whips, plough-handles, rifles. His memory was prodigious; every day, every camp, every event had remained stamped as clear as type on his mind.[2]

The leader of the trek, he said, was Jansen van Rensburg, and forty-seven families took part, plus three single men and two Predikants. Some kind of bargain, he believed, had been struck between van Rensburg and the Governor of the day, Sir James Hayes-Sadler: if van Rensburg would bring up not less than thirty families with their wagons and equipment, they would be leased the land on easy terms.

At Nakuru, this narrator said, the Boers bought native oxen and set to work to train them, while a scouting party went forward on horseback to find a route. To reach the Uasin Gishu plateau they had first to climb a heavily forested escarpment which rose steeply from the valley. There was no road, not even native paths since there were no Africans living on the plateau then. Cecil Hoey used to take safari parties there and testified that the plateau was empty of all African settlements until you reached the Nandi hills far beyond the plain. People called Sirikwa had dwelt here once and had left traces of circular stone dwellings, but they themselves had disappeared. Some local historians supposed that they had been wiped out by the Maasai, others that an epidemic had destroyed them. In places, Hoey had come upon collections of whitened bones which may have marked the site of battles long ago.

The Boers' trek began from Nakuru on 4 August 1908, this old man said. The trekkers halted at the foot of the escarpment while the men hacked a path through the first part of the forest and threw rough bridges over its many streams.

Then they started on the long climb. It must have been a wet year, for soon the wagons were bogged down axle-deep in mud. Two, three, even four spans of oxen (sixteen to a span) were hitched together to extricate the wagons, which sank in again as deeply as before. Up and up they heaved and hauled, up the towering escarpment. I cannot imagine how they got those wagons up; sheer willpower must have powered them besides the half-trained little beasts. It was bitterly cold. Sometimes they made no more than a mile or two in a day.

At last, they drew clear of the forest to the windswept crest of the escarpment and outspanned at over 6,000 feet above sea level, at a camp called Brugspruit, where they thanked God for their deliverance, and a two-year-old girl died. The great plain lay before them with its waving grasses, green now after rain, its trees and rivers and the vast herds of game which gladdened their hearts. This was as the Transvaal once had been and was no longer. Only one man did not rejoice. That was Cecil Hoey, sitting on his rock observing their advance. 'I went back to camp that night', he later recorded, 'a very sad man, realising that the countless herds of game must now give way to make room for western civilisation.'

The emissaries of western civilisation trekked on until they reached the Sosiani river, beside which Eldoret now stands, where they parted company, each family fanning out to find its own bit of promised land. An Afrikaner who had preceded them, one of three brothers called van Breda, had roughly surveyed it into blocks, and each man took up a leasehold of between 800 and 5,000 acres. Each family built a shack from the trees, grass and earth of its new domain, put up fences, inspanned oxen to simple ploughs and turned the first furrows. They sowed wheat, maize and vegetables. It was the wrong time of year, and all those first crops died. They persisted, and the revels of those lions under Sergoit rock were ended. Wheat is more useful to mankind than lions.

When I saw it twenty-five years later, the plateau had been transformed into a prosperous region of wheat and maize fields, fenced pastures carrying grade cattle (native Zebus crossed with pedigree European stock), flocks of sheep and plantations of black wattle trees, with roofs of farmsteads winking at you through trees that had grown up around them. Roads, telegraph wires, reservoirs stocked with fish and used by sailing clubs, all these had come into being in a remarkably short time and despite such setbacks as the First World War, the slump that followed it and then drought and locusts. The plateau and the Trans Nzoia beyond had become Kenya's major exporting area of wheat, maize, wool and wattle bark and one of the granaries of eastern Africa. Tractors crawled like beetles over the rolling plains, and the little scarred, heroic oxen, like the wild animals, had had their day. This was an impressive achievement in a land where, in the words of a historian of the district, 'patient, tough women used to visit Eldoret once a month or took a shopping trip to Nairobi once in a decade, and spent six weeks on the journey.'

All that had changed in 1924 when the railway reached Eldoret, the first train garlanded with wheatsheafs and bearing the Governor of the day, Sir Robert Coryndon. Eldoret had started with a mud-and-wattle hut to house a post office clerk; then came a District Commissioner whose stone rondavel, plus a humbler one for his clerk, together with an office and a store, cost £167 to build. Next came a policeman, then an Indian called Noor Mohamed opened a store, and an ox-wagon brought the Standard Bank of South Africa in the shape of a safe, a brass plate and a manager who became a famous figure round about, J. C. Shaw. The safe rolled off the wagon when it was being unloaded and, as it was too heavy to move, the bank was built round it. Mr Shaw used to take his morning bath in a tub behind its counter, and then stroll in his dressing-gown to Eddy's bar, which had opened up across the way, for a quick one in preparation for the day's business. This consisted mainly of dispensing overdrafts whose limit was one hundred rupees.[3] Mrs Eddy provided the town's water supply by means of an ox-cart service from the Sosiani river and by selling it by the debbi – an empty four-gallon petrol tin.

Eldoret was then called Sixty-four, the number of the farm which became its birthplace. The name was changed in 1911 at a meeting between the farmers and the Governor, Sir Percy Girouard. By then a second Boer trek had taken place, this time on a smaller scale, and British farmers had taken up land. Among them was Cecil Hoey. To cross the Nzoia river he felled a tree which became known as Hoey's Bridge, and so it has remained, though by now a different bridge. This opened the way to the settlement of the Trans Nzoia district, north-west of the plateau. So the rough out-riders of western civilisation, so-called, spread out, and put to use land that had lain for long without a master; and the game fell to their rifles.

All this was described to me by Cecil Hoey, who had seen it all and himself been a pace-maker. What is so interesting about Kenya's history is that events belonging by rights to a bygone century, to the era of covered wagons and the Oregon Trail, should have taken place, albeit on a relatively tiny scale, within the lifetime of people still alive. Cecil Hoey had come to East Africa at the turn of the century. He was a burly man, rather slow of speech, with a quiet humour and strong fixed opinions. Times were to change more quickly than his power to adjust to such changes. Some years later, when a new generation of educated Africans had emerged, he and his wife invited me to stay on his farm on the plateau. Then I received a message cancelling the invitation. I had offended against a code he was not prepared to renounce; I had lunched with an African at a Nairobi hotel. To do this was still liable to offend some, though not all, of the older generation of white people. The African in question was Tom Mboya, one of the first of the new breed, a highly intelligent young man who had been an undergraduate at Ruskin College, Oxford; he wrote a book which contained a telling incident. He had been employed as a laboratory assistant by the Veterinary department and was alone in the lab when a European woman walked in, looked around and enquired: 'Is anyone here?' He replied: 'I am, madam.'[4]

So, regretfully, I never saw Cecil Hoey again to hear more of his recollections – he was a good raconteur. He ended his days on the Coast and, after a lifetime spent in up-country Africa, left instructions in his will that he was to be buried at sea.

There is a postscript to the story of the Boer treks of 1908 and 1911 to the plateau. It is in the shape of an item in the Johannesburg *Argus* dated 23 February 1961, less than three years before Kenya's independence.

Twenty-nine weary trekkers – the vanguard of what they promise will become a mass exodus of Afrikaner families of farmers from Kenya – crossed the Beit Bridge after dark yesterday and spent their first night in their homeland in a Messina rest camp . . . The adult trekkers agreed that they left Kenya because there was going to be an 'explosion' at independence. Mr Piet Olivier, a prosperous farmer in the Eldoret district, said: 'It will be a much worse place than the Congo when independence comes. The only reason why we came now, at the risk of being called cowards, is that we would probably have to leave half our families behind – dead – after independence . . .' Mrs Martha Steenkamp had to sell all their furniture in her 14-room farmhouse for Rand 60 – and the Kenya Government took half in tax.

CHAPTER 3

Nellie's Friends

The track leading uphill from Njoro township to my parents' farm
was so familiar that the years seemed to drop away and nothing to
have changed, except that perhaps the ant-bear holes in the wheel-
tracks were in different places, and the stringy grass in the middle
rather thicker. Small totos in their skimpy cloaks feverishly shooing
herds of bleating goats out of the way; women in goatskin cloaks and
aprons bowed under their loads – one never saw a loadless woman;
an ox-cart rumbling down and drawing into the bush with much
shouting and cracking of whips; all this was the same. And there were
the two umbrella thorn trees bent over the track towards each other
as if guardians of the domain, framing between them the small square
wooden bungalow, its tin roof rusted to a nameless sort of colour and
smothered by a purple-flowering solanum. (Whether the house held
up the creepers or the creepers held up the house, as Nellie had
remarked, was a moot point.)

Before the car bumped to a halt a surge of dachshunds flowed out
to meet me, offering a sea of waving tails and a cacophony of barks.
Then came Karanja in his red fez, scarcely changed at all, and then
Mbugwa, who had changed a lot, having grown from a kitchen toto
into a well-built young man, both of them grinning from ear to ear
and pumping my arm up and down. Dogs, pandemonium, fervent
greetings, and then Jos and Nellie walking more sedately after them.
Neither was a demonstrative person. The evening sun had fallen
behind the dark crest of the Mau hills but the valley far below was
still flooded with honey-tinted light barred by long purple shadows,
and the blue eye of Lake Nakuru winked up at us from the foot of the
long, yellow slope of Menengai. Doves were calling with notes like a
mellow wine dropping from a bottle; green pigeons flew over on their
way to roost, weaver-birds chattered in a thorn-tree just behind the
house, goat-bells tinkled in the distance as flocks were driven in for
the night.

And yet there were changes. Jos and Nellie had aged, of course, but more than I had expected. Life had been hard for them in the intervening years. The farm, Gikammeh – called after the hyraxes that screeched their heads off every night from the trees – lay on the margin of this aboriginal forest which was full of tall, majestic cedars with fluted bark, festooned with grey beards of lichen, and wild olives with their twisted trunks and random branches. Below lay the Rift Valley, bounded on the distant side by the great ranges of the Aberdare mountains. The Njoro river separated our land from the forest. When my parents had come here there had been nothing in the way of civilisation, no human habitations, paths or signs of man, just thick bush, tongues of forest and a number of open glades where creatures of the forest came to graze; buffalo, bushbuck, waterbuck, tiny little suni and others. The only human thumb-print was a flimsy bungalow put there to fulfil the Government's development clauses in the lease. When Nellie first moved in, it had been full of bags of maize belonging to a trader who had used it as a store.

To turn this stretch of Africa into a farm had been hard work, made harder by all the bush and trees. Everything had to be cleared. Just cutting down the trees, or burning them, was not enough; their stumps had to be drawn before a plough could get to work. For this, a labour force was needed. As no Africans were living round about, some had to be recruited from afar. They came, but everything was strange to them, even picks and saws; this was a far country full of dangers, also cold and comfortless, and most of them absconded. There were no tractors then – or rather, Jos and Nellie could not afford one, and the terrain was too rough; the little oxen had to haul and heave at tree-stumps, as deeply embedded as the most obstinate of tooth-stumps in a human jaw.

Gradually, painfully and expensively, trees and their roots were cleared, the bush uprooted and then the small, crude ploughs of the day, some only single-furrowed, were deployed. Maize was sown, fences put up, a cart-track made to the river for water-hauling, storage sheds knocked up, and the round thatched huts of the Kikuyu appeared. Nellie has related how, when she arrived at Njoro in 1923 to start the enterprise (with three dachshunds, two Siamese cats and some basic provisions) she found waiting at the station half a dozen Kikuyu employees who had gone on ahead from my parents' coffee farm at Thika, secretly, ready to accompany her to the new land. She was touched at this act of loyalty and affection, but knew that loyalty and affection were not the primary reasons. Word had got round that there was fresh land, virgin land, with plenty of firewood going free, as well as grazing for cattle and goats. A passionate desire for land was, as it remains, in the very marrow of Kikuyu bones. When it came to giving out new shambas, they wanted to be in on the ground floor.

Now clusters of round thatched huts, each cluster surrounded by a palisade of cedar planks, had arisen. When one Kikuyu family comes, others follow. The half-dozen individuals she had found waiting at the station had mushroomed into a sizeable population, each family with its goats and cattle – and its children, many children. Already Nellie had started a farm school.

The small amount of capital Jos and Nellie had to get the farm established was soon exhausted, because the costs of clearing had been higher than they had expected. The bank was negatively firm. Some other source of cash had to be found. There was much talk at this time (about 1927) of a railway to open up Tanganyika's southern highlands, which lay about two hundred miles south of the line from Dar es Salaam to Kigoma. They were sparsely inhabited, well watered, presumably fertile, and only awaited, in the opinion of enthusiasts, enterprise and expertise to become a land of milk and honey, a 'second Kenya'. Moreover, there were plans to build a railway to link this region with the central line, and surveyors were already at work. Tanganyika's Government was issuing leases on favourable terms, and a minor land rush had started, with several of Kenya's leading figures, including Delamere, involved.[1]

The opportunity seemed too good to miss. Jos and Nellie joined a little cavalcade of battered cars and one lorry which bumped for more than five hundred miles over rudimentary roads, the travellers camping by night beside their vehicles, to the promised land. Jos stayed down there in a half-built bungalow without doors, windows or furniture, living on the most basic kinds of food. He was rather old for this sort of existence, being fifty-three.

Nellie got a lift back in a lorry and returned to Njoro to build herself a mud-and-wattle hut on the plain below Gikammeh on what were called the pipeline farms. This plain was waterless, and part of it had formerly belonged to Delamere – he had called it Equator Ranch. All it needed to be profitably farmed was water. So he laid a pipeline from a river on the Mau escarpment; then he divided the ranch into five-hundred-acre sections, provided each section with a water tank and a patch of wattle trees for firewood, and let it off on very easy terms. This was to further his overriding aim, which was to settle as much of Kenya's highlands as was not in native occupation with farmers of European stock.

The pipeline farms were being taken up; few of the newcomers had experience and equipment for breaking land; Nellie had both. She formed a syndicate with two friends, moved her ploughs and oxen down to the plain (she called her dwelling Piggery Nook) and set to. Being treeless, this land was much easier to break than Gikammeh had been. For company she had the dachshunds and her embroidery – her hands were never idle. She was out supervising the ploughing and harrowing from sunrise to sunset. At one time she had ten teams, each of sixteen oxen, drawing three-furrow ploughs at work on these pipeline farms, and she even acquired two second-hand tractors and trained their African drivers. One of the drivers drove a tractor all the way down to Jos in Tanganyika to help out. Neither man nor tractor returned.

Jos had decided to plant Turkish tobacco, which fetched a higher price than the Virginian kind; with a two-hundred-mile journey by wagon before you even reached a railway, a high price for your produce was essential. But Turkish tobacco plants are not so hardy as the Virginian. His first crop started splendidly, and then was totally destroyed by frost. By this time the prospect of a railway had receded. Moreover Jos's health had deteriorated. (He still had some pieces of shrapnel embedded in his chest, left over from the First World War.) He returned, sadly, to Njoro.

Then came the Depression. No need to labour the point about the catastrophic fall in prices. I know that Nellie sold a number of fat porkers for one shilling each. Neither she nor Jos was a complainer, and only when I returned to the farm did I realise just how hard times had been, and still were. The ponies had been sold, so Nellie walked about the farm, and Sunday morning rides into the forest whch had been so much enjoyed, and games of amateurish polo at the club, were no more. The old Ford had been converted to run on paraffin, which was cheaper than petrol; it spluttered and choked, and its journeys, which were strictly rationed, ended all too often in a call for oxen to come and tow it home for yet another cleaning of plugs and carburettor. When the telephone charges rose to £13 a year the telephone had been removed.

All this did not quench my parents' optimism. Jos was working on plans to start a small hotel on Mombasa island, a plan which really could not go wrong. He had borrowed six hundred pounds from a sister-in-law, and taken on a partner who was supervising building operations at Mombasa. All Jos's previous partners had proved to be broken reeds, and this one was to be no exception.

Nellie took me round the farm to see many new enterprises, several of which were aimed at growing things that no one else had thought of, and for which a market might therefore be found. Almonds were one. Kenya imported almonds – not, it was true, on a large scale, consumption being virtually confined to the needs of three confectioners in Nairobi, but no one in Kenya grew them, so here was a gap that could be filled. Nellie did a lot of research, and the house was full of pamphlets about stocks, varieties, the art of grafting and culture generally. Some sturdy little trees from South Africa were established in a small plantation.

Then there were angora rabbits, attractive bunnies with long, white, silky fur. I forget where she had discovered a market for angora wool, but she had, and corresponded at length with prospective buyers who were prepared to take her crop. The rabbits were in home-made cages behind the kitchen, and in Nellie's little office, full of files and seeds and catalogues and dachshunds and knitting, were carefully kept pedigrees and mating records; it was all done on the soundest scientific lines. The one task she really hated was punching holes in the rabbits' ears for identification. They had long, silky, floppy ears and screamed when these were punched.

Another project, which I think came later, was breeding white mice for the veterinary laboratories near Nairobi. The lab supplied her with foundation mice, and at first they bred prolifically. Then things went wrong, and they began to eat each other. I suppose one might say that Nellie anticipated the actions of the animals' lib movement by some fifty years. Disgusted with the whole affair, she took the white mice into the forest and set them free.

Profits from these and other projects lay in the future; her principal standby in the present was the kikapu trade. (The kikapu is a large woven basket with handles, adaptable to almost any use.) She had always delighted in vegetable culture and grew the most excellent produce under irrigation by the riverside. Once a week she filled a number of kikapus with a selection of vegetables, loaded them into the car and spluttered off to Nakuru where, if she reached it, she delivered the kikapus to the doors of her customers, I think for five shillings a time.[2]

The doyen of the Kikuyu on the farm was Njombo, who had come to us at Thika as a lad, and signed on as a syce, or groom. With the move to Njoro he had changed course, and was now the headman. All the Kikuyu on the farm were squatters: that is, the head of each family was given a shamba of indeterminate size, as a rule about two or three acres, where he built his huts and where his wife, or wives, grew their crops. His sheep, goats and cattle were allowed to graze on the undeveloped parts of the farm, which also provided the family with firewood. All this was free. In return, the squatter undertook to work for six months of the year for the farm's owner, and for the usual wage. This was a low one, but the families were self-supporting on their plots, and if they had a surplus they usually sold it, though they were not supposed to.

This was a system that had grown up spontaneously to meet the conditions of the time, when farms were being made out of bush and there was plenty of land for everyone. It created difficulties later, when undeveloped land grew scarcer and people multiplied. Today it is hard to realise how sparsely populated the country was at the start of British rule. The usual estimate was two and a half to three millions up to the early 1920s when the increase began, slowly at first, then with gathering and now frightening speed, doubling every fifteen or sixteen years.

During my absence Njombo had become an elder, though he was not really old; people, in general, married young, and passed into the elders' grade when their eldest son was circumcised, which normally took place when the boy was between twelve and fifteen years of age. So a man of thirty-five or so could be an elder, and therefore entitled to sit on the kiama, a council of elders who met to settle disputes and impose fines (in sheep and goats) on offenders. The Kikuyu were a disputatious people, so there were many cases, some of which went on for years, for the kiama to hear. A lot of these involved disputes about the bride-price paid by a young man's father to the father of the bride.

Circumcision, bride-price, kiama – the whole social system of the people had been transferred in microcosm from their homeland to European-owned farms. This had advantages for both sides. For the Kikuyu, there was no traumatic break with custom and routine; life went on much as before in a new environment. If the altitude was too high to grow bananas, you switched to potatoes instead. From the employer's point of view, he had a stable and reasonably contented work-force living with their families on the spot, and unlikely to vanish overnight; for certain tasks he could call on women; and the gathering of firewood helped to clear his land.

Where the squatter system could not operate, as for example on big tea and sisal plantations, men had to be recruited on contract, without their wives, housed in 'labour lines' which, though no doubt adequate, looked ugly and dreary, and fed on prescribed rations – an altogether harsher and cruder business for the labourers. The Kikuyu were on the whole reluctant to join recruiters' gangs, whereas people from the Lake Victoria basin, especially the Luo, were more willing to forsake their homes.

Njombo, now that he was an elder, had become more dignified, less prone to laughter, than before. He wore a heavy goatskin cloak trimmed with tiny shells, a great many bangles and charms, and a snuff-horn suspended from his neck by a fine chain made by a Kikuyu smith. I always admired the fineness of these chains made with the crudest of tools, and with a bellows fashioned from the hind leg of a goat.

Njombo's face had become quite wrinkled, and so had that of his wife Wanjui, who greeted me warmly in their round thatched hut with its fire burning in the middle – the fire, lit on marriage, must never be allowed to go out – and three rounded cooking stones. There was no chimney, so the smoke had to find its own way out through the thatch.

Naturally this made the atmosphere inside thick and chokey – there were no windows – and at first your eyes smarted and you coughed. But you got used to it after a while. Smoke had covered the timbers supporting the roof, and everything else inside, with a thick black crust that glistened in the firelight. Wanjui offered me a calabash of uji, a gruel made of home-pounded maize-meal which I had always found dull and rather sour, though herbs from the bush were used as flavouring. I had brought Njombo one or two simple gifts – I think a blanket and a metal cash-box in which people stored their shillings buried in the earthen floors of their huts. We conversed in our basic Swahili, a fine language when properly spoken but alien alike to Europeans and to the up-country tribes, so we did not speak it properly, but used a kind of kitchen version nicknamed Ki-settla. As Swahili was a Bantu language, the Bantu-speaking tribes found it much easier than English to learn, and you could get along in it throughout most of eastern Africa.

While Europeans also found it easy to learn, some did not trouble to speak even the Ki-settla version well. There was a sad story of a man who, about to leave his farm for the day, summoned his headman to give instructions. He had a flock of valuable high-grade sheep of which he was particularly proud, and his final words were: 'Chinja kondoa yote, chinja sana', which he thought meant 'Look after all my sheep, look after them very well.' The headman looked surprised, but replied 'ndio, bwana' – yes, sir – and the farmer returned to find a hundred sheep with their throats cut lying in rows on the lawn. Unfortunately he had confused the word 'chunga', which means 'look after, care for', with the word 'chinja', which means 'kill'.

Njombo had prospered and so had his eldest son, Mbugwa, who was now on my parents' household staff of three, or four if you counted the kitchen toto. Karanja was the cook, Mbugwa was Nellie's personal 'boy' and Jos had, as his, one of the few non-Kikuyu on the farm, a Kipsigis ex-askari. The term 'boy', then in universal use, has come to seem derogatory and insulting, as of course in English terms it is; these were men, not boys. On the other hand French waiters do not object to being called garçons, so far as I know. At the time, no one thought anything of it; it was just the custom; now it is seen as an example of colonialist arrogance.

It might be asked how Jos and Nellie could afford any servants at all, however low their wages, in such hard times. Strictly speaking, perhaps they could not; but to do without them in the circumstances would have been virtually impossible. Firewood had to be hewn, sawn and carried; washing done by hand, often by banging the garments on stones in the river; paraffin lamps cleaned; the old wood-burning Dover stove kept stoked, and so on; there were no labour-saving devices. Without help, there just would not have been time to get through all the work in a day, let alone to run the farm as well. The kitchen was a smoke-filled hovel full of Karanja's friends and relatives looking in for a cup of thickly sweetened tea. Nellie, who enjoyed cooking, had given up worrying about hygiene and become a virtual exile from her own kitchen. Had she cleared it of its shifting population, shockwaves would have spread throughout the neighbourhood, and even beyond.

Mbugwa possessed a wide grin, a lively sense of humour and a stutter. On the first occasion when Gervas came to the farm, he (Gervas) brought with him a trick he had picked up somewhere, a variation of the three-card trick, played with three little bells which you put on a table. One of these bells tinkled, the other two were mute. You challenged your audience to pick out the bell that rang. They invariably lost the bet. Karanja and Mbugwa greeted each failure with incredulous gasps. Then Gervas unfolded the solution. None of the bells had clappers, but on his left wrist, concealed under a shirt-sleeve, was a bracelet with a bell that rang. When he moved one of the mute bells with his left hand, the bell concealed in his sleeve tinkled. The other two bells, moved with his right hand, remained silent. I suppose an experienced three-card-trick player would have spotted the deception, but Karanja and Mbugwa did not. When it was revealed, both of them literally rolled about the floor in ecstasies of mirth. Whenever they saw Gervas after that, even when bringing in a tray of early morning tea, Mbugwa roared with helpless laughter and cried: 'Those bells! Those little bells!'

Gervas presented the bells to Mbugwa and I have no doubt that he grew rich by playing the trick on his many friends and relations – if he managed to keep a straight face. Mbugwa was a most endearing character. Some years later, Nellie told me, he grew a certain variety of potato whose seed she herself had tried in vain to obtain; when he had shown the potatoes to her – they often compared notes on horticultural matters – she had much admired them. The following Christmas, he brought in with the tea-tray a small sack of these potatoes tied with red ribbon, and deposited it on her bed. The characteristic that Nellie found most sympathetic about him, apart from his sense of humour, was that he loved the dogs, and they loved him.

Arrivals and departures at or from the farm were generally regarded as excuses for a party. My arrival was no exception. Njombo, Mbugwa, Karanja and various others decided to organise an ngoma, or dance, in my honour. For an ngoma, everyone dressed to the nines. The attire of the men consisted mainly of intricate patterns painted in chalk on bodies oiled with castor oil, or with fat and red ochre. There were clappers on the ankles, beaded belts and necklaces, and elaborate head-dresses, the smartest ones involving ostrich feathers; the whole effect was exciting and, to our eyes, rather barbaric. These were the warriors and they were meant to look intimidating, even though their weapons had been laid aside. Elders took no active part in the dance itself, but a very active one in the consumption of refreshments. Plenty of beer, made as a rule from fermented maize-meal, was brewed in big gourds with narrow necks that bubbled away by the fireside until the brew was ripe and potent.

Jos and Nellie were expected to contribute a bullock. The selection of the beast led to a good deal of manoeuvre and argument; the Kikuyu had their eye on the fattest, sleekest of the herd, Jos and Nellie were determined that the oldest and scraggiest should be sacrificed. A day or so before the ngoma the herdsman, another Karanja who wore an old felt hat at a jaunty angle, came to Nellie and said: 'That ox Mafutu, memsabu, has become very, very ill. I do not know exactly his disease but he is wasting rapidly and there is only one thing to be done to save him – he must be killed before he dies and his flesh turns so rotten that it cannot be eaten.'

'Then I will summon the vet,' Nellie replied.

'No, no, that would be foolish, memsabu; you would have to part with many, many shillings and then what would you have? A dead ox just the same.' This was probably true, but Nellie stood firm.

'The ox Mafuta looks perfectly healthy to me. It is the ox Goygoy who will be killed for this ngoma.'

Karanja went off shaking his head and muttering at his employer's stupidity, and Nellie knew that the affair was by no means settled. It might well be that Karanja ngombe, the herdsman, would come to her next morning shaking his head again and looking mournful to say that, by some extraordinary misfortune, the ox Mafuta had put his foot into an ant-bear hole, broken his leg and perished in the night. She won that trick by having Mafuta driven into one of the sheds that had grown up near the house and locking it in for the night. There was still the possibility that Karanja would report that a hyena had broken into the shed and savaged Mafuta. She put an extra padlock on the shed's door and hoped that the dogs would give her warning of any skulduggery. Mafuta came through the night in safety and poor Goygoy had his throat cut next morning.

African dances differed from most European ones in that they went on much longer, sometimes for several days and nights, and that the dancers chanted most of the time. The male dancers jumped up and down with tremendous energy and thumping, the ground seemed to shake under their feet, and all the time they chanted a refrain. Drums beat – no other instruments were played – with a compulsive rhythm. The young women, with bunches of grass fore and aft and masses of beads, like the men painted with chalk and smeared with red ochre, also jumped and thumped, but went in even more for swaying and rolling their hips. After a while the dance became what was generally called suggestive; explicit would be a more accurate word. No bones were made about the dance being a thoroughly erotic affair.

The ngoma started at around seven o'clock, and was lit by bonfires; chairs were placed for us on the perimeter, and there we sat, enjoying the spectacle, for about two hours. Firelight threw into relief the leaping figures, red like flames themselves, and flickered on the breasts of the girls which bobbed up and down like corks on a wind-whipped water. Long leaping shadows gave an eerie, almost demonic dimension to the scene. But it was monotonous and, for sedentary spectators, after a while tended to bore rather than to excite. The elders sat around the bonfires getting quietly sozzled and devouring bits of poor old Goygoy, which they roasted on the end of long sticks.

The drumming went on all night, throbbing like an elemental heartbeat in the darkness. There is something savage and disturbing about distant African drums: hints of Conrad's *Heart of Darkness* and of O'Neill's *Emperor Jones*. One thinks of human sacrifice and secret rites, of leopard-men and the 'walking dead' and all sorts of forest mysteries and orgies as one draws the blankets over one's head to shut out that insistent rhythmic throb.

I heard a strange story about African drumming which I believe to be true. A friend of mine was working on an aid project in the land of the Azande, on the border of Zaire and Sudan. The Azande, he said, are particularly skilled at drumming, and send coded messages for great distances which are relayed from village to village. Jonathan, this friend, asked one of the drummers to teach him the technique, but did not get very far with it, and of course the messages were in the Azande language which he did not speak. One day he was idly tapping the drum when he noticed that some sort of pattern was emerging from his taps. When he laid the sticks down, the Azande drummer said:

'Do you know that you have been sending a message?'

'What have I been saying?' Jonathan asked.

'My father is dying. My father is dying. My father . . . '

Astonished, Jonathan noted down the time and date. On his return to England he learned that his father had suffered a heart attack from which he had not been expected to recover. Jonathan's wife, desperately concerned, had consciously attempted to will a message from her mind to his. The time coincided with that on which, in faraway Azande country, Jonathan had unknowingly tapped out, in the Azande code, the message: 'My father is dying.' (His father did, in fact, recover.)

Nellie's party was shorter and more sedate than the ngoma. About a dozen of her neighbours came for a Sunday pre-lunch drink. They were a mixed bag, none of them as glamorous, if that is the word, as the small circle of those who had been dubbed by London gossip column writers the Happy Valley set, and lived some fifty miles away in a valley called Wanjohi running down from the Aberdare mountains. The core was very small, never more than perhaps a dozen individuals. (Nairobi had a temperance society with many more members.) They were visited by rich friends from England with a taste for gambling and for sexual promiscuity – how promiscuous we had no idea, nor indeed did we learn of it until years later; at the time, they seemed much like everyone else.[3] My parents did, in fact, know Lady Idina, the queen of this tiny hive, then married to Josslyn, Earl of Errol, who was murdered nine years later. Nellie went over to their house, called Clouds, occasionally to swap plants, the Wanjohi being a splendid gardening region, and must have been unlucky, for she never struck an orgy; though she did once find one of the visitors, Alice de Janzé, asleep on the floor at four in the afternoon. Jos, my father, knew Joss, the Earl, through the Caledonian Society of which Jos was a strong supporter and Joss the chieftain; they met at Caledonian dinners in Nakuru and no doubt had orgies, of sorts, of their own.

But no such gossip-worthy guests came to our Sunday morning party on the lawn, which was surrounded by herbaceous borders of glorious colour and lush growth. There was a buddleia so big that Nellie had cut a sort of arbour out of it big enough to take a table and chairs. Her closest friends among her neighbours were the Lindstroms, who had arrived from Sweden in 1920 with four small children, a lot of optimism and practically no money at all. They lived in a hospitable and cheerful kind of muddle about two miles away. Gillis, known as Fish – his native name because of his expression – was often absent trying to make a little money out of safari work or managing plantations in unhealthy parts of Tanganyika, leaving Ingrid to take care of the children and to the gradual creation of a farm.

Ingrid possessed a quality hard to define; I would not call it placidity since that suggests a certain torpidness, and she was anything but that; her sense of humour was as lively as Nellie's and in her deep, slow, well-articulated voice she would deliver pungent comments which never crossed the border from shrewdness into spite. In all the ups and downs of life – and the Lindstroms had a good many downs – she remained calm, tolerant and good-humoured; I never saw her fly into a temper or give way to despair.

Both Fish and Ingrid had an easy-going outlook which they shared with Africans, so that a harmonious atmosphere prevailed on their farm. Perhaps too harmonious in one sense; Kikuyu families gathered there in numbers bringing their goats and cattle, so that their farm, not a large one, became overstocked. Also it came to be regarded as a sanctuary by those who, for one reason or another, did not want the eye of authority to be focused on them. I do not mean to imply that it became a sort of thieves' kitchen. Authority did its best to keep track of the country's shifting and illiterate population, almost all of whom had no fixed address and were therefore out of reach of forms and means of registration. Every African who left his reserve to seek employment was obliged to carry, generally in a little metal case suspended from his neck, a piece of paper called a kipande, on which was recorded his name, tribe, and fingerprint, and on which his current employer signed him on or off; and every employer was required to keep a register of the people living on his farm, and to notify authority of changes. Some farmers were stricter than others in complying with these regulations, and strictness was not a Lindstrom *forte*. The extended family system was so far extended that an individual might have a hundred relatives, or more. Family visits were very much a way of life, and there was no definition of a visit; it might last a week or ten years.

At the other extreme from the Lindstroms in their attitude to life and labour was the Harries family, headed by Black Harries, so called because of his swarthy countenance and bushy black beard. He was immensely strong. Nellie related how, when the cattle were going through the weekly dip, a young steer got stuck facing in the wrong direction; Black Harries, who happened to be there, picked up the beast in his arms, turned it round and put it back again.

His attitude towards his labour was the reverse of permissive, and he was on bad terms with some of his neighbours, including Ingrid and Nellie; he conducted against them a war of chits which would arrive at all hours with messages such as 'Your squatters' cattle have broken into my maize' or 'I have reason to believe that you are sheltering one of my boys who has run away and is hiding on your land.' No one paid much attention to these missives. Nellie said that the Harries lived like the pigs they kept, in a sort of gypsy encampment surrounded by discarded bones, but she was prejudiced against them, as she was the first to admit.

On the other hand she loved the Barclays, Hugh and Patsy, who lived on a pipeline farm towards the extinct volcano Menengai that rose above what Delamere had called the cow-town of Nakuru. In a sense, Hugh's farming career had started in the trenches of the First World

War where he had been badly gassed, and subsequently advised to seek a drier air than Britain's for the sake of his lungs. Of all those at our little Sunday gathering I think he proved the most successful in achieving his aims – not great wealth or personal fame, but the creation of a complex enterprise ticking over smoothly and supported by a contented human community, and which he was able, many years later, to pass on to his son. Hugh and Patsy had a reputation for looking after their labour force, and the families thereof, especially well.

For many years holidays overseas were ruled out, but when conditions eased and Hugh and Patsy were able to go 'home' now and again, he pursued the small game of Britain, birds and fish, the big game on his doorstep having mainly been ignored; he was too busy, and later became a conservationist. He specialised in dairying, was the first to import Friesians of Dutch rather than British descent, and became one of the country's foremost breeders. And, on his bit of the 'plain of the rhinoceros without any milk', as the Maasai had called this part of the Njoro levels, he bred Kenya's first two-thousand-gallon cow.

Tom and Kate Petrie were Nellie's nearest neighbours, both true Scots; Tom was more of a trader than a farmer, and Kate an excellent but frustrated cook; Tom was away so much that there was no one to cook for. If she got wind of someone being ill or even off colour, round would come a magnificent cake, and possibly a shepherd's pie or rice pudding. Another Scot was Sandy Wright, who had raised the initial down-payment on his land by shooting buffaloes in the forest and taking their hides to the Kavirondo district where the local Africans prized them for making shields. They paid in cattle, and that gave him a start. He was a convivial extrovert who had recently taken to politics and got elected to the Legislative Council, and he was fond of quoting, rather too often, the maxim: 'days of toil and nights of gladness', the gladness being helped on by liberal tots.

Another of our guests was Reggie Pelham-Burn, a hard-bitten, breezy individual, good at weekend polo when he could borrow a mount, who lived on the pipeline with his half-brother Trevor Sheen and a highly respectable, straightlaced widowed mother who dressed, no matter what the weather, in deepest black. She had led, we were given to understand, a sheltered life in Tunbridge Wells until she had been met at Nairobi station by Trevor Sheen in an ox-cart with a posse of all-but-naked Maasai warriors, and bumped off into a remote trading post in the Maasai reserve where Trevor was engaged in exchanging maize-meal and tobacco for cattle and sheep. Now she had settled in a shack on the plain in one of the clumps of black wattle trees, with wire netting instead of windows, an outside privy (which everybody had) and, one would think, very little to do, unless it was to brush dust or mud from her ankle-length skirts and pleated blouses.

The most opulent of our guests was an American, Billy Sewell, who had commissioned Kenya's leading architect, Jan Hoogterp, to build him a palace near Njoro. And a palace it was by local standards, in neo-Spanish style, with patios and marble-tiled verandas and a red-tiled roof and beautiful furniture, mainly French, kept beautifully polished, and Persian rugs strewn about. Billy loved his furniture and feared that the dry atmosphere of the highlands would warp it, and that it needed periodic refreshment; so once a year – or so the story went – he sent it to the Coast to be restored to health by the high humidity.

Billy had spent part of his early life in China, and had brought with him to Njoro two Chinese servants. When we arrived for dinner they greeted us clad in handsome silk kimonos, and Billy affected one too. He had something of a Chinese look himself, being shortish with a wrinkled face and slightly slanting eyes, and at first glance we were in danger of confusing our host with his manservants. The meals matched up to the very highest gastronomic standards, in marked contrast to our usual tough mutton or scrawny fowl. I remember, even fifty years later, a pudding heaped high with threads of spun sugar, each thread as fine as a spider's web, that shone and glittered in the light of the silver candelabra like a great golden fairy-tale wig. It seemed a crime to plunge a spoon into that crown of filaments and destroy it.

Billy Sewell was a Bostonian, very precise, and with a reputation for stinginess spread, I think, mainly by his wife who, citing that as one of her reasons, had left him for a handsome rancher with a less luxurious way of life. Billy's earlier years had been much less epicurean. He had been one of three partners in a most adventurous little enterprise called the Boma Trading Company, whose object had been to open up trade between Abyssinia and the East Africa Protectorate across the 350 miles or so of the desert that was to become the Northern Frontier District of Kenya. This was a bold idea in 1907 when the company was formed with £1000 of capital, and with Winston Churchill's blessing. The moving spirit was Captain Jack Riddell, who had done some surveying in this dangerous borderland not as yet in the grip of the Pax Britannica, and totally without roads, towns or even villages, where wells and water-holes were few and far between.

Early in 1908 Jack Riddell, Billy Sewell and Freddie Ward, all under thirty, arrived in Addis Ababa to seek the Emperor's permission, without which nothing could be done. This, they were warned, might take a year, and the British Consul advised them not to leave the capital without an armed guard. The Legation's interpreter, however, a Scot who had taken part in the battle of Magdala in 1868, said: 'Give me a hundred pounds and I'll fix it', and within a week handed over a scroll bearing the royal seal, which commanded the governors of the Emperor's distant provinces to aid and abet the three foreigners.

They were intent on buying ponies. Abyssinian ponies were famous for their hardihood and endurance, and would find a ready sale in Nairobi, but the export of horses was forbidden. The three young adventurers hoped that the royal seal would overcome this difficulty. Armed with one rifle and a hundred rounds of ammunition they rode across part of the Danakil desert and bought one hundred horses for the equivalent of £2 a head, but they still had to get permission from the local Ras, or governor, to take them across the border into British Somaliland. This the Ras refused to give, despite the Emperor's safe conduct. 'Bribery and plenty of tej', Billy said, 'did the trick', or part of it; the Ras allowed Riddell and the ponies twenty-four hours to get away. As they crossed the border they saw a long line of horsemen galloping towards them – just too late. They drove the horses through Hargeisa to Berbera on the Red Sea, only to be told by customs officials – this part of Somaliland was then a British Protectorate – that the horses would be subject to an export duty of one hundred rupees a head. A good deal of wangling scraped them over this last hurdle; the horses were shipped via Aden to Mombasa and were sold in Nairobi for £30 each.[4]

The Boma Trading Company's agents established posts in what was to become the Northern Frontier District before the Government got there: these stations were at Marsabit and Dolo, and at Moyale on the Abyssinian border. They opened up a trade in sheep and cattle exchanged with the nomads for cloth, copper wire and beads. But the Government was deeply suspicious of these independent traders roaming about the hinterland and permitted, by an agreement Riddell had secured from the Colonial Office, to carry arms. In 1910 the Governor, Sir Percy Girouard, sent up one of the early administrators, Geoffrey Archer, to take over from the Company their camps, equipment and rifles, and their trading posts became government bomas, as they remain today.

There were others among Nellie's neighbours at her party on the lawn: John and Hilda Adams who sent carnations to Nairobi as a sideline, packing them at night when it was coolest and taking them down to the station about midnight; Len Spiers and his wife Kay who bred and trained racehorses; I cannot remember them all. Most of them (not quite all) were hard-working and optimistic – they had to be – striving to keep afloat on the stormy seas of the Depression as best they could. They lived frugally, the going rate for a farm manager was £10 a month. Nearly all of them did manage to survive, if only just.

The time had come for me to move on to Nairobi to make a start on Delamere's biography. It was sad that, after so long an absence, I could stay for so short a time. How much more sensible, I have often thought, were Africans than Europeans in their treatment of time. Although it could not be ignored altogether, they did not surrender to it as we have done. One day was as good as another; tomorrow would come, and what had been left undone today could be continued then, or the day after, or the day after that. They never invented clocks, the tyrants of our age. Even now, when so many have opted for the western way of life, clocks and Africans have never really forged an alliance. This is often a source of irritation, even fury, to Europeans who have chopped up their days into hours, and grown accustomed to keeping appointments, even sometimes to the minute. Time, for most Africans, flows rather than proceeds in measured jumps. Climate is no doubt responsible and, resourceful as we are, we cannot change climates – except for the worse, it seems, as we are doing, by destroying all the trees. So, back to Loresho I returned.

CHAPTER 4

Adolescent Nairobi

Nairobi was at an awkward age when I returned in the early 1930s: a frontier town no longer but not yet to be taken seriously as a capital city. The Norfolk hotel was much the same, though the hitching posts outside for mules and horses had gone, but the New Stanley was a lot bigger and proudly proclaimed itself to be the only hotel north of Johannesburg with a bathroom attached to every bedroom. Other landmarks remained: Elliot's bakery, Duncan's the Grocer, the Post Office and the DC's office always packed with black humanity, and Whiteway Laidlaw's, Nairobi's first and for a long time only department store. Sixth Avenue had not yet been renamed after Delamere. Vacant lots still yawned like gaps between molars, and wooden bungalows on stilts with rusting tin roofs, hot as ovens, still accommodated many government departments. Blue-gums with peeling bark and narrow rustling leaves, mostly planted by John Ainsworth, the town's first Commissioner, cast pools of shade along Government Road, which had been tarmac'd. Rickshaws had been replaced by box-body cars.

To make a box-body, you got hold of a second-hand chassis and built the super-structure out of planks, roofing felt and wire netting. Canvas curtains at the sides were rolled up to be secured by straps, and lowered when it rained. Wire netting was often stretched across the open back and sides to keep in dogs, luggage and the African passengers who crowded into every vehicle that moved. These passengers were hard on the springs, and carrying them was not really altruistic, for when you got stuck they would all leap out and push to the accompaniment of a rousing, rhythmic chant culminating in cries of 'sukuma! sukuma!' (push, push) which seemed to generate sufficient power to lift the vehicle right out of the ruts. My father, who was prone to feeble puns, called them pushengers.

When I left in 1925, most of the pushengers were clad in a light-weight blanket knotted on one shoulder in the manner of a Roman toga; now nearly all wore tattered khaki shirts or trousers, or sometimes a thick, heavy khaki overcoat left over from the First World War. The women had resisted change. They streamed in every morning from shambas outside the town bent double under heavy loads of produce, generally with a little black head, shiny as a billiard-ball, bobbing about on top. So distended were the mothers' ear-lobes that blocks of wood six inches in diameter could be inserted, or even an empty whisky bottle. Only now and again did you see a girl in a shapeless cotton 'mother hubbard' dress, signifying her attachment to a Christian Mission. European attire was more colourful; the fashion was for brightly coloured corduroy trousers and silk shirts for both sexes, and for broad-brimmed hats sometimes adorned by strips of leopard-skin.

'A cross between a dust heap and Lyons' Corner House' was how the town appeared to Daphne Moore, wife of the new Chief Secretary (number two to the Governor) who arrived in 1929. Her first impressions were unfavourable. 'The atmosphere is one of intrigue, suspicion, dishonesty and unkind criticism ... The Service is underpaid, disgracefully housed, and given no encouragement to do honest work.' Governor Sir Edward Grigg, she wrote, was universally distrusted and ran the country in cahoots with two scoundrelly accomplices, Hugh Martin, the Commissioner for Lands, heavily in debt, of dubious honesty and seldom sober, and Grigg's private secretary, Eric Dutton, a devious plotter. The Moores had come from Nigeria, where things were much better ordered. 'Talk is the curse of this country. Even the man who comes about the electric light talks and talks while I stand on leg after leg and finally subside on to the dust-bin.' Grand dinner parties were no better. The food was much too lavish and pretentious – asparagus, lobsters, foie gras in aspic – the conversation boring and the women kittenish, except for Glady Delamere who was 'charming and clever and suggests Elinor Glyn and sofas strewn with tiger skins; the cats in the village say that she has never recovered from her great success with the Prince of Wales.'[1]

Daphne Moore was also far from kittenish – more like an asp, at least as regards her tongue. She was intelligent, well-read, and had considerable talent as a sculptor. I found her alarming, and others felt the same, but her hiss was worse than her bite.

Like most colonial civil servants posted to Kenya, the Moores had been warned against the wiles of the wicked settlers and advised to keep them at arms' length. At first they followed this advice faithfully, but as time went on her reactions became less prickly and she wrote: 'We are not likely to get into the pockets of the settlers, but it seems silly to both of us to take up a snooty attitude to them socially; it doesn't help matters officially for one thing.' Even the Governor earned words of praise. He was informal and unpompous, and 'I have never before met a Governor who neither walked first into a room nor was served first at meals. He is most genial and easy to talk to.' She attended a dance at Government House in honour of the Neville Chamberlains, but they got stuck on the plains and failed to arrive; meanwhile Tich Miles, the senior aide-de-camp, had invited all the people normally barred from Government House on moral grounds, and a good time was had by all.

If Daphne Moore was unkind to Eric Dutton, he had only himself to blame. He deliberately cultivated a pose of boorishness and enjoyed his reputation for ill manners, while at the same time ingratiating himself with the nobs of this small colonial world. He was the sort of man one could imagine tapping a Minister on the shoulder and, with a knowing smile, whispering into his ear a piece of scandalous gossip. But the image he projected of himself was only half true. He was a brave man, for one thing; so badly had both legs been smashed in the war that he was obliged to wear heavy iron calipers and to use a stick; nevertheless he climbed Mt Kenya and got to within five hundred yards of the top. At that time, in 1926, only Sir Halford Mackinder and his Swiss guide had reached the summit, in 1899, so even for a fit man this would have been a considerable achievement.

Beneath his off-putting manner and homely appearance lay a vein of creativeness which found expression, when opportunity could be manoeuvred into offering, in designing buildings, gardens and parks. When Sir Edward Grigg, Governor from 1925 to 1930, invited Britain's great imperial architect, Sir Herbert Baker, to design a new Government House in Nairobi, a smaller version in Mombasa and other public buildings elsewhere, Eric Dutton sat at Baker's feet and acquired a good working knowledge of the trade, as well as the friendship of the brilliant but erratic Hollander, Jan Hoogterp, whom

Baker put in charge of his East African building programme. After Dutton moved on to Northern Rhodesia, he summoned Hoogterp to create in that country's barren bush a complete new capital to replace the inadequate little township of Livingstone at the southern tip of the Protectorate. Dutton, with great relish, organised the planting of a nursery of thousands of indigenous trees and ornamental shrubs with which to adorn it. 'There was something spellbinding', he wrote, 'about seeing row after row of trees, each labelled with the street or avenue where they would take up permanent residence, and knowing that they would go on growing and giving their shade and their magnificence for years to come.'² After crippling set-backs and prodigious exertions, the future tree-lined capital of Zambia, Lusaka, was officially opened on 31 May 1935.

Sir Edward Grigg had been appointed to his governorship on the understanding that Kenya, Uganda, Tanganyika and Zanzibar were soon to be united in some form of federation, that Nairobi was to be its capital and that he, Sir Edward, was to become its first Governor-General. The old bijou residence in stockbroker's black-and-white that had hitherto served to house the King's representatives was clearly no place for a Governor-General, and a grandification was planned. Grigg, a big man with big ideas – he was one of the *Round Table* school founded by Milner's Young Men – would have no truck with merely adding on an extra wing or two, so behind Baker's stately white columns and imposing portico arose a splendid edifice which swallowed the old one like a whale ingesting a krill. By Kenya's frontier standards the cost was outrageous, some £80,000, and its taxpayers – the white and brown ones – squealed indignantly and talked of *folies de grandeur*. Their anger rose to boiling point when a large ballroom was added at top speed to be ready for a visit by the then Prince of Wales.

There is a thesis to be written on the legacy of royal visits to colonial possessions. Such visits were intended to strengthen loyalty to the Crown and the cohesion of the Empire. Their on-the-spot effects were more down to earth. In many a far-flung outpost of Empire a gleam came into the eye of many a district officer as he reached for a file in which was embalmed a cherished project clobbered by a Treasury veto. Now at last the chance had come to achieve that longed-for road, to improve that unhygienic market, that inadequate district headquarters, dispensary, school, shed for drying hides in, seed farm or ghee-making project. How was Royalty to get from A to B along a road without bridges? Should a Princess be exposed to the squalor of a makeshift native hospital without an operating theatre? How were chiefs and elders to present their Loyal Address in seemly fashion in a dilapidated court-house whose roof had fallen in? A reluctant Treasury scraped the bottom of its barrel, road-gangs wielded picks with a will, lorries bumped through the bush loaded with corrugated iron, cement and tins of paint, district commissioners purred with delight. I know of at least one rutted track, passable only in dry weather, that had been converted into an all-weather road to enable a Princess to lunch with a remote farmer whose dwelling (in which a loo had to be installed) commanded a spectacular view. As a result, local farmers were at long last able to get their produce to the railway station during the rains. In time, along came international agencies with tarmac and machinery, and the track became a scenic highway, possibly a strategic link as well.

The Griggs made a notable impact on the raw Colony. 'They raised the tone' I was told. King George V took a lively interest in the conduct of his East African subjects, and was pained by rumours of the white farmers' slovenly habit of dining in dressing-gowns and pyjamas. Sir Edward was instructed never to allow such behaviour in his presence. In Nairobi the situation did not arise, but when the Griggs visited up-country farmers they found the royal ukaze an embarrassment. Some of His Excellency's hosts, requested to change into suits, thought his attitude stuck-up and pompous. Queen Mary had issued her own Royal Command to Lady Grigg: no divorcée was to be received at Government House. Ned Grigg wrote in his memoirs[3] that this injunction was strictly obeyed, but when I asked his widow about it she laughed and said 'Nonsense!' Perhaps some divorcées slipped in while he was away. Those were the days of 'guilty parties' taken in adultery by a hotel chambermaid bringing in the early morning tea; the wronged spouse was perhaps exempted from the royal ban. But Happy Valley-ites were not invited to Government House, despite their high rating in Debrett's.

Lady Grigg, Joanie to her friends, was as strong a persoanlity as her husband. Young, handsome, full of energy, and equally determined to set the mark of progress on the country, she saw that the wellbeing of women and their babies had been sadly neglected. Not a single maternity hospital for Africans had been established, nor had a single African nurse been even partially trained. Medical missionaries had done what they could, but for the most part African women had their babies as they had always done, in dark, unventilated, smoky huts shared with sheep and goats, attended by old women who had never heard of disinfectants, sterile instruments or even soap and water. If things went wrong, the witch-doctor was called in to appease with incantations and spells the offended spirits who had caused the trouble. The fact that nearly every girl had been circumcised, which left scar tissue that impeded childbirth, made matters worse. It was no wonder that infant mortality was high, and deaths in childbirth common.

So, in trying to change all this, Joan Grigg faced a daunting task, at first almost single-handed. Neither the women themselves, ultra-conservative in outlook, nor the tribal elders, wanted change. On the contrary, they resented interference. In order to receive even the most basic kind of training in midwifery, a girl would have to leave home, live amongst strangers and learn new ways utterly at variance with those of her own people. Most likely she had been pledged from childhood to a husband, and perhaps the first instalment of the bride-price paid. Her father could scarcely be expected to welcome the overthrow of ancient custom and the disruption of his plans.

It was not only Africans who shied away from innovation. Many Europeans doubted the wisdom of 'forcing the pace', the official phrase for taking action of almost any kind. African resentment against interference was like an unexploded bomb that might go off at a touch. It very nearly *had* gone off when the Church of Scotland Mission had tried to abolish female circumcision amongst the Kikuyu. In 1929 a sixty-three-year-old woman missionary (a Miss Stumpf) had been forcibly circumcised and left to bleed to death. Unrest had been such that the Government had backed away from any active attempt to discourage the custom. Time and education, they said, must be the remedy.

So, no money was available with which to build even the simplest of maternity hospitals, to train nurses or to open clinics for women and their babies. Starting from scratch, Joan Grigg set out to raise the money. She appealed, cajoled and bullied, set up committees and relentlessly chivvied commercial firms and business men, trusts and people like the Aga Khan, whose generosity was proverbial. The culmination of the appeal was a mammoth Child Welfare fête at Government House. Not everyone enjoyed being chivvied. The future writer Karen Blixen, then living on her coffee farm at the foot of the Ngong hills, wrote crossly to her mother of 'Lady Grigg's confounded fête' which she thought 'crazy and barbaric'. People were being 'pumped and badgered' to give objects for sale. Faced with a request to supply roasted almonds for the tea pavilion, she doubted whether her cook remembered how to do them. (Not difficult, surely?) In a fertile flight of fancy she compared Joan Grigg's fête to the actions of the mayor of a French provincial town who, at a cost to his citizens of 100,000 livres, had presented Madame de Montespan with a barge with silken sails in which to proceed down a river.[4]

The fête itself she found 'utterly exhausting', the only bright moments being visits to the cocktail bar where, she wrote, drinks were concocted from 'about twenty different left-overs'; no wonder these gave her 'instant strength'. However, the fête made over £3,000, and in time the Baroness became reconciled to the Griggs. They could be 'tremendously pleasant', she wrote, in contrast to most of the British, whom she found bourgeois, dreary, ill-bred and philistine. But with the Griggs she could discuss Shakespeare and the Old Testament. Despite a horror of everything to do with childbirth she allowed herself to be conducted round Joan Grigg's newly established maternity home, where she pitied a young woman being wheeled into the labour ward – 'how nice it would be if one could sit on an egg'.

Maternity services had fared better in Uganda, where the hospital started by the great missionary doctor Albert Cook had been training girls as nurses for some time. He loaned two of them to staff the cottage hospital at Mombasa that Joan had raised funds for and had built, which opened its doors in 1926. To start with, no one came. Then a single African woman braved the unknown and was safely delivered. This was the start of a trickle that became a flood. A second hospital was built in the Pumwani district of Nairobi; now enormously enlarged, it is still in business nearly sixty years later. Nor did Joan Grigg confine herself to the welfare of Africans. An Indian maternity hospital followed, Indian girls were coaxed into training, and a hostel for European nurses was built.[5]

Joan Grigg's was a remarkable achievement, and her name is commemorated in the Lady Grigg maternity home in Mombasa. But malice directs the gods, the fates, or whatever it may be that orders, if anything does, our human destiny, and many of our virtuous aims lead towards disaster. To save the lives of babies and mitigate the suffering of mothers must be seen as a great and Christian Good. Death by starvation of tens of thousands, eventually millions, of people, and especially of children, can be seen only as a great Evil. Yet the first creates the second. Kenya's birthrate is now the highest in the world; the average family size is eight and a half children. This flood of babies is drowning the resources of the country, over-population has become the greatest threat to the nation's stability. Would it have been kinder in the long run to have let nature continue that cruel and ancient culling method to which every species must submit, lest it overwhelm the others? Goodness knows.

A very different regime at Government House followed that of the Griggs. Gone were the grand parties, the French chef, a certain panache and imaginative, if costly, gestures – the visiting Prince of Wales was supplied every morning with fresh trout flown from a farm in the Aberdare mountains in time for breakfast. Sir Joseph Byrne, a former Royal Inniskillen Fusilier, had risen by way of the post of deputy Adjutant-General in Ireland to command the Royal Irish Constabulary, and to be rewarded by the Governorship first of the Seychelles, then of Sierra Leone, and finally of Kenya. His cautious approach to decision-making led to a frequent response of 'yes, but–' and hence his local nickname Butty Byrne. With her usual asperity Daphne Moore wrote: 'I have listened to the damn man telling me the same dull stories about himself every time I meet him.' But he had his human side too. On New Year's Eve, 1932, Glady Delamere gave a party at Muthaiga Club which included the Byrnes. 'The Haldemans were there. Lady Idina [formerly Hay, formerly Gordon, formerly Wallace] got herself introduced to H.E. and the whole club held their sides to see Kenya's most notorious vamp clasped in the arms of the King's representative who was apparently making the most of it.'[6]

Butty Byrne went on leave soon after my arrival in Nairobi, and it was to Daphne's husband, Chief Secretary Henry Monck-Mason Moore, that I applied for permission to use the secretariat library and to see as many of the files as possible that related to Delamere's career. Research into colonial history was very amateurish in those days. Proper archives, public record offices, embargoes, fifty (later thirty) years' rule and all the rest were lacking. You just asked questions and borrowed papers and, at least in the provincial and district centres, no one seemed to mind whether you returned them or not. There was little sense of history then, no idea that these records might interest generations to come. When – this was some years later – I visited Meru, north of Mount Kenya, and asked to see the district record books, I was told that the last DC, in a fit of tidyness, had burnt the lot. Luckily some records have survived and so have personal diaries, and much has since been saved, classified and made available to students in the Rhodes House library in Oxford and elsewhere.

But things were different in Nairobi's secretariat. Delamere's role as a goad prodding the Government's backside naturally had not endeared him to the senior officials, and their attitude was evasive, not to say obstructive. Then, unexpectedly, there came a softening and a change. I was given a desk in the secretariat's library and shown most of the files I had hoped to see. I had no idea what had brought about this change and only later discovered that I owed it, in the main, to the current deputy head of the Treasury, George Sandford. He nursed a good deal more impatience with bureaucratic constipation than most of his colleagues, was interested in Kenya's history, and, most unusually, had edited the *East African Standard* for several years before returning to the Colonial Service. He had known and admired Delamere and thought that the full story should be told. I remember him as a slightly built, sandy-haired man, bright-eyed and with a twinkle, who gave out a bird-like sense of eagerness and interest in all that went on. Eventually he climbed the ladder to a minor governorship (Bahamas) and a knighthood.

Delamere had first reached East Africa in 1897, and ever since his life had been so closely intertwined with the country's development that I was clearly committed to a history of white settlement as well as a biography. Of white settlement only, not of all aspects of the country's story set in its historical perspective. That was a task for professional historians and beyond my powers. I called the book *White Man's Country* because that phrase was a summary of Delamere's political aims, and one he often used. It was not intended as an historical assessment.

Curiously enough, when people argued as to whether Kenya was, or was not, a white man's country, they were not then making a political judgment. They were making a medical judgement. Some held that people of European stock would not be able to establish a healthy, self-perpetuating population on the equator, and at an altitude of over 5,000 feet, because the actinic rays of the sun, combined with the rarefied atmosphere, would sap the vitality of the European stock and lead to its degeneration. Several doctors took this view, but Delamere and others disagreed. Ironically, those who believed that Kenya would prove to be a 'white man's country' on this basis were probably right. Insofar as we can tell – and there are third and fourth generations of white Kenyans – the stock seems able to maintain its vigour, though perhaps four generations, and on so small a scale, is not enough on which to base a judgement. I do not think it occurred to anyone that politics, not health, would decide the issue.

Loresho provided me with an ideal base. It was a comfortable, creeper-covered stone bungalow with the usual deep veranda, built around a central quadrangle with a fig tree, sacred to the Kikuyu, in the middle. Glady had her own separate cottage, and a nanny with her three children lived in another. The altitude was higher than Nairobi's, the air crisper and cooler and, after the rains, filled with the orange-blossomy scent of creamy-white flowers that burst out all over the coffee bushes surrounding the house. Indoors, a scent of madonna lilies hung upon the air. Glady had been thirty years younger than Delamere, whom she had married as his second wife in 1928 when he had less than four years to live.

Glady was a very hospitable person with a wide and varied collection of friends, and you never knew whom you might find breakfasting on the veranda, having arrived overnight from some distant farm or outpost. She had the art of mixing together different kinds of people and keeping conversation on the boil. In argument she could be aggressive, but then she would disarm her guests with a deep throaty chuckle and a sudden unexpected turn of phrase. Sometimes, after dinner, everyone would go on to dance at Torr's hotel to the rhythmic, sentimental tunes of the thirties – Smoke Gets in Your Eyes; Dance, Dance Little Lady; Poor Little Rich Girl; Bye, Bye Blackbird; These Foolish Things – all rather doom-laden songs, love was never a carefree experience. For lunch there was a small restaurant, Chez Gaby, newly opened in Government Road by a genuine Frenchman where the food was excellent and cheap, especially sea-food brought up overnight from Mombasa packed in ice.

Like Joan Grigg, with whom she had been friends from childhood, Glady was much concerned with good works, as well as with social life and local politics. She was canvassing for a seat on Nairobi's Municipal Council, elections to that body having recently been introduced. These elections were for whites only, the Indian members being nominated by the Governor: no blacks, but then there were no black rate-payers. The Council, closely modelled on the British pattern, elected its own mayor and deputy. The numbers on the voters' roll remind one of English parliamentary elections before the Reform Bill: Glady was duly elected in 1934 by 236 votes to 80. She became an able, energetic councillor, and four years later was elected mayor, and then twice re-elected to that position.

Welfare among Africans in Nairobi's shanty-towns, and a charity that helped distressed Europeans, also took up a lot of Glady's time. As the Depression deepened, farmers and business-men went bankrupt in all directions and their fate was grim. There was no social security, no insurance, no dole, nothing between them and starvation but the kindness of still-solvent friends, and, as a last resort, classification as Distressed British Subjects – provided that they *were* British – when they were shipped at government expense, penniless and steerage class, back to Britain. The *East African Standard* was full of pathetic pleas for help. 'Steady worker, do anything for keep only.' One John Hickey of Ruiru, declared bankrupt, 'had lost all his money in a coffee shamba, an old man now penniless with no means even to get to Court that day'. Anyone with cash in the bank could pick up marvellous bargains. 'Farm Sale. Kilima Logi estate, 998 acres, 381 planted in coffee with factory, stores and two houses, sold for £1,000 to pay the mortgage.'

Glady was involved in a charity which helped as many of these destitutes as much as it could, but more of her time was spent at Pumwani in an African clinic, washing and weighing babies and trying to persuade their mothers that a diet of almost undiluted carbohydrates based on maize-meal and cassava did not build the best babies.

All this invokes an image of Lady Bountiful dispensing soup to the poor, and that was more or less the position. In the towns – and there were only two to speak of – the gap between the relatively rich and the evidently poor was wider even than in Europe, and roughly corresponded to the gap between the races. So the Lady Bountifuls were white and recipients of the soup were black. But this did not apply in country districts. Some of the Maasai, for example, were richer than the very richest Europeans – a single family might own several thousand head of cattle. They kept their wealth on the hoof instead of in banks, and felt no need to spend it on consumer goods. Few, if any, Indians either dispensed soup or received it. Their two separate communities, Hindu and Muslim, looked after their own and did not invite outside interference.

Glady as Lady Bountiful weighing African babies at a welfare clinic does not at all accord with her image as others have presented it. She has been depicted as a bossy, bitchy and emotionally unbalanced woman, endlessly carousing at Muthaiga Club with Happy Valleyites, and so possessively in love with Lord Erroll that she was even suspected of having shot him – 'He was her man, and he done her wrong.' This may have been a true portrayal at the time of the Erroll murder case in 1942 – I last saw Glady in 1938 – but I doubt it. When I knew her, while she certainly caroused quite often at Muthaiga Club, the Happy Valley was not her scene.

Joss Erroll had casual affairs with a great many women and Glady was probably among them, but he was not the man she loved and hoped to marry when he was free to do so; he was separated but not then divorced from his wife. When war grew imminent, Alistair left East Africa and she realised that the affair was over for good. When he got his freedom, he married someone else. Her antidote to despair was non-stop war-work, mainly in canteens for soldiers and airmen who flocked to Nairobi when it became the Allied base for the Ethiopian campaign. In this she was tireless, her life became frenetic and if at times she seemed unbalanced, this was because she needed to fill every minute and did not dare to stop. She burnt herself out. A stroke followed and she died, aged forty-five, in 1943.

Had Glady been quite the over-bearing and promiscuous character some of those who never knew her believed her to be, I doubt whether she would have enjoyed the friendship of the Taylors, Charles and Kit. They were pillars of respectability. Charles was jovial, rubicund and avuncular. He had been the pioneer of coffee growing in the Thika district and had helped my parents to establish their own plantation. 'Mr Taylor came up' runs an entry in Nellie's diary for a day in April 1914. 'Planting coffee all day, busy counting etc: Finished in evening, total 33,278 trees planted 9 x 9, 54 acres about.' Members of this small white community starting their plantations went on calling each other Mr Taylor, Mr Gooch, Mr So-and-so (not many Mrs's) until the First World War broke it all up, and the men rode off to Nairobi to join the East African Mounted Rifles. Charles Taylor survived four years of bush campaigning in Tanganyika in pursuit of von Lettow Vorbeck and his elusive army.

After his return from the wars, Charles became a boardroom farmer as well as a practical one; his was the moving spirit in founding the Coffee Board of Kenya which organised the marketing of the entire crop; he sat on the boards of various banks and companies, oversaw the management of many plantations, and lived to be the Grand Old Man of coffee to whom everyone came for advice. He had been one of Delamere's trustees, and could not have been more helpful to me, as I think he was to everyone.

Kit Taylor was tall and thin, grave in manner, precise in speech, orderly in mind, Christian in outlook, and given to good works among Africans. An unobtrusive sense of humour underlay the gravitas which was one's first impression, and she was (and is) an excellent mimic. The Taylors dwelt in a cottage at Loresho with their only child, Kathini, called after another coffee estate. Kathini inherited Charles' business acumen and Kit's stalwart spirit, and, after the white farmers' diaspora, was to become the founder and boss of a successful property agency in London.

Kit had reached East Africa in 1904 when her father had been appointed Nairobi's first Town Clerk. Ted and Helen Sanderson had started their new life in tents with two camp beds and sleeping bags, two trunks to sit on, a folding table and very little else. Hyenas howled all round, their whoops and chuckles mingling with the thump of native drums. Later, they moved into a wooden bungalow so rickety that it shook when their terrier ran across the veranda; their bedroom had no windows but five doors. When Helen bought some real china cups at a sale, having hitherto made do with chipped tin mugs, she felt 'uplifted'. Amid these primitive conditions – 'we could not get a candlestick so we made a hole in a potato and cut it flat, and it did quite well' – the ladies dressed to the nines when they dined out. In August 1904 a party of eighteen invited to Government House sat down at a table decorated with pink roses and silk mats, and arches of asparagus fern embellished the doorways. After dinner everybody sang, Ted's 'Fairy of the Ring' winning several encores. At a luncheon party at the same venue Helen, properly corseted, wore a white satin and lace blouse, a white scarf and a broad-brimmed black hat. Afterwards they all went to the races where the principal event, a steeplechase, had three entrants; Sir Claud de Crespigny won in a canter. There were only about twelve horses in Nairobi, so the racing must have lacked variety, if not incident. (Meinertzhagen recorded that a rhino had had to be shoo'd off the course before one of the races could start.)[7]

One hundred guests, a sizeable proportion of Nairobi's white population, picnic'd with the Governor and his lady in the forest, played games until tea-time, and then danced the Lancers in the open to the music of the Kings' African Rifles' band. That evening was something of an anti-climax, however; the Sandersons dined with the bank manager, the cook got plastered and howled outside the door until the host went out and thrashed him, when he howled louder than ever. Helen Sanderson attempted to drown the uproar by pounding on a piano, but when a snake was found under Ted's chair the hostess understandably went off into a fit of hysterics. In that legendary Nairobi, you could buy six pounds of mutton for one rupee, about seven pence, and pay your somewhat unreliable servants – they seemed to get drunk a great deal – the equivalent of about 28 pence a month.[8]

CHAPTER 5

Cockie, Blix, and the
Prince of Wales

Almost every 'early days' account of Kenya brings in Jim Elkington, a resplendent figure who rode handsome horses and imported a pack of English fox-hounds with which to pursue jackals and small antelopes on his farm, Masara, about six miles from the centre of Nairobi. Sometimes the quarry led hounds and hunters into the nearby Kikuyu reserve, and Nellie, freshly out from England where she had pursued the fox over green pastures, was startled to hear a view-holloa followed by the cry: 'There they are, running like hell among the bananas!' That was in 1913.

The bungalow in which the Elkingtons had lived in, I think, 1905 was still there when I was at Loresho. So was Mrs Jim, as she was always known, a stoutish, respectable old lady, and her only child, Margaret. The resplendent Jim, who had a roving eye, had died of gunshot wounds believed to have been self-inflicted because a married lady had refused to go off with him, but there was a rumour, probably no more, that the gunshot wounds had been inflicted by the lady.

Masara was such a perfect example of the Early Colonial style of settler dwelling that I wished it could have been preserved as a folk museum, complete with bleached and horned animal skulls lining the walls, a veranda that ran all round the ramshackle wooden bungalow, littered with riding crops and bits of saddlery; with dog-bowls lying in wait to trip you up and the dogs themselves waddling about, fat dachshunds as I remember; with a population of cats, and a caged parrot so positioned that it gave early warnings as to the nature of callers who approached the bungalow's steps. If they had black faces the parrot would call: 'Tafuta pesa! Tafuta pesa!' meaning 'look for money' – the assumption being that the caller was offering bananas, eggs or some other commodity for sale. A cry of 'Just coming! Just coming!' greeted white-faced visitors. But I suppose the bungalow was too far gone in white-antery to have survived much longer. Coffee bushes reached almost to the veranda steps. Most of the furniture had been bought at auction sales about thirty years before and looked it.

The Elkingtons had brought up their daughter on strict Victorian lines, sending her to bed at six o'clock until she was seventeen or eighteen years old. Margaret never went to school, and grew up to be rather simple-minded, but knowledgeable about horses and their breeding. Her youthful playmate and companion had been a large black-maned lion named Paddy, an amiable beast raised from a cub who roamed the place at will, uncaged. Then one day instinct erupted and he seized a visitor, a young girl named Beryl Clutterbuck, by the leg. A posse of syces headed by Jim brandishing a whip came to the rescue and Beryl was freed, and recovered, but Paddy was caged for the rest of his life. All stories about potentially dangerous pets end sadly in one way or another.[1]

Regardless of the whims of fashion, both Mrs Jim and Margaret continued to dress in ankle-length skirts made of khaki drill, blouses buttoned at the neck, and black button boots, though Margaret wore a divided skirt for riding. After about thirty years at Masara, they decided to replace their tin hip-bath, filled with debbis carried in from the kitchen, by a modern porcelain appliance filled from taps. With considerable reluctance, Margaret agreed to take the first plunge. Like the dachshunds, she had by then grown somewhat portly, and the bath must have been a small one: she found herself stuck. Her mother was unable to dislodge her. A frantic search ensued for some garment with which Margaret could be covered before help could be called in. Mrs Jim found an old sou'wester oilskin in which she swathed her daughter; houseboys were summoned and, amid rousing cries of 'pull! pull! pull harder!' Margaret was extricated. She never used that bath again.

In all the years they had lived in East Africa they had never once been 'home'. Then came the coffee boom of the 'fifties and, after about half a century, they took the great decision to see England once again. Their own ways had not changed, and they did not expect England's to have done so either. At the last moment, Margaret rebelled; she could not face a parting from the dogs and cats. But the fares had been paid, and she was almost dragged into the aeroplane in floods of tears. They planned to stay at Brown's hotel in Dover Street, to hire a car with chauffeur, visit such relatives as survived, and buy new outfits. When Mrs Jim went shopping, she was appalled: the shops were full of horrible, indecent garments she would rather die than wear. Fortunately she found a dressmaker who agreed to copy exactly the garments she had brought with her. There was a long chase, eventually fruitful, after button boots.

Nevertheless, the visit was not a success. There were too many changes; Margaret was homesick and wrote a postcard to the dachshunds every day. They cut short their holiday and were thankful to be back again. Had nothing in England, a friend enquired of Mrs Jim, altered for the better? Yes, she said, after some thought; London was quieter. The friend was surprised. London's roaring traffic could hardly be described as quiet. 'Quieter than flys and omnibuses,' Mrs Jim replied.

Mrs Jim died not long after this excursion and Margaret never left East Africa again. The dachshunds grew fatter and more sluggish, the cats sleeker, the house dirtier, curtains and covers more frayed, but Margaret's horses thrived and won a satisfactory number of races. She died in 1976, aged 81.

Soon after my arrival in Nairobi the famous Laura Corrigan appeared: famous for her wealth, derived from her husband's steel mills in the United States; for her lavish hospitality; and for her dedication to the pursuit of people of title, and wherever possible of royal blood. The most distinguished among the guests at her dinner parties, held in the former home of Mrs George Keppel, would, after enjoying a meal prepared by (it was said) the best chef in London, receive a costly gift – a gold cigarette case, say, or a diamond wrist-watch. Game, set and match went to the hostess who entertained the Prince of Wales, and in time she achieved this ambition.

An African safari was on the list of recreations. Early in 1933 Laura Corrigan left Nairobi for the bush accompanied by the Vicomte de la Rochefoucauld, Count and Countess Paul Munster, two white hunters, a French maid, and Cockie, one of Nellie's oldest friends. She and I, then aged eighteen, had travelled together to England in 1925 in a small, slow, cramped and scrupulously clean Dutch vessel whose plump and jovial captain had ogled Cockie outrageously, and shared with her many quips and sallies which made him shake like a jelly. He stood us both van der Humm liqueurs every evening after dinner. Cockie declared that I lost my passport three times, once at each port of call, but of this I have no recollection. On our arrival in London she had taken me on a shopping spree among entrancing dress materials whose names I had never even heard of – crêpe de chine, georgette, triple minon (incredibly light and fine) – and then on to a 'little woman round the corner' from Belgrave Square who had fashioned them, for next to nothing, into garments considerably more presentable than the khaki shirts and shorts or trousers in which my life had hitherto been spent.

Cockie had come to Kenya immediately after the First World War with her husband Ben Birkbeck, hoping, as all the soldier-settlers did, to make their fortunes. They soon ran out of money and Ben went back to England to raise some more. This left Cockie homeless. 'Nellie invited me for a weekend and I stayed for three months,' she declared. They laughed for much of the time. Cockie had a repertoire of music hall songs described in those days as risqué. 'You don't know Nellie as I do, said the naughty little bird in Nellie's hat', was a favourite because of my mother's name. No one knew how it went on, but several versions were invented.

It was during Ben's absence in England that Cockie met the Baron Bror von Blixen-Finecke, husband of Tania, or Karen, author of *Out of Africa*, who later was to write under the name of Isak Dinesen. The Blixen marriage was already on the rocks. Tania's famous love affair with Denys Finch Hatton was under way and the Baron, Blix as he was known, had been expelled by Tania's family from the management of their farm at Ngong. The farm was heading for the rocks too, though not yet actually on them. Blix, possessed of much charm but no money, was living a kind of gypsy life in the bush with no fixed abode, existing on tick, and dodging his creditors. There was a shop in Nairobi called The Dustpan, kept by a Mr Jacobs, where Blix got his bare necessities. Mr Jacobs was patient, but there came a time when Blix was threatened with imprisonment for debt. He was in despair. Cockie offered Mr Jacobs her pearls in settlement. Mr Jacobs refused the pearls, saying: 'The Baron will hear no more of this little difficulty.' And he did not.

Blix and Cockie worked out an unusual way to make their assignations. They concealed their messages in the barrel of Blix's rifle, which was taken to Tania's farm manager, who acted as go-between. 'It must be our secret,' Cockie said of their affair. One day the manager's wife discovered the ruse, informed a furious Tania, and Blix wrote: 'It is our secret no longer.' In 1922 Tania and Blix were divorced, thankfully on his part and somewhat reluctantly on hers. Despite Blix's extravagance, fecklessness and philandering, the hearts of neither friends nor wives ever hardened against him. Cockie's divorce from Ben followed two years later. 'I hope you'll both be very happy,' said a friend after their wedding. 'So do I,' Cockie replied, 'but that may be difficult, literally without a penny.' The friend's response was to offer Cockie £800 a year to go to Tanganyika, locate some land whose lease he had been granted, and plant coffee.

So they set out in a rickety old lorry with a tent, basic supplies and two African servants. Their destination was Babati, a small cluster of dukas lying about a hundred miles south of Arusha, northern Tanganyika's bush-capital. They set to work to clear the bush and build themselves a shack with a corrugated iron roof to catch rain-water, which at first was all the water they had in the dry season; the land lacked a spring or river as well as almost everything else. When the rains broke they had a great deal too much water; floods surrounded them on all sides and cut them off for weeks at a time.

'They were the happiest years of my life,' Cockie said. Yet she was nothing if not gregarious. Had they no neighbours, I enquired? One, she replied, a Doctor Popp, not a medical doctor but a learned Rhodes Scholar. He had a charming young wife, who left their home once a year to have a baby in Arusha. 'That was her annual holiday.'

Arusha consisted of two streets lined with Indian dukas, a couple of banks, a post office and the New Arusha hotel. To reach it, after a hundred jolting miles, was as great a thrill, Cockie said, as she had formerly experienced on approaching Paris. Arriving after nightfall, they were beckoned by a distant blaze of lights, or at least a twinkle, and drew up at the hotel to luxuriate in a four-course meal, a real bath, news of the outside world, a proper bed, and the anticipation of collecting their mail next morning. There was even a telephone and you could ring up Nairobi, though you could not count on getting through.

Soon after they had settled at Babati, Blix was summoned to Arusha by Denys Finch Hatton, who was in charge of an important safari. The client was the Prince of Wales. Blix was invited to join the safari as second hunter; Cockie went back to Babati, only to be awakened from her sleep by the arrival of five weary, hungry and bedraggled travellers: Blix and Finch Hatton with the Prince and two aides, the Hon. Piers Legh and Alan Lascelles. They demanded food, but Cockie told them that the meat-safe was empty. 'You must have *something*,' said the Prince. 'Only eggs.' 'Well then, scrambled eggs.' They scrambled the eggs together. 'Is Blixen leaving you all alone here?' the royal guest enquired. Cockie said yes. 'Then you'd better come with us.' So Cockie did.

The hunters' main objective was to shoot a lion. Plenty of lions were about, and the best chance of success was to rise before dawn and hope to find one or more still feeding on an overnight kill. The Prince liked to sit up late talking and playing his accordion, thus rendering everyone unfit for early rising, sharp-eyed tracking and a steady aim next morning. Protocol demanded that the Prince should make the first move to go to bed. The hunters persuaded Cockie to break it by pleading weariness and retiring early. The others sprang briskly to their feet and did the same. Left alone, the Prince played his accordion to himself until two o'clock in the morning, and at dawn was just as bleary-eyed as ever. Nevertheless, he did get his lion.

The safari was abruptly ended by the news of King George V's dangerous illness. The night before the Prince started on a dash to his father's bedside by car, train and finally naval destroyer, he remarked: 'To think that in a few days I may be King of England!' 'And what, sir, will you do then?' 'I shall do exactly what I like!' was the reply. Cockie felt a trifle apprehensive. He added that he would put back the clocks at Sandringham and Windsor, Edward VII having kept them half an hour fast to counter his consort's habit of always being late.

In the Prince's character, Cockie recalled, self-indulgence and consideration for others were curiously blended. Even when on safari, he would abandon the chase after animals to chase almost any personable young human female who crossed his path. At Dodoma, he turned up several hours late at a formal dinner party, after disappearing into the night with the wife of a very junior official; and when in Nairobi he invited two young typists to Government House (Cockie said), filled them with the Griggs' champagne and persuaded them to indulge in that old Nairobi pastime of dancing on the table. On the other hand, Cockie had admired an ice-making machine he had brought on the safari. 'I'll send you one,' he told her. She thought no more of it, but several months later the device arrived at Babati with the compliments of the Prince of Wales.

This was a relaxed and cheerful party, with the Prince in an easygoing frame of mind. But you never knew just how far you could go (Cockie said), no matter how close the relationship. One of the Prince's oldest and closest friends was called G. Trotter. After the advent of Mrs Simpson, at the time when everyone concerned was trying to keep the affair hushed up, Trotter suggested to the Prince as tactfully as possible that he should not, in public places, allow Mrs Simpson to take his cigarette from his lips and place it between her own. 'I hope, sir, I know you well enough to say this,' Trotter added. 'G, you do *not* know me well enough,' the Prince replied, and he never spoke to Trotter again.

The Blixens' idyll at Babati ended. The coffee did not thrive and the enterprise was closed down by its owner. Cockie started a dress shop in Nairobi while Blix turned back to hunting for his livelihood, and also resumed his pursuit of attractive ladies. He was in turn pursued by a lady who had never met him but had heard so much about him in their native Sweden that she had resolved to become the third Baroness Blixen. So she set out for Africa, arrived at Babati, where Blix had his safari base, and announced that she had come to stay. And stay she did.

For a while Blix, African-style, enjoyed the company of one wife in the bush and another in Nairobi; but when a friend invited him to stay and he accepted with the rider: 'I shall bring both wives,' Cockie responded with the edict: 'You will take only one.' He took Eva. So the marriage ended.

Cockie took as her third and last husband the handsome Hollander Jan Hoogterp. They moved to Johannesburg, where living was expensive and entertaining on a lavish scale necessary, Hoogterp believed, in order to secure commissions. It was difficult to entertain lavishly when cash was short, but Cockie hit on an ingenious method of doing so. 'You pack your guests in so tightly that no one can move. Then you say to everyone – *do* help yourself, the drinks are at the other end of the room. Practically no one can reach them. That way, all you need is one bottle of gin.'

It was while in Johannesburg that Cockie had the unusual experience of reading her own obituary. Eva was killed in a motor accident in Baghdad and the leading newspaper muddled up the Baronesses von Blixen. The editor, on learning of the mistake, rang up to apologise. 'Don't mention it,' Cockie responded. 'I'm returning all my bills marked Deceased.' The editor insisted that a correction must be published, in any words Cockie cared to choose. 'Any words?' Certainly, the editor confirmed. Cockie dictated the correction. 'Mrs Hoogterp wishes it to be known that she has not yet been screwed in her coffin.'

Her real name was Jacqueline but her father, when she was a baby, had called her coq-a-leeky after the soup, and the abbreviation remained after nappies had been discarded. He was a banker, though hardly a conventional one; Cockie remembers an especially appealing Christmas present: a pair of bantams, which were allowed to sleep under her bed. 'For goodness sake,' a friend wrote to her before she married Hoogterp, 'don't make a third mistake.' Events proved that she had. The real love of her life was Blix.[2]

But at the time of which I write she was married still to Jan Hoogterp, living mainly in Nairobi and acting, intermittently, as a kind of social secretary to Laura Corrigan. An occasional crumb from the rich lady's table fetched up at Njoro. 'Cockie arrived with lobster and Corrigan champagne,' says my diary on a day in 1933. 'Had a party.' It cannot have been a large party with only one lobster, but perhaps there was more than one bottle of champagne.

When Delamere died at the end of 1931, the obvious leader to succeed him was Ewart Grogan. He was experienced in local politics, well versed in finance and economics – he had at one time been the financial correspondent of *The Times* – and a fluent public speaker. Grogan himself expected to be chosen, but the elected members of the Legislative Council preferred Lord Francis Scott, a post-war settler with much less political experience but who was generally liked and trusted. Grogan had made enemies, in part through his cavalier treatment of his wife, and was never really trusted by his fellows, who thought him too clever by half and with eyes too firmly fixed upon the main chance.

Francis Scott was a less pugnacious man than Delamere, less impetuous and eccentric, but he shared the same imperial ideas and could be just as quick-tempered and impatient. This was generally attributed to a war wound in the foot that caused him constant pain until it was amputated, but in fact the wound had paralysed the sciatic nerve and his leg was numb rather than painful. Tall and distinguished-looking, fair and with ice-blue eyes, his perfect manners befitted a former officer in the Grenadier Guards who had been aide-de-camp to the Viceroy of India, the Earl of Minto, and had married the Viceroy's daughter. He was a younger son of the Duke of Buccleuch and had eighty-four first cousins.

At Rongai, about 120 miles up-country, the Scotts had built a two-storeyed house, something hitherto unknown in farming regions, called Deloraine. It was, for those days, an imposing edifice in local stone shaped by Indian masons, with lofty upstairs bedrooms encircled by a wide veranda, and proper plumbing. The Scotts had brought from Britain many of the trappings of civilisation – good silver and china, linen, family portraits, books, valuable furniture and comfortable mattresses. They lived in some style, with a lady's maid called Loder and a Scottish nanny, later replaced by a succession of governesses to educate their two daughters. Loder was a forthright, uncompromising cockney lady who ordered the houseboys about in a manner one would have expected them to resent – 'them black bamboos' she often called them, bamboo being her version of the Swahili word for bloody fool, pumbafu – but she removed the sting by solicitude for their health and frequent cups of tea liberally sugared. Bamboos later graduated into bastards. She outlived her employers and became housekeeper at Muthaiga Club, where she never pulled her punches when commenting on those members who did not, in her opinion, behave as ladies and gentlemen should. 'Airpins in 'is bed again,' she would announce in disapproving tones.

Eileen Scott lingers in my memory draped in chiffon scarves, clasping a French novel and a gaily coloured parasol, and uttering at intervals bird-like cries of 'Oh, François! François!' when some domestic mishap stung her husband into an outburst of irritation. Setting forth on an expedition in their battered old T-model Ford was quite an undertaking since, as well as the dogs and novels, Eileen surrounded herself with a quantity of props such as cushions, towels, a tin of Keating's flea powder, a first aid kit, a picnic basket, a bottle of smelling salts and a parasol, and wore beige cotton gloves. She was seldom without her parasol, and would hold it aloft when riding about the farm on her pony.

In politics, Francis was a good and steady leader whose judgement was said to be sound – rather a damning word perhaps, but it implied that he did not make inflammatory speeches about birthrights and Christian civilisation, and would never have led a mob of angry settlers to the steps of Government House shouting 'Resign! Resign!' at the

Governor, as Delamere had done in his salad days. In fact, Francis
Scott was a 'moderate'. The eleven members elected to Legislative
Council by the Europeans had a 'Left Wing', also called 'Progressives',
consisting of a Captain Cotter and a fiery Irishman from Eldoret
named Tommy O'Shea. Their aims would not be labelled left wing or
progressive today. They were hell-bent for full and unrestricted self-
government, i.e. government by a small white minority freed from all
Colonial Office control.

As there were then some 40,000 Europeans and about three million
Africans in the Colony, this idea did not commend itself to any British
government, of whatever complexion. Indeed it had been the Duke of
Devonshire, Colonial Secretary in a Conservative Government and
hardly a rip-roaring radical, who had set his signature in 1923 to the
white paper which had laid down that: 'Primarily, Kenya is an African
territory, and H.M. Government think it necessary definitely to record
their considered opinion that the interests of the African natives must
be paramount, and that if and when those interests and the interests of
the immigrant races should conflict, the former should prevail.' You
could hardly be more definite than that. Although the next paragraph
administered a soothing pat to the slapped faces of the Europeans –
everyone's interests would be safeguarded, there would be no drastic
policy reversals – this statement continued to be the bedrock of British
policy in Kenya until independence came just forty years on, when
drastic reversals of policy did indeed occur.[3]

Francis Scott and his 'moderates' realised self-government by whites
to be immediately unattainable, but it still remained, despite the 1923
white paper reinforced by another in 1930, their ultimate aim.
Meanwhile they pressed for closer association of the settlers, who were
the mainstay of the country's economy and its principal tax-payers, with
the processes of government – an aim that 'government by agreement'
during the Grigg régime had partially, but only partially, achieved.

If the settlers' demands often seemed absurd and their voices strident,
one of the reasons was the irritating, at times infuriating, habits of
bureaucracy. If that bureaucracy is not only permanent and immutable
but also centred six thousand miles away, frustration can build up a
powerful head of steam. Bureaucratic delays, nit-picking and com-

placency can be bad enough in a democracy where at least the citizen can vent his fury by writing to his MP and, if that way inclined, march with banners. A white Kenyan could, certainly, write to his Elected Member, but what could that Member do? LegCo had a large, permanent majority of officials who could, and on important issues did, outvote all the unofficial members combined. The Governor, advised by an Executive Council, could at any time direct the votes of his officials. He in turn was under orders from the Secretary of State for the Colonies, who in *his* turn was the agent of whatever political party was in power in the United Kingdom. Thus the chain of command stretched from Westminster to Nairobi and beyond, down to the junior district officer in his boma at the bottom of another chain which stretched up to the Chief Secretary, who was directly responsible to the Governor. So it was government by bureaucracy down to the African herding his cattle in the bush and the white farmer filling in forms for whatever board or commission organised the marketing of his produce.

The Colonial Office was, in those days, a very curious institution indeed. A young man who chose the diplomatic service for his career would be posted to some foreign capital and spend the next twenty-five years or so moving from embassy to embassy, with spells at head-quarters in between. So no one could reach the rank of Under-Secretary in Downing Street without knowing what went on in foreign parts, nor become an Ambassador without knowing what went on in Downing Street.

Not so with his counterpart in the colonial sphere. Either he joined the Colonial Service, was posted to an outpost of Empire and spent the rest of his working life overseas, or he entered the home Civil Service, chose the Colonial Office for his province (having failed to get into the Treasury or the Home Office, almost every entrant's first and second choice – the Colonial Office came low in the pecking order) and spent his working life in Whitehall. So he could retire to enjoy his knighthood and his pensioned ease in Godalming or Sevenoaks without having set foot in any of the countries whose destiny he had directed. So, also, a district officer could rise to the rank of Chief Secretary or even Governor with no first-hand knowledge of the Office that ordered his career. Home is home and overseas is overseas and never the twain shall meet seemed to be the basic principle.

They did meet sometimes, of course, especially after aeroplanes replaced ships, but only briefly. Senior Colonial Office men would appear from time to time in colonial capitals, stay at Government House, confer in the secretariat, buy curios for their children and depart, little the wiser as to what went on in the outback beyond Government Road. They feared, it seemed, contamination by uncomfortable notions and ideas that might compromise their impartiality. Detachment was the aim.

I came across an instance of this point of view during the Second World War, when the colonies were virtually cut off from Britain. Only very occasionally did someone overcome the various obstacles to travel and find a way to London. I was employed at the time by the news department of the BBC. It had occurred to someone that these rare visitors might have interesting tales to tell about the war effort in the Empire overseas that would hearten us all in our beleagured island. So I was temporarily attached to the Colonial Office to trawl for any such stories as there might be.

One day there came into my office a young man from Mauritius who had, on his own initiative, set up a radio station to broadcast pro-Allied news to Madagascar, which was believed to be providing a base for German submarines. He was full of enthusiasm for the Allied cause, and it occurred to me that, as no other Mauritian had been seen in Britain, so far as I knew, for nearly four years (this was in 1943), the man in charge of the Mauritian desk, whoever he might be, would be interested to meet this visitor and hear his story. The gentleman in question, located in a small dark room in the inner recesses of the Office with a smallish carpet – rank in the hierarchy could be measured by carpet size – glared at me when I entered his lair as if I had been something nasty escaped from a zoo. I explained the situation. 'Has he an appointment?' the gentleman icily enquired. I had to admit that he had not. 'I do not see anyone without an appointment,' he replied, taking up his pen to inscribe another minute in the file. I had to report to the young man from Mauritius that unfortunately the head of the relevant department was engaged in an important conference and could not be disturbed.

It would be unfair to suggest that every Colonial Office man shut himself in his bureaucratic burrow. Now and again a tall, bulky, red-haired individual would stride into my office and pace the small room (small carpet) like a caged tiger, gesturing freely and letting flow a spate of talk, often original and stimulating but sometimes rather out of control; he did not seem able to stop. This was Andrew Cohen, a brilliant intellectual, left wing in his politics (in the British, not Kenyan, sense) with a Cambridge double first in Classics. He was ambitious, impetuous and accused by some of arrogance, which I think was justified, but he had considerable charm, a lot of drive and was clearly a man to be reckoned with.

In 1940 he had been sent to Malta to organise supplies during the siege of that island, and there was a story, true or not I do not know, that his duties had included the prosecution of a baker for breaking the law about the composition of his bread. An offending loaf was one of the exhibits. Launched on a tirade about the wickedness of those who tampered with the staff of life, Andrew Cohen seized the loaf to add point to his oratory, and absent-mindedly began to tear off bits of it and chew them as he warmed to his theme. By the time he reached his peroration, he had eaten the evidence.

An exceptional man, he became an exception to the tradition I have mentioned of apartheid between home and overseas. He persuaded the current Colonial Secretary, Arthur Creech Jones, to let him go out and govern Uganda, not with the happiest results. In 1953 he fell out with the Kabaka, king of the Buganda people, and had him deported to England, only to find himself obliged, two years later, to welcome back the young king with due pomp and ceremony and restore him to his kingdom. It was a short summer for King Freddie Mutesa, thirty-fifth Kabaka of his line. After independence, Uganda's first President, Milton Obote, ordered his troops to occupy the Kabaka's seat of government, a show of force intended to crush an alleged Baganda plot to secede from Obote's unitary state. Tanks rolled in and flattened the Baganda's ancient seat of government and the Kabaka's palace with its sacred associations, and the graves of former Kabakas guarded day and night by relays of old women, and the fire that never went out. King Freddie escaped over a wall, fled to London and died there miserably five years later, ostensibly of alcoholic poisoning; the rumour was that he was murdered, though this was never confirmed. The name of the army commander who took in the tanks was Idi Amin.

CHAPTER 6

Umbrellas, Tea-birds
and the Nandi Bear

African journeys were best started in the early mornings when everything was mint-fresh and sunlight mild and gentle as it slid down the boles of trees, and you did not need to screw up your eyes. Heading north-west from Nairobi you met streams of people coming in to work or market on foot and on bicycles, and flocks of goats herded by thin-shanked boys in wisps of cotton cloth. A blue smoke-haze seeped through thatch, goat-bells tinkled and warm greetings sounded like water gurgling over rocks. It is the smells that one remembers: wood-smoke, red dust, Kikuyu body-smell compounded of castor oil and red ochre, cowdung, then some aromatic scent from the bush, and once, driving through a tongue of forest, a whiff of jasmine.

The main up-country road has altered its course several times since I first knew it. If you go back far enough, much of it followed the old caravan route from the coast to Uganda, a foot-slog of some seven hundred miles. Then came a wagon-track, and the first motor-cars bumped along it. The wagons took a different route but re-joined the so-called motor road at the bottom of the escarpment, near a little stream where everyone paused to take on water. On the way up, the water in your radiator always boiled and you had to stop at intervals, pause until the boiling subsided, cautiously remove the cap and fill up. If you didn't pause, a fountain of boiling water flew into your face.

The main roads were surfaced with a red laterite murram which had, and still has, the habit of forming into corrugations, like a sheet of asbestos or galvanised iron roofing. This made your vehicle bound about like a jellybean and shake itself to death. There was a trick, however: if you drove at a certain speed, generally about forty miles an hour, your tyres skimmed along the crests of the corrugations and over the valleys, and you could enjoy a comparatively smooth passage so long as you didn't have to slow down. When the corrugations reached a certain stage and the frequent pot-holes deepened into caverns, a grader was deployed to smooth it out. A recently graded road was a dreadful hazard. Either you slithered about in thick red dust that blotted out your visibility, or you skidded uncontrollably in deep mud. On the escarpment there was a precipice on óne side. A lot of dead vehicles were strewn about the rocks and bush on that wall of the Rift Valley. You were sure to have punctures. Altogether a road journey was quite an adventure and took a long time. Nairobi to Nakuru, about a hundred miles, took five or six hours or more. Nairobi to Mombasa was a three-day journey, with one night spent at Kajiado in the Maasai reserve and the second at Moshi in Tanganyika.

I was bound for Elmenteita, a lake set among rocks and low craggy hills and flat-topped acacias, fringed with a thick crust of rose-pink flamingos. It was here that Delamere had had his ranch, Soysambu, and his simple home on a ridge overlooking the lake. A belt of tall umbrella thorn trees imparted, with a bit of imagination, something of the look of an English park; instead of deer, herds of impala and eland, waterbuck and zebra, gazelle and hartebeest grazed beneath the shade of the trees. Delamere had allowed no shooting on his ranch except when this was essential to protect his pastures and, in the case of predators, the lives of his domestic stock.

In 1905 and 1906 he had bought and put together a number of undeveloped leaseholds in this waterless stretch of the Valley's floor as a refuge for his flocks and herds, which were dying in droves on his Equator Ranch at Njoro. The Njoro land had looked fertile and promising and was quite unoccupied, simply waiting for development. Delamere stocked it with sheep and cattle, but instead of thriving they wasted away. The Maasai, who had grazed their livestock all along this section of the great Valley, had given these Njoro plains a wide berth. It was not until years later that scientists working in Scotland discovered a shortage of minerals, notably cobalt, to be the cause of the trouble.[1]

At Soysambu I stayed with the Dempsters, the manager and his wife. He and two young men, John Byng-Hall and Frank Howden, ran this 40,000-acre ranch. Starting with tiny, humped Zebu cattle and equally small, hairy Maasai sheep, by crossing them with imported pedigree English bulls and Australian rams, and then crossing their progeny again with pedigree animals, Delamere and his staff had built up herds and flocks many times more productive than their forebears. The trouble was that these graded-up animals were also highly susceptible to disease, and had to be driven at least once a week through arsenical dips. Another trouble was a shortage of water. Only one river ran along one of Soysambu's boundaries and that sometimes ran dry. Delamere had laid a pipeline from springs in the hills some twenty miles away to feed troughs installed in his paddocks, and this needed constant policing and repair.

Ticks were the main carriers of disease. They came in many sizes, from tiny red ones, pepper-ticks we called them, that made you itch like fury, to big purple ones that swelled like balloons as they engorged themselves with blood, and went pop when you squashed them. De-ticking the dogs was a daily ploy, and we used to keep an old cigarette tin full of paraffin to drop them into.

At Soysambu, tea came with the dawn, and by sunrise I was away with one of the managers whose first task was to hear herdsmen's reports, inspect sick animals or the corpses of dead ones, and give instructions for the day's work. Sometimes disease or accident had killed an animal, and quite often lions or hyenas had enjoyed a night-time meal. Ewes would be mustered and put with the correct rams, others would be dosed, pastures inspected, flocks moved and herdsmen consulted. Then back for a late breakfast on the Dempsters' veranda. No meal has ever tasted more delicious, with an appetite sharpened by fresh morning air and by that sense of expectancy and wellbeing that tingled in the blood at the start of each new day on these open savannahs.

Distances seemed endless. The plain stretched away for miles and miles but always you could see mountains, scoured with ravines as if raked by lions' claws and ridged with forest. Soysambu's western boundary reached to a hump of hills called Eburru where hot steam spouted among the rocks. This was a harsh, wild, empty land where no one had ever lived and settled, only migrated according to the seasons, seeking fresh green grass that sprang up after rain. All the herdsmen were Maasai. They lived within their fenced manyattas in long, low, sausage-shaped mud huts, windowless and roofed with withies.[2] You had almost to crawl on all fours to enter one, when you would find yourself plunged into thick smoke from the cooking-fire. I have always been amazed that people, especially babies and tots, could live and thrive in this atmosphere without becoming human kippers, their lungs coated with tar.

The young warriors with mops of red pigtails were free-striding, graceful, arrogant and proud, but when they stood still, often with one arm draped around another's shoulders, there was a curiously soft, moulded, feminine look about their greased and well-proportioned limbs and torsos. Certainly there was nothing soft or feminine about their behaviour. From infancy they were trained for war, in the shape of raids to capture their neighbours' cattle and sometimes women. You could say they were the fascists of East Africa, not to mention racists, but because of their physical beauty, their bravery and their uncompromising pride in themselves, a kind of Maasai-worship prevailed among many Europeans. Delamere had not worshipped them, but he had indulged them, forgiven their misdeeds and listened to their opinions. One of his forms of indulgence was a free issue of umbrellas once a year to his herdsmen to shelter them from the sun. The herdsmen preferred spears.

From the administration's point of view, the Maasai were tricky. A District Commissioner at Narok called Hugh Grant was speared to death by the infuriated owner of a favourite black bull included in a batch of cattle confiscated as a fine for some breach of the law. Some time before this event, Nellie, Jos and I stayed at Narok with Clarence Buxton, a district officer, who was thought by his colleagues to be a bit mad. He was an idealist who believed that you could change human nature, and especially African nature, for the better. I suppose most white people believed this, and that 'for the better' meant 'more like us'. But Clarence — a descendant of the Buxton who had been Wilberforce's right-hand man in the campaign to abolish slavery — chose unusual ways to effect such changes. How to turn Maasai warriors, as specialised in warfare as thoroughly as cacti are specialised for dry habitats, into peaceful, law-abiding, hard-working citizens? Clarence believed that one way to do this was to substitute manly sports for cattle raids, and cricket bats or polo sticks for spears. The Maasai kept donkeys, and Clarence had a plan to induce the warriors to play polo mounted on these animals. He also had a stadium built and tried to interest them in football.

The more conservative among his colleagues did not really want to see the Maasai changed. At heart, I think, they envied these young men's apparent freedom,[3] their status, their physique, the spice of danger in their lives and their sexual opportunities – the warriors could take their pick of lovers among unmarried girls. In fact they had just about everything a young man could want, so why try to turn them into disgruntled, trousered clerks?

That was the 'zoo policy', Clarence insisted. You couldn't, and shouldn't, fence the Maasai off and treat them as interesting and picturesque anthropological specimens. Sooner or later they would have to join the twentieth century and, if they put it off too long, people of tribes they despised would take all the best jobs and lord it over their former enemies. (As indeed was to come about.) The Maasai would become human dinosaurs, he said. Polo on lethargic donkeys might seem a peculiar way of trying to break the tribal mould, and it never caught on, but Clarence did succeed in getting the Maasai to do something just as contrary to custom – to handle picks and shovels. He got the warriors to make roads.

He also got himself into trouble. The warriors were highly excitable. On very little provocation they would work themselves into a state of frenzy that induced a fit of quivering all over like a bowstring, a preliminary to going into battle. The road-making was going on quite smoothly when we were there, but soon afterwards there was an 'incident', which nearly resulted in disaster. The road-makers were in a particularly inflammable state, having only recently been circumcised and passed from boyhood into the warrior age-grade; custom demanded that they should now prove their manhood by blooding their spears. Two sections of this age-grade challenged each other to defy authority and attack its representative. The first thing Clarence knew about it was the approach of forty or fifty frenzied warriors armed with spears and clubs. They must have been a terrifying sight, with sunlight flashing on their spears and on their red greased bodies, although they were without the tall head-dresses made of lions' skin and the war-paint with which the Maasai normally went into battle. In the defence of the boma Clarence had two armed police constables and four members of the tribal police who did have rifles, but very little training in their use.

Clarence waited until the warriors were within a hundred yards before giving the order to fire over their heads. I do not know whether he could see the whites of their eyes but he did see 'no trace of *homo sapiens*, no light of sense or reason', as he wrote in his report, but an expression of 'demonical insensate savagery' as they came on.[4] The volleys checked them, and Clarence stepped out and started to harangue them in their own tongue.

The moment was fragile. There was a double hazard, that the warriors would come on, and that the policemen would panic and fire into the mob. Clarence was a tall, imposing-looking man and, miraculously it seemed, he held them. They lacked a leader and protective medicine which only the laibon, their witch-doctor-cum-priest, could supply. Their frenzy subsided as suddenly as a switched-off kettle ceases to boil. When everything was sorted out the Maasai resumed their road-making and there was no more trouble. But an undertow of protest remained. When a Maasai sees a shooting star, Clarence told us, he will say: 'Away with you, and take all the Europeans with you.'

Clarence Buxton's own story ended sadly. Despite his attractive wife and their four children his eye roved, and he was named co-respondent in a suit for divorce heard in Nairobi. The wronged husband was another official, but very much junior in rank and status – in fact, the government analyst. This raised some unkind smiles, since Clarence not only had rather grand connections (son of a baronet) but had been looked upon as a model of rectitude. Such lapses were severely frowned upon in the Colonial Service. Clarence was not dismissed, but transferred to Palestine, the next worst thing. Two years later he resigned and returned to his farm at Limuru, having been divorced and re-married to the government analyst's former wife.

All this has taken us a long way from Soysambu and its Maasai herdsmen. Most of these were not warriors, but men who had passed through the Eunoto ceremony when their pigtails had been shaved and they had become elders free to marry, procreate and take a share in the governance of the tribe. They had shed excitability with their red locks.

From Soysambu I moved further along the Valley to Nderit on the shores of Lake Nakuru, where Delamere's former manager lived. Boy Long and his wife Genessie were a handsome pair. He had dark, curly hair, a ruddy complexion, lively dark eyes and looked like an English country squire with a dash of the cowboy, accentuated by a broad-brimmed Stetson hat and a bright Somali shawl (tomato red or electric blue) thrown across his shoulders. He once rode his horse round Glady Delamere's nursery clad in this attire. Women adored him. He was said to be one of the best stockmen in the country; he would not have been employed by Delamere for fifteen years had it been otherwise.

Boy – his real name was Caswell – went to great trouble to write down for me his recollections of those days. These included an episode when an American called Paul Rainey had kept a pack of bear-hounds at Soysambu to hunt lions. When the hunted lion turned to face the baying dogs, the hunters would gallop in with rifles to shoot it from the saddle. In fifteen days' hunting they killed twelve lions. Then luck turned against them, and a man called Fritz Schindler was knocked off his horse by a lion and killed.

Genessie Long was slim, elegant and rich; she wore long pendant ear-rings, had a well developed sense of drama and was tougher than she looked. She had come to Kenya as a bride in 1923 on safari with her first husband – Blix was their white hunter – and fallen in love with Africa, the safari life and the prospect of adventure. Subsequently she also fell in love with Boy Long, and they married. She bought the ranch Nderit on the shores of Lake Nakuru, where she designed a splendid house with enormous rooms built round a patio with a fountain playing in the middle. Even larger stables accommodated, she told me, about seventy horses. She was an accomplished horsewoman and a good shot. A semi-tame hippo used to share the cattle's drinking troughs.

Boy and Genessie lived in style and entertained generously. The standard dress for house-boys was the kanzu, a long robe like a nightshirt, generally white and sometimes rather grubby; grander employers added an embroidered waistcoat of the kind worn by Arabs and Swahilis at the Coast, but Genessie went one better and dressed her house-boys in dark red kanzus with beautiful gold-embroidered waistcoats and scarlet turbans.

She had a penchant for travel in the world's remoter regions, inspired by Rosita Forbes, and an ambition to ride to Petra on a camel. By then Petra had ceased to be remote and mysterious, and people reached it by car. This she did, and then hired camels, a guide, a servant and two Circassian policemen and proceeded, on her own, to Shobak and two Crusader castles, sleeping in the open or, sometimes, in the women's quarters of hospitable, if unhygenic, desert Arabs.[5]

In those days this was a bold achievement for a woman, and I listened enthralled to her descriptions, but when I re-told some of them to Nellie, she was unimpressed. Nellie reacted with suspicion to anything that smacked of what she called swashbuckling. There was an occasion when Genessie arrived for lunch with mutual friends in Nakuru clad in beautifully cut white jodhpurs and a white silk shirt, a neat little revolver with a mother-of-pearl handle tucked into her belt. Nellie, eying the revolver coldly, asked Genessie whether she had found it useful when shopping in Nakuru. 'Oh, yes,' was the reply. 'I've just shot a cobra in the drive.' Nellie looked at her with scepticism, and was somewhat abashed when a dead cobra was brought in.

By this time, Genessie had married Lord Claud Hamilton, a tall and handsome former Guards officer whose taciturnity was a perfect foil to her lively eloquence. They had taken over Nderit, and Boy Long had also found another wife.

The time had come for me to move on. Gervas arrived from South Africa and we planned to fly back together after spending a few days at the tea plantations of Kericho on the way. So, after a short stay at Njoro, we borrowed Mbugwa and Jos's old Ford and drove over the escarpment to Kericho, which lies on the western flank of the Mau hills in a lush and fertile region where rain falls almost every afternoon. This had been another of those buffer zones between two hostile tribes that had been given out for white settlement. It separated the Kipsigis, then called Lumbwa,[6] who lived in the hills, and the Luo, who occupied part of the flat, hot, steamy basin of Lake Victoria lying below. Just as the warlike Maasai descended with spear and club upon the Kikuyu, so did the Kipsigis, who were no less warlike, descend upon the Luo, and also upon the neighbouring Kisii.

Part of this buffer zone had been leased after the First World War to a group of partially disabled officers who formed themselves into a body known as BEADOC — the British East Africa Disabled Officers Cooperative. Each man was to have his own block of land, but marketing was to be centrally organised and so was the purchase of implements, seeds, fertilisers and so on.

This seemed a fine idea on paper – compassionate might be the word used today – but in practice it was crazy, even cruel. Scarcely any of these men possessed experience of farming, nor had they any of the practical skills needed by pioneers. They received no training. Few could raise much capital, and their disability pensions were miniscule. Nothing had been made ready: they had to start by clearing bush and putting up shacks to live in. They spoke no African language, though most of them had picked up a smattering of Swahili on the voyage out. The nearest railway station was twenty-two miles from Kericho along a track which was impassable for a great part of the year. Kericho itself was a small government boma with a DC, a post office, a police post, a few dukas and little else. Malaria was rife, and other tropical diseases of which little was known were endemic. The nearest hospital was at Kisumu, nearly sixty miles by rail from Lumbwa – if you could get to Lumbwa.

So, in 1919, at this remote spot there had arrived between seventy and eighty war-damaged men, some one-armed or one-legged, some on crutches, some with sight or speech impaired, others shattered by shell-shock, and all inspired by a belief that here in a new land they would make for themselves a new life of action. Poverty and unemployment in Britain were already destroying the hopes of men back from the trenches and reducing some to hawking matches and shoe-laces on city pavements. In Africa, they believed, sunshine, highland air and wide horizons would heal them, and tasks beyond their damaged capabilities would be done by able-bodied Africans.

The scheme was doomed to failure, and it failed. Yet, despite all that was stacked up against it, the Beadoc men might have succeeded had it not been for a catastrophic collapse in the price of flax. I have never understood why this happened so suddenly and completely at this time (1922). You would have thought that people would have gone on wanting linen. But seemingly they did not; the price plummeted almost overnight, and expensive machinery that had been imported to process the fibre was never used. The settlers had already suffered various setbacks and this was the last straw. Beadoc went into liquidation, the disabled men dispersed, and the land, some 25,000 acres, was put on the market for an asking price of £3 an acre. No one wanted it.

There is an ironic ending to this tale. A couple of years later the manager of a tea estate in southern India visited Kenya on holiday, heard the story, inspected the land, reported favourably to his employers, and in 1925 some 20,000 acres were bought by James Finlay and Company of Glasgow. The rest of the Beadoc holding went to Brooke Bonds. That was the start of the tea industry in the Kericho district, though not of tea-growing in Kenya; a few small plantations had been established at Limuru for some time. The irony was that this Kericho land proved to be some of the very best in Kenya. Fortunes have been made out of tea, now one of the country's most efficient and productive enterprises. If the Beadoc settlers had planted tea instead of flax, and provided that someone had taught them how to deal with it, tihey might have survived.

Some of the Beadoc men refused to be beat. Years later, I met in a Gloucestershire village the widow of one of the disabled men. In 1915 he – William Dawson – had been blown up by a shell and sustained such terrible head wounds that he spent three years in hospital and suffered one operation after another. He had other injuries as well. After Beadoc's failure he managed to get a job on the railway supervising the building of bridges, saved a few pennies, went into partnership with another Beadoc man who had only one leg, and bought some undeveloped land in the Sotik district. Here they planted coffee which did not thrive, so they scrapped it and replaced it with tea, which did. William Dawson married, bit by bit enlarged his operations, raised a family and prospered in a modest way. 'We thought we were going to live there forever,' Sylvia Dawson said. Forever turned out to be thirty years. Shortly before Kenya's independence they were bought out by the Government for just enough to enable them to buy a cottage in an English village. Kipsigis farmers took over the land.

By the time we visited Kericho in 1933, Anglo-Indian expertise had turned about one-fifth of the original Beadoc land into tea plantations and built an imposing factory to process the leaves. This was the achievement of William Lee who, with his wife, had exchanged the comforts of a prosperous plantation in Travencore for pioneering in the bush. No one had warned them, Mrs Lee told me, of the cold; at first the office was in a tent, and she had relays of hot-water bottles to keep her hands warm while doing the accounts. Labour had been the greatest problem. 'The Kipsigis would cut the bush all right,' Mr Lee said, 'but they wouldn't dig.' (Women's work again.) Mounds of seeds kept arriving from India before the nurseries were ready. No sooner had the first plantations been established than the world depression struck, resulting in the international scheme, in which Gervas was involved, to restrict production and increase demand.

Few Africans had as yet acquired the tea-drinking habit; but might they not be persuaded to do so? Instead of putting all their tea into chests for export, the companies started to put some of it into little packets, a couple of ounces at a time, which could be sold for a few cents and which Africans could afford. Brooke Bonds chose the name Simba (lion) for their product, and had a lion printed on the packets. African Highlands, their principal rival, baulked of the lion, chose a Crested Crane and called their tea Ndege, meaning bird (or aeroplane). They were delighted when subsequently an African, observing a flock of cranes, exclaimed: 'Look – tea-birds!' Tea drinking was encouraged by the medical authorities because it involved, or should involve, boiling the water, and the habit spread.[7]

While Gervas and I enjoyed our visit, Mbugwa took a poor view of it and was anxious only to shake Kericho's mud off his feet. He had fallen, if not among thieves, among Kipsigis, which from his point of view was worse. So he welcomed our departure, but encountered a new peril. Our route lay up the forested escarpment and towards the Nandi hills where there lurked a savage monster known to Europeans as the Nandi bear and to local Africans as the chemosit. The name, that is, was known, but the creature itself remained elusive. Many sightings had been claimed but descriptions varied and, despite many attempts, no one had succeeded in securing a specimen. Traps had been set and sprung but only tufts of hair found at daylight; shots had been fired and hits claimed but no corpse retrieved. People had heard its blood-curdling cry at night and found evidence of its ferocity: dead sheep, and other animals, whose skulls had been cracked and brains removed. It seemed to have a penchant for brains.

An extra-large hyena; an outsize baboon; an aardvark or ant-eater; a giant ratel; survivor of a vanished colony of chimpanzees; these were among the theories advanced as to its identity. The Nandi and the

Kipsigis drew on their imaginations when describing it. The historian A. C. Hollis recorded in 1909 that the Nandi believed the chemosit to be 'half man, half bird, to have only one leg but nine buttocks, and his mouth, which is red, is supposed to shine at night like a lamp'. Possibly the prototype of Edward Lear's Dong with the Luminous Nose? On the other hand the DC at Kabsabet, who had actually set eyes on it, described it as 'about three feet high to the back, round and even pudgy, with a small pointed head'.[8]

We were heading for Kapsiliat, which I was tempted to think almost the most beautiful of Kenya's many beautiful farms. It belonged to old friends, the Ridleys; Mervyn had kept a pack of foxhounds at Makuyu, not far from our Thika coffee farm, and we had enjoyed many weekend hunts over the plains in pursuit of jackals or steinbuck. One day in 1923 the Governor, Sir Edward Northey, had taken part in such a hunt, and it occurred to me that the *East African Standard* might accept a brief account of this event. Governors were always news. Copying out the composition in my best handwriting, I sent it off, and anxiously awaited the arrival of the next weekly edition of the newspaper. A week or so later I rode in trepidation the five miles to Thika to collect our mail, and back again not daring to open the package. Perhaps I expected some exclamation from my parents such as 'Look! They've printed a bit about our run last Sunday week.' No such comment came. Nevertheless, tucked away on a back page was my effort – in print. Some weeks later I got a postal order for five shillings. I was hooked.

Now Mervyn and Sybil were living with their daughter Susan at Kapsiliat on a flank of the Cherangani mountains in a long, comfortable bungalow built of local brick and timbers and roofed with cedarwood shingles. Tall native trees surrounded it, the lawns were green and smooth, the borders full of colour, and the whole place had a tidy, cared-for look about it, the farm an air of ticking over happily. There were well-groomed ponies, pedigree bulls, proper fencing, fine-woolled sheep. Mervyn was a large, broad-shouldered, jovial man whom everybody liked.

Many British emigrants to Africa carried in their hearts an ideal of what they wanted to create, and that was a little piece of England, Scotland or Wales as it ought to be, not necessarily as it really was, and as they thought it had been in their childhood days. It was a feudal vision. The squire rode among his smiling peasantry who touched their caps or doffed them, inspecting his beasts and crops and returning to a well-ordered household where cooks were roasting venison, still-room maids baking cakes, gun-dogs wagging their tails and ale always on tap. It was, of course, an absurd, romantic and outdated dream impossible to translate into reality; in Africa the smiling peasantry could be sullen and thievish, crops droughted and rust-ridden, beasts diseased and cooks drunk, but here at Kapsiliat the dream seemed more nearly to be realised than in most places. It was such generous country, towns with their discontent and squalor so far away, and the Ridleys' rule benign. But then, we only stayed there for a couple of days. And I believe that stock-thefts inflicted on the enterprise a running sore.

We drove up through the forest along a winding track – not a glimpse of the chemosit – to the crest of the Cherangani hills, where a staggering prospect hit us like a thunder-clap. Beneath our feet lay a sheer drop of over four thousand feet into the Kerio valley, parchment-coloured, shimmering in the heat, speckled with bush and patterned by cloud-shadows. Down far below the Kerio river found its way towards the Northern Frontier deserts and Lake Rudolf beyond. Across the valley rose its other wall, the Kamasia hills. It was as if some primeval god had split a great slice of his creation with a colossal scimitar.

A dry-weather track ran along the crest, and we followed it for some way, encountering from time to time small parties of women carrying loads, and men carrying spears. They were Elgeyo people, travelling to distant markets, and had a coppery, Maasai look about them. The women were bright as macaws in wide, stiff collars made of coils and coils of copper wire, and heavy ear-rings made of blue and scarlet beads stitched on to strips of leather. The wire was wrapped so tightly round their limbs that their flesh bulged out above the coils. How could they endure these hot, heavy embellishments like tourniquets, and why was their circulation not choked? The quantities of wire wound round their limbs, and of their bead ear ornaments, were measures of their husband's wealth – status symbols, like diamond rings, emerald brooches and mink coats in our society. At least our symbols are more comfortable.

From Kapsiliat we drove past fields of withered maize and clouds of dust over the Uasin Gishu plateau and on across the Trans Nzoia to the slopes of Mount Elgon, and next day inspected that mountain's famous caves. I believe they are the only caves in the world frequented by elephants, who come to eat the mineral salts with which the rocks are impregnated, picking a path delicately in the darkness to avoid crevasses, and feeling their way with their trunks. They use their tusks to scrape off chunks of rock.

These ancient caves were also used by Africans who drove their cattle in to lick the salty rock; as nesting sites by swallows and swifts; and as roosts by great colonies of bats: furry-faced, soft-bodied, hanging upside down like fruits of darkness, and emitting a constant suspuration of squawks and squeaks. Their eyes looked red when we shone our torches up at them. Bats, I am sure, are amiable animals, marvellously equipped to navigate by echo-location and so avoid bumping into things, devoted to their young and thinking no evil; their faces, when you can see them, are appealing with big, sad eyes. In ancient China, I have read, they were a symbol of long life and happiness. So the weakness is in me that I find them repellent. Such great communities seething overhead are mysterious, beyond comprehension. These were fruit-bats, *Rousettus aegyptiacus*, one species of many. At dusk they emerged in swirling clouds to feed on the fruit of various forest trees. I think it is excess that one finds so unnerving – termite castles alive with their scurrying inmates; relentless armies of siafu, the terrifying soldier ants; great, evil swarms of locusts – and close-packed crowds of nameless humans. Suppose something were to spark off a surge of hatred and anger? However, these fruit-bats were friendly, but smelly, and it was a relief to emerge into the sunshine and shadow of the forest with its rich scent of moss and fallen logs and spent leaves, and to see overhead the flash of a turaco's wings and the graceful leaps of Colobus monkeys.

So, back to Njoro for a few days, and then the time came for our return to London. Imperial Airways' Croydon to Cape Town flight was just over a year old. Nairobi to Croydon took six days and a bit. You flew in four-engined biplanes of the Hannibal class that looked like ugly metal sausage-beetles, and came down every few hours to refuel, and then for the night. On this occasion we started off by train to break the journey at Entebbe, where we stayed a couple of nights with the Mitchells. I had met him in Nairobi when he was Chief Secretary in Tanganyika; now, in 1936 he was governor of Uganda, a country then basking in peace and prosperity – 'the pearl of Africa', it had been called. Kenyans envied it for its affluence, good roads and other amenities but considered it smug and full of thieves, while Uganda, for its part, looked with mingled disdain and irritation at its neighbour which, in their view, was full of uncouth settlers and down-trodden natives, and kept a stranglehold on Uganda by reason of its control over the Railway, the landlocked Protectorate's only outlet to the sea.

Philip Mitchell was possibly the ablest of the Governors who had come and gone in East Africa, up to that date. He had spent the whole of his career in Nyasaland and Tanganyika, so was a professional colonial servant, in contrast to the Army and Air Force commanders, varied by an occasional politician, who had been tossed a governorship to sweeten their retirement, or to get them out of the way. He was tall, good-looking – a little florid perhaps – outspoken and incisive, realistic and far-sighted, a perfectionist who did not suffer fools gladly – 'a complete feckless nonentity' was his verdict on a Governor under whom he had served. He kept fit by playing golf and riding every morning along the lakeside and among the shambas, which appeared as forests of banana trees, talking to passers-by in his flawless Swahili; and very handsome he looked in his well cut white breeches and open-necked shirt on a thoroughbred pony brought from Kenya.

Government House had a pillared portico, spacious rooms kept cool by overhead fans, and view to the Lake over green lawns set with shady trees. The atmosphere was business-like and informal, and I felt sure that Lady Mitchell would see to it if any gubernatorial pomp was allowed to intrude. She was an oddity: short and tubby, almost as broad as long and, while not at all unfriendly, without that veneer of manner that can ease encounters between strangers. I can see her now, sitting on a chair too high for her, her feet dangling some distance from the floor, clutching a whisky and soda in her hand and looking like an amiable frog. The story was that Philip Mitchell, on departing to take his leave in South Africa, announced that he would marry the first woman who beat him at golf. Lady Mitchell, then Miss Margery Trywitt-Drake, did.

He took us to see the college that had recently started to arise on Makerere hill just outside Kampala. It was one day to become, he said, a university serving the whole of East Africa, the seedbed of an African élite whose men and women would take over the leadership of their country and take their place on equal terms with people of a wider world. Higher education for Africans was a cause dear to his heart. 'They have it in them', he wrote, 'to become as civilised as any other race of men.'9 The college, when we saw it, had ten tutors and 156 pupils drawn from all four territories, fifteen of them girls. One of Mitchell's aims was to equip the future university with a single chapel for Christians of all denominations, which would help to bridge the gulf, still deep and wide, between Protestants and Roman Catholics. In this he was disappointed; two chapels were to arise.

It was during our visit that the question came up of literature for a new and growing reading public of Africans. Mitchell had identified a serious gap in the educational system. Every year the schools were turning out more and more adolescents who could read, but only just; few had received a secondary education and their English was rudimentary. Apart from the Bible and primers issued by the various Missions, there was practically nothing in their own vernacular tongues, or in simple Swahili, for them to read. Mitchell foresaw that, if no action was taken, this gap would widen, and widen dangerously; all sorts of folk with axes to grind might step in, using cheap hand-printing presses, to spread their opinions, and often lies. 'We don't want a vacuum filled with hot air' was his comment. A generation for whom new fields of knowledge were being opened deserved something better.

This conversation was to have repercussions for me nine years later. War intervened. In 1940 Mitchell was summoned to Nairobi to co-ordinate the East African war effort, then on to Ethiopia to set up a civil administration after the Italian defeat, then on to govern Fiji and serve on the staff of South-East Asia Command. In 1944 he was transferred back to Nairobi, and soon afterwards invited me to report on the situation in all four East African territories as to the provision of literature for Africans, and on what could and should be done to improve it. So, in October 1945, I set out on this daunting task.

There was already in existence a Literature Bureau set up by the Nigerian Government to print simple books and booklets in the Fulani tongue for the Muslims of the North. It was arranged for me to have a look at the set-up on my way, so I proceeded, in the uncertain conditions of air travel just after the war had ended, to Zaria, where the Bureau had its headquarters under Dr Rupert East. After a week there and a few days in Kano, I continued my journey to Khartoum in an ancient Anson of RAF Transport Command, and then more briskly in a Lockheed to Kisumu where we were dumped, as Nairobi airport was closed to civilian traffic. However, there was a train.

I spent the next two months talking to, or being talked to by, all sorts of people: school teachers and directors of education, missionaries and information officers, and many others, including George Turner, the new principal of Makerere University College as it had by then become, whom Mitchell had enticed from Marlborough College and who was to inspire the budding university with his forward-looking, humane and Christian spirit.

Sir Philip had returned from the wars an exhausted man, having had no leave for seven years. He was on the verge of a nervous breakdown. I remember how, one evening at dinner, talk flowed from him as it often did – he could be a brilliant conversationalist – but scarcely made sense, like an engine racing away while not in gear. Shortly afterwards he went on three months' leave and returned apparently restored, but I do not think that he was ever quite the same again. The cutting edge of his intellect had been blunted, and that was why (I believe) when tremors of the impending Mau Mau crisis began to shake the country, he insulated himself from their shock, brushing aside the warnings he received from his subordinates, and why he ended his career in 1952 under a cloud instead of in the bright sunshine that his former achievements deserved. He was a sincere Christian who did his best, I think with reasonable success, to live up to the Founder's teachings, and a patriot of a kind now all but extinct, who wrote of King George V: 'He was a living personality to me and my generation, an inspiration and an example . . . the one sure foundation of honour and justice, of security and of devotion.' Mitchell added that he had cried like a child as he listened on the radio to the King's funeral service in St Paul's Cathedral.

At the end of 1945 I submitted a report suggesting the lines on which an East African Literature Bureau might be set up, and what its main objectives should be. Nothing happened for a while, except approval of the report in principle. The problem was to find someone to run the proposed Bureau, a difficult task calling for an unusual set of qualifications. It is seldom that a round peg can be found to fit exactly into a round hole, but in this case it was, in the shape of Charles Granston Richards. He had reached Nairobi in 1935 as a member of the Church Missionary Society to develop book distribution among Africans through the C.M.S. bookshop there. By 1947 this bookshop was known throughout East Africa for its service to an African reading public which was rapidly expanding. Charles Richards was already beginning to develop local publishing and had himself written several short books in Swahili. The Church Missionary Society agreed to release him by stages, and on 1 April 1948 he opened the Bureau with headquarters in Nairobi. It came under the East Africa High Commission, which had been set up in 1947 to co-ordinate the various services common to Kenya, Uganda and Tanganyika – the nearest these three countries ever got to the federation that for over twenty years had beckoned them on like some phantasmagoria in the sky towards a unity that never came, in the process spilling into the sand untold billions of words uttered and printed by commissions, committees, enquiries, reports, proposals and conferences.

Charles Richards remained director of the Bureau for fifteen years and built up a most impressive enterprise, including a library service whose 'book boxes' were delivered to bush schools from the border with Sudan to that of Zambia and fed from up-to-date central libraries. He set out to train his staff in all aspects of book production and distribution, so that when he left in 1963 the whole Bureau, from his successor downwards, was staffed by Africans.

I had no more to do with the Bureau after writing my report, so cannot tell its story here, but three of its aims were, I think, especially important. One was the training programme I have already mentioned. Another was to stimulate the writing of fiction by indigenous authors. Before the coming of the missionaries in the nineteenth century, the only written East African language was Swahili; but, as with other pre-literate peoples, there was a strong oral tradition of folklore and stories, nearly all of which involved the supernatural. When the Bureau launched its magazine *Tazama* (meaning Look!) and invited readers to submit stories, the centre-pieces were often ogres. The staff of the magazine introduced more up-to-date heroes and heroines. Instead of ogres there were businessmen, head teachers and the like, and the ogresses became air hostesses whose adventures were more sophisticated than meeting nasty apparitions in the forest. Gradually, new African writers emerged. A prize was offered for the best original work of fiction, and it was through this contest that Ngugi wa Thiong'o, today a widely read author, became known outside East Africa.

The third aim was to get Africans writing and reading about their own histories, traditions and their natural world, drawing on their own environment for images and examples. Many of the books previously on offer had been translations from British or American texts; it made little sense to read about primroses or skylarks or the wives of Henry VIII if you had never seen a primrose, heard a skylark, or seen anything remarkable in a powerful king having six wives.

Finally, there was the question of what language to publish in. East Africa has over two hundred, most of them spoken by too few people to make their use in publishing a viable concern. In the end, the number of languages used was narrowed down to twenty-seven, including English and French.[10]

The Bureau flourished until the break-up of the East African Community (which succeeded the East Africa High Commission), in a welter of recrimination and ill-will, in 1977. Kenya and Tanzania then carried on with their own separate Literature Bureaus. Uganda's branch had already sunk beneath the blood-stained waters of the regime of Idi Amin.

At Entebbe Gervas and I boarded an Imperial Airways aeroplane – the Horsa, I think – and continued our homeward journey. Bumpier and bumpier it got, hotter and stuffier, paper bags constantly in use especially when coming in to land, which we did at Malakal, Kosti and Khartoum, where the temperature at midnight was 110°F. Off next morning in the dark, down at Atbara for a repellent breakfast, on to Wadi Halfa where an uneatable luncheon smothered in flies awaited us in a tent which was even hotter than Khartoum. At Assuan we spent the night in a horrible hotel, and proceeded at daybreak to Cairo.

Here we abandoned our Horsa to embark in a much more comfortable flying-boat. Our hours were still erratic. We were called in Alexandria at 3.30 a.m., had breakfast at 4 a.m., and were airborne in Sylvanus well before dawn. This was the best part of the flight, over the sea. Above Corfu we flew low over two parallel lines of grey, majestic warships of the Royal Navy's entire Mediterranean fleet. Here was Britain's seaborne might, and might it was, very reassuring; we had no inkling that soon it would be seen no more. We parted from Sylvanus at Brindisi to catch the night train to Milan, and so to Le Bourget and the last lap across the Channel. A strong head-wind reduced our speed to that of a fishing vessel just below; we raced it neck-and-neck until we reached the English coast; the fishing vessel just won.

We cannot really have enjoyed this six-and-a-half day trip, and yet all the memories that linger are good: crossing a silky Nile at dawn to see the Tombs of the Kings, the whole bowl of the sky aflame, unbearably dramatic above an infinite desert; cool drinks at evening in hot places with fellow-passengers and crew, consisting then of five young men, all cheerful and friendly; stretching cramped legs under the shady trees of Khartoum's small zoo before nightfall; the good food and comfort of the wagon-lits. And it was still an adventure. We were to fly this route many times again and note its progress from discomfort, heat, airsickness, improvisation and the unexpected – we once spent nearly two days in the desert, sheltering under a wing of our stranded aeroplane, while waiting for a spare part – to a stream-lined, non-stop, eight-hour flight in air-conditioned comfort, meals on trays, stewards and service and no paper bags – and impersonal, uneventful dullness, with the gloomy prospect of an international airport at the end.

CHAPTER 7

Livestock Barons of the
Rift Valley

Three men between them owned a large chunk of the Rift Valley, transformed its dusty veld into thriving ranches, and became legendary figures to a younger generation. These three were Lord Delamere, Galbraith Cole and Gilbert Colvile.

Only the first of the trio took to politics, to become the spokesman of the white community and to win a name beyond the borders of East Africa. A good deal has been written about Delamere's political life and about his career as a pioneer but his character, I think, has remained an enigma.

I can remember him only dimly: a short, stocky figure in a big mushroom hat with long greyish hair (he was then in his fifties) and a beaky nose, clad in a mud- or grease-stained brown cardigan, glimpsed in Nakuru's single street. His name was revered in East Africa, and I was startled to learn, when engaged on his biography, that his relatives in England, far from admiring him as an empire-builder, condemned him as a renegade who had ducked his responsibilities as a landowner and drained his Cheshire estate of its resources in order to finance wildcat schemes in a remote part of Africa that was nothing but a burden to the British taxpayer, and had been much better left to its primitive tribesmen and savage beasts.

His first wife was Florence Cole, a daughter of the Earl of Enniskillen. She had all the charm, wit and sparkle expected of the Irish, as well as generosity of spirit and loyalty to a husband who, while not unkind or probably unfaithful, gave more of his heart to his dreams and schemes for the growth of his adopted land than to his wife's happiness. After a gentle upbringing at Florence Court in County Fermanagh, she was dumped down in a mud hut without doors or windows amid wild animals, Maasai warriors and herds of cattle, far from telephones or doctors or any contacts with what we call civilisation, and left alone for weeks or even months on end to act as farm manager. This was the lot of many European wives and few complained, while some relished its dangers and responsibilities. Certainly Florence Delamere did not complain, but she must have lacked companionship, she was never strong, her health suffered and she was separated at an early stage from her only child.

Her life became rather easier when Delamere moved to Soysambu, his first enterprise at Njoro having failed, and built a somewhat more substantial dwelling. Even so, there were few comforts. After her death, her brother Galbraith wrote of Soysambu: 'There's something about it that always depresses me and I can't help thinking that my sister must have hated it. There's somehow a sort of bareness about D's surroundings that I can't explain.'

Two of Florence's brothers, Galbraith and Berkeley Cole, aged twenty-two and twenty-one respectively, arrived in East Africa in 1903, fired by Delamere's enthusiasm, to settle there for the rest of their lives. Galbraith had the ranch next to Soysambu called Kekopey, meaning in Maasai 'the place where white comes through green' – a reference to deposits of diatomite later to be mined by the Coles. Galbraith wrote of his brother-in-law: 'I think he is the most brilliantly clever person I know, marvellously quick to understand things, but he shuts his mind to all things except those which have to do with the material side of life with the utmost determination.' This resolve left 'a sort of gap, a something rather hollow in his company. He's the sort of person to whom you would hesitate to express a thought that perhaps seemed a little far-fetched – not that he wouldn't understand it, he would, no one better, but he would dismiss it probably with ridicule. His keen wit, his perception and an amazing faculty for, so to speak, detaching himself and *never* giving himself away, make him very strong in dealing with most people, and all sorts of material things . . . He won't be known but he likes to know others. It's rather like "take all and give nothing" with him.'[1]

A good prescription, perhaps, for the armour of a politician but not for the companionship of a spouse.

This wall of privacy had existed even when he was a young man. At the end of 1896 he had left Berbera on the Gulf of Aden at the head of a large caravan, marched southwards across barren deserts sparsely occupied by ferocious nomads for nearly two thousand miles, and reached Kenya's highlands just under a year later. His companion was a young doctor with whom he had already spent some time elk-hunting in Norway and recovering from a serious accident sustained while fox-hunting in Cheshire. During the whole expedition they were continually in each other's company and became good friends. Delamere was then twenty-six years old. Not long before he left England, he had become engaged to be married. Yet not once, Dr Atkinson told me, during the whole expedition, did Delamere mention his fiancée's name or speak about her, and it came as a surprise to hear that his companion had married.

There were, I think, two Delameres. There was the dedicated farmer who in his early days lived sparsely and austerely, indifferent to comfort, seeking for company his Maasai herdsmen – he was a fluent speaker of their tongue – and for reading matter pamphlets about liver-fluke in sheep or white papers on government expenditure; and there was the roisterer renowned for his parties at Muthaiga Club or Torr's hotel when champagne flowed and thick heads followed in the morning. His hospitality, when these festive moods took him, was unbounded. Rose Cartwright, who knew him well, told me that she used to avoid him when she met him in Nairobi. 'I knew I'd be swept into a party if I didn't,' she said 'and much as I enjoy parties now and then I don't want them all the time. But up-country he was quite different: generous and nothing was too much trouble if you were in a fix of some kind.'

Had Florence lived, her influence might have found ways to breach the wall erected to repel invaders of his privacy. Instead, her death in 1914, when she was only thirty-seven, strengthened the fortifications. Delamere formed no stable relationship with any other woman until his second marriage fifteen years later. Then he wrote to Glady: 'I believe that you and the future of Kenya are the only two things I care for.' Within less than four years, he was dead.

Galbraith Cole had set eyes on Africa at the age of nineteen when his regiment had arrived at the Cape to take part in thc Boer War. While the regiment was resting, he used to ride off on his pony with a horse-blanket to sleep in the open, and in the early dawn 'wander about looking at all sorts of things, small buck, merecats, birds, everything . . . the bold rugged scenery, the exquisite clearness of the atmosphere, the amazing beauty of the starlit nights impressed my imagination . . . '

With Delamere's help, he secured a grant of 50,000 acres, later exchanged for 30,000 acres adjoining Soysambu in the Gilgil district. There were then no woolled sheep in East Africa, only the longhaired native kind. He bought 2,000 Maasai ewes for five rupees each (about seven shillings) and sent to New Zealand for twenty-eight merino rams to cross with them. At first nothing went according to plan. In the initial breeding year, ninety out of every hundred lambs died. Most of his Kekopey ranch was waterless, and only about one third could be put to use. Galbraith had water piped from a river in the hills and installed tanks. Zebras came and helped themselves, and thousands had to be shot. Lions broke into the enclosures where cattle were driven for the night and killed and stampeded the beasts. 'How can you make a country and an industry and feed a lot of lions at the same time?' Galbraith demanded. 'If I had my way I would gas all the vermin and game that got in the way of development.' Few farmers were conservationists then.

Less than twenty years later, Galbraith possessed on his two properties – he had acquired another one, even larger – over 30,000 merino sheep and several thousand head of cattle; the death rate from all causes was, in a normal year, down to under seven per cent, and his wool was fetching satisfactory prices in London.

Meanwhile there had been a personal disaster. As well as lions, zebras and diseases, stock-thefts were a major worry. One white policeman and a small force of askaris stationed many miles away were impotent to stop marauders from stealing Galbraith's sheep and eating them on the spot. The law having failed him, he took the law into his own hands. One night he came upon a hut hidden in the bush and surprised inside it three Kikuyu men skinning a sheep of the merino, not the native, breed. The men fled; Galbraith fired two shots after them and one of the men was fatally wounded. Galbraith failed to report the matter to the police.

He was tried for murder, for which the penalty was death, by an all-white jury, and acquitted. There had been instances before when all-white juries had returned questionable verdicts in cases involving fatal injuries to Africans. The Government decided to make an example and the Governor, on orders from Whitehall, issued a deportation order on the grounds that 'the Hon. G. L. E. Cole is conducting himself so as to be dangerous to peace and good order in East Africa and is endeavouring to incite emnity between the people of East Africa and His Majesty' – a charge which would have been difficult to substantiate. Galbraith left the Protectorate in ignominy and with no prospect of return. This was in September 1911.

In the years that remained to him, Galbraith was to suffer agonies from a particularly vicious form of rheumatoid arthritis, and it was generally believed that he had contracted this during his exile. But the first stages of the disease were already with him, for he had been invalided out of the army before he ever reached East Africa. His exile worsened his condition. Bitterly resentful and frustrated, he could settle nowhere. He tried 'German East' but could not abide the Germans – 'too beastly for words to express' – and wrote that he was 'like a storm-tossed ship without a helm and so must drift before the wind . . . I keep fairly well on the whole but still get these bouts which wear me down, especially when I am on short rations . . . I shall have to disguise myself in the end and go back to look at my own place.' Disguise himself he did, as a Somali, and got back to Gilgil, but only for three days – he had to 'hustle out of the country again very quickly'.

War had broken out by then and his brother Berkeley had been put in charge of six hundred goats which, for some reason, the Government wished to send to Zanzibar. He engaged Galbraith as an 'assistant stockman' under the name of Egerton. When they reached Mombasa, Berkeley was recalled and 'Egerton' instructed to take goats on to Zanzibar. He did so, at government expense. The deportation order was still in force, but war came to his rescue. His mother pleaded his cause with Lord Harcourt, Secretary of State for the Colonies, and in October 1914 he was back at Kekopey.

It was at this period of Galbraith's life that the writer Llewelyn Powys became his unlikely but congenial manager. Powys was a consumptive who had come to Africa to join his younger brother Will in the hope that the clean highland air would purge him of the disease. Will and Llewelyn were sons of the Rev. Charles Powys and his wife Mary, who reared eleven children in their vicarage at Montacute in Somerset.

Mary claimed the poet William Cowper as an ancestor and, more remotely, John Donne. Of her six sons, three became writers of distinction; although not widely read today they have a faithful following and a journal devoted to their works, and in their time stood high in the estimation of literary cognoscenti, if not on lists of best-sellers. These three were John Cowper, Theodore and Llewelyn. Of the daughters, Gertrude became a professional painter, and Marian a world authority on lace. Theirs was an intellectual, vital and exceptionally close-knit family. Most of the men enjoyed striking good looks; they were tall and well-built with fine-cut, positive features and tightly curled hair.[2]

Will, the youngest son, had the family good looks, but nature and the land appealed to him more than the arts. As a schoolboy he reared orphan lambs (his sister told me) in the orchard. His father obtained for him the tenancy of a farm on the Montacute estate, and he was happy there until lured away by the prospect of adventure in the wilds of Africa. Family tradition holds that too much time spent following the Blackmore Vale fox-hounds had something to do with his change of intention. If that was so, he made up for any neglect of duty by an almost obsessive devotion to it later on.

Early in 1914, at the age of twenty-six, he set sail for East Africa with practically no money and no plans save to visit an old friend called Barry who had a farm near Eburru in the Rift Valley. Barry had no job for him but lent him a mule on which to go and look for one. On the Kinangop, he wrote, 'I met a wild-looking man, Seymour, on a motor-bike. He gave me a job at once for my keep, but he did not like it much because I ate a pot of jam a day. I spent my time digging wells for windmills.' He was also instructed to round up any stray livestock he could find and drive them on to the government farm near Naivasha with whose manager Seymour had a feud.[3]

Will Powys moved on to work for the East African Syndicate whose huge block of land, almost all undeveloped, stretched from Gilgil to Thomson's Falls (now Nyandarua). Most of it was high, cold and wild with a good deal of forest, and it was here that Llewelyn joined his younger brother just after the start of the First World War. Llewelyn, still coughing blood, barely had time to pick up a smattering of livestock knowledge and Swahili before Will rode off on a mule to join the East African Mounted Rifles, leaving his brother in charge of two thousand head of cattle, fourteen thousand sheep and a virtually untrained labour force.

Anyone more unsuited to the life of a farmer in Africa it would be hard to imagine. Llewelyn had been a schoolmaster and had tried his hand at essays and sketches, up till then with scant success. His cast of mind was intellectual and aesthetic, his nature sensitive and sweet. The Powys good looks and charm of manner were his in full measure and, despite his illness, he seemed to overflow with zest for life and vitality. Women inevitably succumbed. 'His face had the beauty of an apple orchard under the sun,' wrote one of his mistresses, Alyse Gregory, whom he eventually married. Even when he lay dying in a Swiss sanatorium the novelist Ethel Mannin testified 'I have never known such charm – charm that kindles the senses like sunlight.' 'Lulu is in love with life and the visible world,' wrote one of his lovers. 'Those were his real paramours.' He was a pagan with a deep religious sense, a hedonist who shrank from hurting others. 'Deliberate cruelty is the only unpardonable sin, and personal fulfilment the principal virtue,' he wrote,[4] summing up the philosophy of the intellectual pace-setters of his day, before cruelty became a commonplace and personal fulfilment a justification for selfishness and greed.

To maroon such a man among the crudities of African farming was rather like pitching a maestro with a Stradivarius into a village brass band. He hated the cruelty and indifference to human life he saw in his surroundings, and the uncouthness of those Africans, and the coarseness of those Europeans, he encountered; hated them and feared them, yet responded to the country's beauty. One day, riding in the forest, he came upon a young and all but naked Kikuyu girl filling her water-gourd at a pool. Beguiled, he returned to assignations with her beside the pool and 'the long, lonely years I had passed in Africa made my whole being cry out for something to love, for some romance, for it is exactly this that is lacking in the great dark continent'. He contemplated a retreat from civilisation's complexities into a romanticised primitive world, and proposed marriage, African style. The girl's father named a bride-price but she herself shrank from so traumatic a step. So Llewelyn 'never again looked into the provocative eyes of this rare hamadryad of the African forest.'[5] He may not have looked into hamadryads' eyes but it was not in his nature to live for long without women. 'I see in the background three Kikuyu girls from far away,' he wrote to his brother. 'I shall perhaps select one when I come back to dinner tonight.' But the local women soon disillusioned him. He had been docking lambs' tails with a red-hot iron, an operation at which 'I am not very deft . . . even the black women give me small compensation – great black Gilgil trots poxed for the most part and without modesty.' In another letter he complained: 'how they lie and steal and deceive you – what duplicity behind their dusky skins!'[6]

After the East African Syndicate changed hands, he moved down to Kekopey in the Valley where life was rather more civilised. He and Galbraith Cole took to each other, though with reservations; in character and outlook they were poles apart. Galbraith (Llewelyn wrote) might be 'as hard as flint and crafty as a snake, and cold as ice, but by Jove he has a brain and one can say anything to him, and he will switch his brain on to it and ferret it out. He has more intelligence than anybody else in East Africa and more distinction of mind. He will discuss after our manner, and if he was not a Spaniard with the heart of an inquisitionist he would be a very delightful and illuminating companion.' Never in his life before, Llewelyn added, had he met so strong a character. That character had been forged in solitude and tempered by pain. 'I've lived much alone in my life and utterly alone in my thoughts,' Galbraith wrote in 1917. 'For sixteen years, ever since I thought at all, I've been in Africa and in some ways it's a hard country. One is constantly at war with nature and this must needs leave its mark on one's thought and ideas. Few people I've ever met would care to know the things I think and fewer still would sympathise or understand them, so I've shared them with the trees and the hills and the stars in the sky more than with people.'[7]

Galbraith regarded his new manager with wry amusement. 'When he first came, he used to ride furiously from one point to another and except to get a series of crashing falls he effected very little, but now he has learnt a lot and is really very good. He used to say, I don't know why I get so many falls while riding around looking at the meringoes, as he used to call them. I used to say, I should go a bit steadier if I were you, but still used to see him going like the wind over pig-holes and stumps as if there weren't any.' Llewelyn was 'not a lover of big silent places. He likes a walled garden where he can sit under an apple tree and have "exciting conversations" . . . He is so innately good that he is quite incapable of living up to his own theories.'

For Llewelyn, Africa was 'a country frequented by clawed creatures with striped and gilded pelts, where nettles sting like wasps and even moles are large as water-rats'. Worse than that, it was a continent where 'the sun, naked as when it was born, sucks out one's life blood, and nourishes savagery long since made dormant by the pious lives of one's ancestors'. 'Kill! Kill! Kill! is the mandate of Africa' he wrote in *Black Laughter*, one of two books of sketches based on his African experiences. 'Blood! Blood! Blood!' is the title of the last chapter, in which he relates how, on the shores of Lake Elmenteita – which he called Lake Elemental – the vultures, 'that host of godless hooped fowls', were drawn to him by his blood-red shirt, the shirt of a 'renegade stockman who, go where he might, was destined to carry upon his back until the day of his death the shocking striped band of Africa'.

In 1916 Lady Eleanor Balfour, daughter of the second Earl of Balfour and niece of the former Prime Minister, braved the submarines to spend a few months with her cousin Alison who was married to the Principal Medical Officer of the Protectorate, Dr Milne. Her fiancé had just been killed in France. She was young, tall, blue-eyed, fresh-complexioned, vivacious and attractive, endowed with intelligence, enthusiasm for good causes, a strong sense of duty and the heart of a lion. Galbraith hated what he called the 'peculiar vulgarity' of Nairobi and never went there unless compelled to do so by business. On such occasions he stayed with the Milnes, who kept open house for up-country folk. Under their roof he fell precipitately in love with Lady Eleanor. She went on safari with the Milnes, and stopped a few days at Kekopey, where Galbraith took her out in his car to shoot a buck, lending her a light rifle. She took careful aim at an impala and shot it through the heart. 'I did not know until months later,' she wrote, 'how much hung on that shot. Galbraith had said to himself "If she kills it, our friendship will ripen; if she misses, it will come to nothing." Well, I killed it all right.'[8]

After she returned to England, he continued his courtship by letter. In the following year he went 'home' to seek treatment for his rheumatism, and in December he and Nell were married in London. Her uncle, Arthur

Balfour, gave them the wedding breakfast. They returned to a scene of disaster. Drought had so shrivelled the pastures that nearly half the sheep had died. What hadn't shrivelled had been devastated by fires so ferocious that Delamere had had to drive his car on to his veranda to escape the flames. Rinderpest was decimating the cattle. Delamere had come over to inoculate Galbraith's beasts, had broken a precious syringe but managed to jab a thousand head with an old and blunt instrument. On top of that, East Coast fever, a tick-borne disease, had broken out. There was no dip for the cattle to go through at Kekopey, and one was hastily built. To crown it all, Galbraith collapsed with an attack of dysentery which very nearly killed him, and his arthritis revived in an acute form. Nell wrote: 'Galbraith is absolutely on the rack and can't last much longer in that pain.' He got no sleep, and acute colitis and toxaemia developed. 'I don't know how it will all end but if he can't get relief soon it will kill him.'

In this extremity, Dr Burkitt was sent for. Although there was little he could do, he had (Nell Cole wrote) a 'life-giving personality' and his mere presence did Galbraith good. Nurses came from Nairobi, and their neighbour Lady Colvile, who was French, volunteered to come and cook invalid dishes. Then came Spanish 'flu among the labour force, smallpox among the herdsmen, and Delamere's cook died of bubonic plague. 'My house is overrun with plague-carrying rats,' Llewelyn wrote. 'I am now trying to catch them and in one day have caught thirty.' The fleas that transmitted the infection were only supposed to be able to jump two inches, but 'not a few have had spring enough to reach my trousers, where to my great content I have caught and killed no less than three of these naughty insects'. The trials of Job were re-enacted in this beautiful but seemingly lethal Valley. Lady Colvile turned out *not* to be a good cook. Spanish 'flu put the railway and post office staff out of action, so an instrument needed to lance a painful abscess Galbraith had contracted failed to arrive. The nurse had to return to Nairobi. 'A serval cat got one of my turkeys,' Nell wrote, 'the boys are breaking all my china and I can't get the motor to go.' Over four thousand sheep died that year.

Gradually, painfully, Galbraith pulled round. He and Nell went off on safari beyond Laikipia to look for land free of the ticks that were destroying their sheep. There were no roads, and rhinos were so plentiful that in three days they saw twenty-one which they scared off with whistles. Galbraith kept going on twenty grains of aspirin a day. They found the land they wanted, and another stretch of open plain, almost waterless, was added to their estate.

There were credit items on this ill-starred ledger. Two sons were born. On the birth of the eldest, Galbraith sat on his veranda and thought of David's future. 'The apparently unending plains I see before me make me hope that his outlook will be as wide and free as those plains. I set little store by achievement. I would have him with a faculty for discrimination and for observing and appreciating all beautiful things and with a mental outlook that had no limit; if he had these, I should be content.'[9]

When at last the war ended, Will Powys came back to Kekopey after many adventures. He had captured six Germans, Llewelyn reported: 'the bullets whizzed round him but he did not care, when he got to their camp he ate a Hovis loaf and a great fat sausage.'[10] Later he had been put in charge of buying cattle in the Belgian Congo and transporting them to the armies in the field, and had been awarded a Belgian decoration. His return released Llewelyn to sail thankfully back to the civilisation to which he belonged. Time softened his memories of that unblest continent. Some years later he wrote to Galbraith's widow: 'Think of your being back at Gilgil again! Some day we will be seen walking together as we were fifteen years ago – our ghosts. What days they were! How odd that it should have been from you and you alone that I learned so many of the ways of life. I am glad I outlived him, glad I can still know like any spurfowl when the sun rises. Think of you having seen the sun rise in Africa again!'[11]

After four years of marriage, Galbraith wrote to Nell: 'The joy you bring me completely transcends all the pain I have suffered, ever.' But the pain did not abate as arthritis intensified. First he was obliged to walk with sticks, and once hobbled into the bush after a lion, and shot it. Then he was forced into a wheel-chair. The decision was made to retreat to England and a house was bought in Gloucestershire, but Galbraith felt exiled once again and longed for his own land, his sheep, and his servants, especially the Somali Jama Farah, who had been with him for many years and nursed him with great devotion. Galbraith lost the sight of one eye. 'I sit here watching the clock as if I were in prison . . . I want to die where I can hear a zebra barking.' He and Nell returned to Kekopey, where he sat on the veranda looking out across the lake and the plain with his one good eye while his flocks were driven past for inspection, and plans put before him for a new wool-shed and manager's house. The pain did not abate.

One day in October 1929 Nell loaded his revolver and took the dogs for a walk. Jama Farah supported his arm while he raised the revolver to his head. 'There is nothing sad about the spot where Galbraith lies,' Nell wrote. 'Its beauty is so exquisite it takes one's breath away.' And 'he lies there,' a friend related, 'looking out across the plain, watching the buck, watching the changing lights upon the lake and the sun going down over the Rift Valley.'

Galbraith's age was forty-eight. His brother Berkeley had died, unmarried, four years earlier, at the age of forty-two. Florence Delamere had also died young.

Nell took over the active management of Galbraith's two big ranches, with their many flocks and herds and Maasai herdsmen. She also became a moving spirit in the Moral Rearmament movement which swept through Kenya in the late 1930s. Known to begin with as the Oxford Group, it had been started by Frank Buchman with plenty of American showmanship and evangelical gusto. 'Absolute honesty, absolute purity, absolute unselfishness and absolute love' were the cornerstones of its doctrine. Those who sometimes faltered in pursuit of these aims foregathered periodically at 'house-parties' to confess their sins. At the MRA headquarters at Caux in Switzerland, super 'house-parties' were held to which the chosen were invited with all expenses paid, and it was rumoured that cakes and ale were more to the fore than sackcloth and ashes – probably this was merely a malicious rumour. I am sure that Nell Cole, like many others, was wholly sincere in her conviction that human morals stood in urgent need of reform and that the place to make a start was in one's own life and character, here and now.

Special efforts were made to persuade Africans to join; a number did, and when the Mau Mau revolt broke out in 1952 they refused, with great courage and at the risk of their lives, to take the oaths that were enforced with much obscenity to kill, maim and destroy white people and their livestock and property. In the three years that followed, Mau Mau adherents killed many more of their fellow tribesmen than of their designated foes. MRA supporters used the technique of group confession to bring to repentance men and women held in detention camps for Mau Mau offences, and to 'cleanse' them from the undoubted impurities of their revolting oaths.[12]

It was the Church of Goodwill which Nell built beside the main Nairobi-to-Nakuru road at the foot of the escarpment, on a corner of Kekopey, that was the cause dearest of all to her heart. It was built as a memorial to Galbraith, and as a thank-offering for the safe return of her two sons from the wars. Also, she wrote, she wanted to 'make a physical, visible demonstration of what I stood for – that is, Christianity'.[13] It stands today, a charming little church built of stone and timber from the estate, modelled on an old Mission church in Zanzibar. It was built, with many difficulties, at first by Indian and then by African artisans, and paid for entirely by Nell. The first service was held on 6 November 1949.

In age, Nell became rather a formidable figure – I suppose an arduous life, heavy responsibilities and a position of command had left their mark. But she was always kind and generous, quite without false pride or pettiness, and had memorable blue eyes with a look in them of candour, innocence perhaps, and now and then a glint of humour. She was an accomplished public speaker with a clear brain and an enthusiasm that kept her young in spirit, and was one of the first Europeans to become after independence, legally that is, a Kenya citizen. Kekopey she handed over to her younger son Arthur and his wife Tobina, daughter of her old friend Rose Cartwright, and her other property to David, who became the Earl of Enniskillen. She ended her days, indomitable and sanguine to the finish and rising ninety, in the home for the elderly established in Nairobi by the East Africa Women's League.

The third member of the trio of livestock barons I have mentioned – all were old Etonians – was Gilbert Colvile. Of the three, he was the least gregarious and the most single-minded in his devotion to his sheep and cattle. His father, Sir Henry Colvile of the Grenadier Guards, had been a distinguished soldier with a great array of medals. He had taken part in the relief of Khartoum in 1885 when General Gordon perished, and won a medal for his successful conduct of a campaign in Bunyoro while he was assistant Commissioner of Uganda from 1893 to 1895. Unfortunately his military career ended ingloriously in the Boer War when he was relieved of his command by General Roberts after an operation that had gone wrong. He met his end neither in battle nor in bed, but by being knocked over while on his bicycle near Bagshot in Surrey.[14]

His country seat was Lullington near Burton-on-Trent, and he took to wife a French lady, daughter of Pierre Richaud de Préville, who had a château in the Pyrenees. Gilbert was their only child. Probably he would never have settled in East Africa had he not blown off several toes while shooting rabbits, which disqualified him from taking up the commission in his father's regiment that he had gained on leaving Sandhurst. Soon after his father's death in 1907 he and his mother came to East Africa on the usual shooting trip. Gilbert so much liked what he saw that he gave up all idea of the army and decided to become a pioneer instead. After Lullington was sold he was joined by his mother, but she did not share his dwelling. Like Delamere and Galbraith Cole, Colvile became a Maasai addict. He learned their language, respected their independent spirit, admired their physique and tapped their expertise in cattle management. He also shared their indifference to comfort, and lived in a shack overrun by ill-disciplined dogs and furnished with the skins of wild animals imperfectly cured, and therefore smelly. As he acquired more land he ran up more dwellings; the living room of one of these was panelled with the skins of lions.

Lady Colvile built a more substantial house at Gilgil, near the railway station – too near; passenger trains stopped there at two o'clock in the morning to refresh their engines, and passengers often woke her up to ask for cups of tea. This prompted her to build a hotel where she installed a manager, and thereafter slept undisturbed. She died in 1930 on her way back to France and was remembered as a convivial, hospitable lady, cheerful and fond of good food, not at all misanthropic like her son. But apparently the Somali, or at any rate one Somali, disapproved; he thought it infra dig to keep a hotel, considered her to be seedy, and told the writer James Fox that she used to carry milk on her head. This seems extremely unlikely, but then the Somali was prejudiced, and disparaged Gilbert too because he used to travel with a Maasai herdsman clutching a spear in the front seat of his car.[15] Colvile lived like a Maasai, the Somali said, which put him quite beyond the pale.

I remember Gilbert Colvile as a smallish, wiry, rather wizened man, reserved but not unfriendly, who willingly answered my questions about Delamere, his neighbour and friend. In later life he looked rather like a tortoise. His Maasai name was Nyasore, meaning the lean man. 'When he was hunting he would go all day with only an egg and a cup of tea in his stomach,' one of his servants told Mirella Ricciardi, daughter of the Roccos who lived at Naivasha. 'Nyasore was a Maasai like us. There has never been another white man like him.'[16] He was a great hunter, especially of lions, and kept a pack of mongrel dogs who bayed the quarry until Colvile came up and shot it; I have been told that he destroyed over 250 lions in this way. He could be as hard on his dogs as on his men. One of his managers recalls seeing him draw his pistol and shoot a dog that misbehaved itself during a lion hunt. To protect himself from thorns he wore a jacket and trousers made from the skins of antelopes he had shot and cured himself.

His initial ranch was Ndabibi, lying to the north and north-west of Lake Naivasha and eventually covering 40,000 acres. His neighbours, the Carnelleys, were ardent conservationists, which Colvile most emphatically was not. He accused Stephen Carnelley of harbouring lions that devoured his, Colvile's, cattle, and then returned to sanctuary on Carnelley's land. As a result the two were not on speaking terms. Colvile was a dangerous enemy. Stephen Carnelley owned two small islands in the lake and kept them as a sanctuary for birds and hippos. Colvile set fire to them, destroying the bird life and forcing the hippos to seek new homes.[17] An odd quirk in Colvile's character was a passion for fires. Most people dreaded them, but Colvile liked nothing better than to set a match to a stretch of dry grass or a bush-clogged gulley on one of his ranches and watch the blaze roaring away. But first he always checked the state of the firebreaks and the direction of the wind, and estimated the chances of rain.

His mind and heart were centred on his cattle. To start with he followed the current fashion by importing pedigree bulls, but soon realised that their big-boned progeny needed a high-protein diet, and failed to thrive on sparse and fibrous veld grass; also they were more susceptible to disease. So he got rid of his imported beasts and replaced them by Borans, hardy Zebu cattle from the north. In this way he built up one of the country's best and largest herds of beef cattle. So he made money, a lot of money; on his death he was said to be worth over £2½ millions. 'To meet him you would think he had no money at all. He was very hard on his managers,' one of them told me, 'and very mean as well.' Despite this, most of them stuck to him, one for over thirty-four years, another for nearly twenty. Those who stood up to him did best. 'When I was appointed,' one of them said, 'I went round his estates and presented him with a long list of things I thought should be done. He said no to all of them, so I told him there was no point in having me as general manager if he was going to turn down all my suggestions. He said: "Don't be stupid, Romer, I always say no to start with, now begin again and give me reasons." He then agreed to everything, and I got on well with him after that.'[18] Like many rich people he would swallow a camel and strain at a gnat. He would buy an expensive tractor without a second thought but quibble at the cost of half a dozen pangas. Nor did he provide umbrellas for his Maasai herdsmen.

Everything he made he put into buying more land and breeding more cattle, until he possessed five separate properties totalling about 265,000 acres. (The largest, Lariak on the Laikipia plains, covered 160,000 acres.) His beef herd numbered about 20,000 head. In order to expand the sale and improve the quality of local beef, he started a cold storage company, and was one of the founders of the Kenya Meat Commission, and its first chairman. This entailed visits to Nairobi, and his shabby appearance – a rather dirty bush shirt and trousers, no tie and no socks – caused raised eyebrows among some of his tidier colleagues. Michael Blundell found him rude. Once, at a meeting, Michael addressed the chairman as Gilbert. 'My name is Colvile' was the frosty reply.

Politics held no appeal. 'We used to have quite lively meetings at Naivasha,' recalled a former DC, 'but Gilbert never came. He was out in the bush with the Maasai.' There was a streak in his nature of choosing to be 'agin the Government', even when co-operation was in his own interests. During the Mau Mau troubles, the DC I have quoted said: 'His place was absolutely crawling with very subversive fellows. The moment we pinned something on them, he hired an expensive lawyer in Nairobi who got them acquitted – Kapila I think, a very clever Indian who ran rings round the local magistrate.'[19] Colville avoided women, and took no part in Muthaiga's revels. Austere in habit, he did not smoke and touched no alcohol. Maasai snuff, raw and strong, seemed to be his only indulgence.

Then, at the age of fifty-five, came an extraordinary volte face. In 1941, Sir Delves Broughton was tried in Nairobi for the murder of Josslyn Hay, the twenty-second Earl of Erroll. The white community of Kenya was not prone to making moral judgements, but in this case the protagonists had gone too far. After Broughton was acquitted, both he and his much younger wife Diana, whose affair with Erroll had provoked the murder, were ostracised. Even at Muthaiga Club they found themselves unwelcome. After an interval Sir Delves Broughton, a broken man, returned to England, where later he committed suicide. Diana was left homeless, unhappy and with few friends. Colvile felt sorry for her and wrote to tell her so. She was a beautiful woman, elegantly dressed, fond of jewels, sophisticated, chic – a far cry from Maasai manyattas, lion hunts and cattle yards.

In a gesture which seemed quite out of character, he bought for her a mansion on the shores of Lake Naivasha whose Moorish look, with white crenellated walls and a minaret, had earned it the title of the Djinn Palace. Oserian was its real name. It had been built by Major Cyril Ramsay-Hill for his wife Molly, who had subsequently married Joss Erroll. Despite her wealth, which Erroll quickly squandered, her life with the handsome but unscrupulous Earl was unhappy. She sought consolation in drink and drugs and died miserably, leaving Erroll what was left of her fortune. James Fox wrote in his book that there is a portrait of Molly, Countess of Erroll, in the hall at Oserian, reclining on a canapé, which must be an interesting sight.[20]

To everyone's amazement, Gilbert Colvile and Diana Broughton married. Her acquaintances were as surprised as his; they had not cast her in the role of the wife of a rancher, least of all a rancher like Colvile. He was said to be the richest man in Kenya – probably several Indians were considerably richer – and known to be a recluse. The marriage appeared to be a happy one and lasted for twelve years. Gilbert taught Diana to ride about the plains, sustained by Maasai snuff, and muster cattle, while Diana weaned Gilbert from some of his Maasai ways and, when she could, from some of his more parsimonious habits. When one of the managers was in conference with the boss, she would have his car driven round to the pump and its tank filled with petrol. There was tragedy: a son was born, and lived only for a few days.

Diana was twenty-five years younger than Colvile and as sociable by nature as he was solitary. Soon after Tom Delamere, after a successful business career in London which enabled him to settle what remained of his father's debts, came to Soysambu to live, he and Diana met and fell in love, and amicable divorces for both Diana and Tom Delamere's wife were arranged. Colvile stayed on at Oserian, keeping a close eye on his cattle at Ndabibi and on his other estates. He remained on good terms with Diana and Tom, who sometimes came to stay at Oserian, and all three would be seen together at Nairobi races; but his life was, in the main, a lonely one. He had few friends. He and Diana had adopted a daughter, but she was away at school or else with her mother. His austere habits scarcely changed, and an excellent cook was sadly under-used. He reverted to one former custom: almost every evening his Dorobo headman, oddly named Swahili, would squat down on the living-room carpet and converse for an hour or so with his employer in Maasai. His constant companion was a pug called Peggy, a present from Diana. Peggy was buried beside him at Ndabibi after he had died in a Nairobi hospital, following a stroke, in August 1966, aged seventy-eight. His infant son lies there also, with Tom Delamere as well. He left Diana all his property, together with his mother's jewels. 'He was a hard man,' wrote a manager who had served him for many years, 'and did not suffer fools gladly, but believe me he was a clever man too.'[21] A younger manager, who knew him only in his later years, added: 'He was aloof and shy and enigmatic and peculiar but he was kind to me.'

CHAPTER 8

A Man of Big Ideas

Away to the north-west of the great Valley, on the crest of the escarpment which forms its western wall, lived another rancher and farmer, one with bold, original and sometimes hare-brained ideas. Like Galbraith Cole, Powys Cobb had fought in the Boer War and subsequently travelled north to spy out the land, and had fallen for the rolling open downs interspersed with belts of cedar forest, the chilly dawns and windswept uplands of the country round Molo. This was too high for small-scale cultivation or for Maasai cattle, and so was untouched by the mark of man.

He had picked out an area of 30,000 acres, named it Keringet after a river, and persuaded a friend to join him. John Hill-Williams with his wife and two small daughters went ahead in 1908, and Powys Cobb followed shortly afterwards at the head of a cavalcade consisting of his wife and two young children, a nanny and her husband, four bulls each of a different breed, six thoroughbred mares and a stallion, two bloodhounds – Prospero and Prosperine – two kittens and an assortment of ducks, geese, turkeys and hens, together with trunk-loads of clothes, furniture, saddlery, tools and general possessions. At Mombasa they paused while railway wagons were fitted with screens to protect the livestock from tsetse flies en route. From Molo station they proceeded by ox-wagon and on foot to the site of their new home where, Mrs Cobb had been led to believe, a substantial house awaited them. She had even brought soft furnishings from Heal's with which to equip it. It was typical of her husband that the house existed only in his imagination.[1]

While in some ways a practical man, Powys Cobb was also a dreamer, and the germ of this adventure lay in a dream. A lover of the sea, he had formed an ambition to buy an ocean-going vessel and equip it as a floating school for boys from poverty-stricken homes; then to sail to distant ports in search of adventure, and to inspire his pupils with a vision of the scope and grandeur of the world. While not a poor man, he was not nearly rich enough to finance so ambitious a project, and in the undeveloped highlands of East Africa he thought he saw the answer. There he would make a fortune, and return to England to devote it to the realisation of his dream.

I did not know all this when I first met him, as I was not yet eight years old. This was in 1914, when I had been despatched on a visit to the Hill-Williams, whose daughters were round about my age. The partnership with Powys Cobb had not lasted long, and by then the Hill-Williams had their own chunk of Africa called Marindas lying up against the forest boundary at an altitude of over 9,000 feet. Mountain streams rushing down from the forest were icy cold, and on their banks grew wild delphiniums, purple bog violets and, at certain times of year, drifts of dwarf gladioli. Maidenhair ferns stooped over the water, and the white flowers of an especially strong-scented jasmine starred the tangled undergrowth. Gertrude Hill-Williams had surrounded their cosy little thatched house made of rough-cut cedar planks from the forest with a garden full of English flowers — roses, extra-tall delphiniums, phlox, peonies, larkspur, tiger-lilies were there as well as daffodils and narcissi, and other bulbs of the English spring.

I loved Marindas, and especially picnics in the forest, sometimes beside 'rhino falls', so-called because above it was a dead tree used by rhinos as a scratching-post. To reach the little waterfall we followed a narrow path that twisted about among rocks and passed a cave said to be the home of a leopard. Hilda and Tuppence, the Hill-Williams children, told me that they sometimes kicked aside bones that the animal had gnawed. We were escorted by a young Nandi carrying a spear and by the nanny, Emily Bull, who feared nothing and rode about, side-saddle, on a mule. They were a wonderful breed, those nannies, plucked from the orderly routine of well-off English house-holds to find themselves surrounded by semi-naked tribesmen speaking strange tongues who dwelt among goats in (by nanny standards) horribly insanitary huts. The nannies were not much better off themselves in flimsy shacks with leaking roofs, lizards running up the walls and a possibility of snakes above the ceiling (when there was one) and scorpions crawling into boots. They had, as a rule, only their employers and their charges for company, and had to put up with male, black, alien nursery-maids. All this for very little pay, ten or twelve pounds a year. They took it in their stride, and some married farmers and became ladies of substance with nurseries of their own.

We saw a good deal of the Cobb family, whose standards of dress and behaviour were considerable higher than those of my own. Dorothy Cobb, who was two or three years older than I, envied me because I wore shorts, whereas she was clad in clean and tidy dresses, and her younger brother Tom in sailor suits. He possessed a most enviable little blue cart which was harnessed to a pet lamb. We stalked pigeons with bows and arrows copied from those of the Dorobo, but I do not think we ever hit anything. To begin with, both Dorothy and Mrs Cobb had ridden side-saddle, but they soon gave that up and rode astride like everybody else. Years later, Dorothy told me that I had taught her to tie shoe-laces; I suppose it had been done for her before that.

The Cobbs' labour force was drawn from several different tribes, and each tribe had its own village and headman. Maasai were employed to tend sheep and cattle, Kiksigis to serve as grooms, Kikuyu for the cultivations, and men from the Nyanza province near Lake Victoria to be trained in iron-work and carpentry. There was a foundry, a sawmill, a brick kiln and a carpenters' shop, in fact a miniature town up on those downs. Self-sufficiency was the Cobb objective.

I remember an alarming pack of large dogs in the care of Coley, the nanny's husband, who did the butchery – every worker had a regular ration of meat. The Maasai reserve was less than a dozen miles away, and the Cobb's high-grade cattle were an irresistible temptation to the warriors. Parties would come through the forest to frighten the herds-men and drive away as many of the cattle as they could. The dogs would be put on their trail and bay the animals until Powys Cobb or one of his assistants arrived to put the warriors to flight. The hounds themselves never attacked the rustlers. They were descendants of Prospero and Prosperine; and bloodhounds, fierce as they look, are gentle, sloppy-sentimental creatures. They would never go in for a kill. But lions and hyenas had also to be dealt with, and some of the bloodhounds were crossed with mastiffs, who introduced the needed strain of ferocity.

Until war came in 1914, a number of young Europeans were intermittently employed at Keringet, for Powys Cobb, like Delamere, was a strong believer in the white settlement of the highlands. He saw Keringet as a training ground for pioneers, much as the floating school of his dreams was to train young seafarers. Pupils used to pay for their apprenticeship then, rather than the other way round. Obviously this custom was open to exploitation, but, equally, a young man straight from school in Britain with no Swahili or farming skills was of little or no value to his employer for a year or so, and sometimes a liability.

Ned Powys Cobb had a passion for machines, the larger the better, and with great expense imported a pair of enormous steam engines which broke the flimsy bridges between Molo station and Keringet, and sank into the rivers. Once extricated, he stationed one on each side of the block of land he wished to plough and connected them by a cable and winch. A plough with six discs was then drawn to and fro between the engines. In theory, this greatly speeded up the cultivation, since a two-furrow disc plough was the most that oxen could manage. In practice, the engines often broke down, an untrained labour force got the chain and winch hopelessly tangled up, and the engines, which were wood-burning, needed a labour force of their own to keep them supplied with logs.

Once a year, the whole Cobb family migrated to the Coast, where Ned could indulge his passion for the sea. He also started there a sisal plantation. A safari into Jubaland – then part of the British Protectorate, later ceded to Italy – persuaded him that cotton would thrive on the estuary of the Juba river. Only a large plantation would do, to be worked by the most up-to-date plant. So machinery of gargantuan proportions arrived from America at Kismayu, on the mouth of the river. Kismayu was a very minor port indeed, attuned only to dhows. Somehow the machinery was got ashore but there it quickly, and irretrievably, sank into the mud. Great big dredgers and other colossi lay about in attitudes of abandonment and despair for many years, and may lie there still for all I know.

Many years were to pass before I again saw Marindas and Keringet. Both the Hill-Williams and the Powys Cobbs had gone. Despite his age and the aftermath of a serious injury – he had fallen into the blades of a mower, been gashed to the bone and stitched together by Powys Cobb – Jack Hill-Williams re-joined the army in 1915 and, two years later, died of cerebro-spinal meningitis contracted in Dar es Salaam. Hilda and Tuppence were then at school in Nairobi. They stayed for half a term. They were old enough to help their mother on the farm, and there was no money for school fees.

At Marindas their lives were solitary; all the younger folk had gone to the wars. They all but lived on their ponies, became proficient stockmen and mechanics, and grew to adulthood almost without contact with other white children. Africans were their companions, Swahili and a smattering of Kipsigis and Kikuyu their foreign tongues. They were much more scared, Hilda told me, of other European children their own age than of lions and leopards, which were all about. Their mother carried on their education by means of a correspondence course, and managed always to have books in the house. Determined to keep her own mind from rustication, at the end of the day's work she made time for serious reading; Hilda remembers that Gibbon's *Decline and Fall* was one of her favourites. Not until 1921, when they were nineteen and seventeen years old, did they leave Africa for an introduction to the civilisation of Egypt, as a start, and then of Europe.[2]

The fortunes of the Cobb children took a different course. The family returned to England in 1915, Powys Cobb wishing to re-join his regiment despite his age, forty-three. But he was found unfit for military service and went back to Molo, leaving his wife and children behind. They never re-joined him. All the pupils and managers had gone from Keringet, and help was badly needed. An acquaintance of the family heard about the situation and volunteered to fill the gap. She was young, intelligent and enterprising, the daughter of a successful architect and niece of a painter who became president of the Royal Academy. The moment Ethel Dicksee set eyes on Keringet she fell in love with it, and in due course its owner fell in love with her. After an interlude, she became the second Mrs Cobb.

But Keringet did not long survive the many wartime difficulties such as the disruption of markets – two hundred fattened pigs, for example, were killed and buried on the same day – followed by the currency débâcle of 1922, which increased the Cobbs' overdraft by fifty per cent. This broke him, and his bank foreclosed. He and Ethel salvaged thirty-seven heifers and, each riding one pony and leading another, drove them to the far end of the Mau escarpment, where a block of land called Mau Narok had not long since been released for white settlement. Like Molo, it was unoccupied, high and cold, and the Government considered that, if developed, it would act as a buffer-between the Maasai and the Kikuyu, who were already moving into the Rift Valley. Here Powys Cobb acquired another 30,000 acres. How he managed this when a penniless bankrupt I cannot imagine, but he did. He and Ethel went back to tents and oxen and, bit by bit, on borrowed capital, built up another enterprise and made another home.

Many waters cannot quench love, and bankruptcy did not quench Powys Cobb's passion for grandiose schemes. The shipping of produce to distant markets was unreliable and expensive; Powys Cobb decided to build his own fleet. For a reason it is difficult to fathom, plans were made to lay the keel of the first vessel on the shores of Lake Naivasha, by rail nearly four hundred miles from the Indian Ocean. How it was eventually to have reached the sea was never revealed. An American engineer called Thaxton arrived to take charge. He, Ned Powys Cobb and Ethel stayed for some days at Kekopey while the project was being launched, an experience that the vessel itself was never to enjoy. Nell Cole was unsympathetic. 'I never met a man who could talk rot so unceasingly,' she wrote. 'Galbraith says he is like a buzzing mosquito that one longs to catch in a net.' Others, however, thought him an excellent raconteur who could keep his audience in fits of laughter.[3]

Delamere, too, thought kindly of him. The rains in 1930 were exceptionally heavy, and ruined seven hundred acres of the Cobbs' barley which rotted on the ground. Prices were slumping and the rest was not worth harvesting. 'I'm afraid it means their selling the developed part of their farm and starting again on another bit,' Delamere wrote. 'Rather hard at Cobb's age to start all over again, and for her after making their home so nice. But it has happened to all pioneers in all the countries they have made. Their joy is in the creation of something out of nothing.'[4] Powys Cobb himself made the same point. 'One works because of the fascination of it, because each furrow turned, each calf born, is a tiny step towards a distant goal.' But in a disillusioned moment he exclaimed: 'Africa is a sink!' With restored confidence, he quoted the saying: 'Farming is more than a living, it is a way of life.' One of his Molo neighbours, Jack Lipscomb, adopted as his maxim: 'Live as if you would die tomorrow, farm as if you would live forever.'

Mau Narok was not far by crowfly from my parents' home at Njoro, although some distance by road. One day Nellie, on impulse, decided to pay a call on the Cobbs by walking along the crest of the escarpment which rose steeply above her farm. So far as anyone knew there was no path, only thickets of giant heather and even taller brambles, with slithery tufts of coarse, reedy grasses growing in boggy ground in between the thickets. We planned to camp on top and make an early start so as to reach our goal before the sun grew fierce. The Cobbs, we thought, would give us lunch and we could make our way back to camp in the cool of the evening.

The plan did not work out like that. We loaded up a donkey with our gear and, taking Mbugwa and several dachshunds, clambered up through the cedar forest, then through a belt of bamboos, then out on to the moorland with its dripping heather and squelchy turf, and found a spot relatively sheltered from a chilly wind for our camp. On one side lay the Maasai reserve stretching down to the Tanganyika border and beyond, on the other side the Rift Valley, but we could not see either because of the giant heather and, at daybreak, a clammy mist. The only wildlife we saw, apart from a pair of mountain francolins, was a solitary eland. Cockie had come with us and next morning, over an early breakfast, suggested that we might stay the night at the Cobbs. Colonial hospitality seldom failed, and they would be sure to have a nice warm fire and a good dinner. So we started later, taking toothbrushes, and Cockie wore her pyjamas underneath her shirt and trousers. The dachshunds came too.

Mau Narok, which means the black mountain, turned out to be much further than we had expected and the going a good deal worse. We had to keep changing our direction in order to avoid bogs, steep ravines or patches of especially thick bramble and heather. The dogs leapt over and among the tussocks like so many porpoises; they kept on gallantly but, when we paused, cast us reproachful glances. Nellie was nervous lest they might lag behind and come upon a leopard, or the leopard upon them, and it was far from unlikely that we might encounter a herd of buffalo; nor were rhinos out of the question.

Hours went by before, footsore and weary, we sighted thankfully the first sign of human habitation – a fence. Then came a cart-track of sorts and at last a shingle roof rising above a grove of young trees. Too late for lunch, we feared, but no doubt we should be offered something. Cockie congratulated herself on her foresight in bringing her pyjamas. No one was at home.

We dug out of his hut a surly house-boy who led us to a spacious sitting-room lined with cedar slabs and bookshelves, with large windows commanding a tremendous view, and with great cedar rafters supporting a lofty roof. It was well furnished, nothing shoddy; gone long ago were tables made from petrol boxes and amerikani. I dimly remember, after so many years, a big, polished gateleg table standing beneath a large window, and sprinkled with magazines and journals, many of them scientific, proceedings of learned societies and the like. Archaeology and astronomy seemed to be the favoured subjects – the past and the stars.

There was a long wait before the owner appeared, summoned from the wheel-side of an ailing tractor and in no mood for colonial hospitality. He was a smallish man with very pale eyes, no noticeable eyebrows and a trim pointed beard like that of General Smuts, whom he somewhat resembled; in fact, I think he had taken the General for his model. He told us that Ethel was away and his cook on holiday, and offered us a cup of tea. It was an exhausted little party, human and canine, that limped back to camp with blistered feet and aching limbs through a misty drizzle and a fading light.

That was my last glimpse of Ned Powys Cobb. In thirty years he and Ethel between them with their African labour – I think Ethel was the real driving force – created a better, more productive, more successful enterprise than that at Molo, which had passed into the hands of an Italian family. Thousands of bags of wheat and barley jolted down to the station, cream to the creamery, pigs to the bacon factory, fat beasts to the slaughterhouse, wool to the London auctions. More white farmers came to the district, and so did many Kikuyu families with their goats and cattle and ever-growing families. Ethel had no children. In his eightieth year, in 1952, Powys Cobb sold most of his farm to the European Agricultural Settlement Board, which was buying land from white farmers and dividing it into smaller units for lease or sale to immigrant newcomers. He kept back what he called 'a foothold' of 5,000 acres for Ethel.

His youthful ambition to go down to the sea in ships had been shelved, not forgotten. 'I want,' he wrote, 'to end my days in freedom, and only the sea can give that.' He bought a yacht, and he and Ethel cruised for several years among the Greek islands and around the

Mediterranean. But he was no longer able to sail his own vessel, and a hired master was not the same. So he retired again, this time to a houseboat on a mere in Holland, where he died in 1959.

Ethel returned to her 5,000-acre 'foothold', and turned it into a well- stocked, well-organised and fruitful farm. At the same time, and like Nell Cole, she created a lasting memorial to her husband – a church. This she designed herself from start to finish, built it with the aid of semi-skilled masons, and carved with her own hands the altar-rails and other features. It was a replica of an English village church in every detail, and of no mean size. Her neighbours looked on with a certain wry amusement, for Ned Powys Cobb had often proclaimed himself an atheist.

Like most of the white farmers, those of Mau Narok were almost completely insulated from the political tremors that could have warned them of the earthquake to come. 'I have just heard,' Ethel wrote in 1961, 'that there is a plan afoot for Government to buy the whole of our lovely Mau Narok and place Kikuyu squatters on it with ten acres to each family. It is a terrible thing . . . ' She had, she wrote, one thousand acres under crops and large flocks of sheep; 'the farm is very nearly developed to its capacity and looks so lovely, it breaks my heart.' Twenty-nine other white farmers in the district would have to go. And 'what will become of our old employees, some of whom we've had for thirty years? I simply don't know how I could possibly leave my lovely little church to its fate. I feel I *must* try to stop and look after it.'

But two years later she said goodbye forever to the church, the farm and her employees and to her home, and bought a couple of acres on the Isle of Man. Farming was in her blood, and it is an infection for which there is no known antidote, not even failure. Soon she had one hundred and seventy acres and was keeping sheep and cattle again. Also she designed and had built a number of self-contained flats for the elderly, and when she died in her eightieth year in 1975 she left most of her remaining property to provide for the upkeep of Ballycobb, as she had named her modern almshouses.

And the little church? The faces of the congregation have changed colour, but there are many more of them than before, and the church is well maintained. A simple inscription in the porch commemorates the name of Edward Powys Cobb.

CHAPTER 9

Under the Mountain

Only dwellers in a country often pulverised by drought would have written: 'I will lift up mine eyes unto the hills, from whence cometh my help', because that is where help does come from, from springs and storms. Help for the livestock barons of the Rift Valley came mainly from the Aberdare mountains, rising darkly to the east, mantled with forest and moorland and frequently muffled in mist and cloud.

One night a long time ago my parents, a young syce called Chegge and myself emerged from the dripping forest on ponies stumbling with fatigue to see a light winking at us through the trees, a sight as welcome to us as a safe den to a hunted creature, for we were cold and hungry and had lost our way; the night was resonant with menacing noises, Nellie had broken a stirrup, Jos had lost his compass, Chegge kept muttering about evil spirits, and a boil on my bottom was giving me hell.

We had arrived at a low and rambling log house beside a stream, and were greeted with surprise – for we had come unannounced and by an unusual route – by Captain Ernest Fey and his wife Mary. Above their outpost, forest rose to the summit of the Kinangop, the southernmost of the Aberdares' three peaks – like all these names, a Maasai one, derived from a phrase meaning 'those who live in the mists of high places'. Below lay a sweeping open plateau, bare of trees and creased by an occasional gulley, ending in an escarpment dropping into the Rift Valley.

Sometime in 1906 a curious procession could have been seen setting out from Naivasha station beside the lake of that name. In the van walked Captain Fey and his son Jim followed by Mary in a sedan chair borne by four hefty Africans. Beside it walked their daughters Nell and Norah clad in the long, tight-waisted skirts and blouses with mutton-chop sleeves of the day, and creaking along behind was an ox-wagon piled high with all their gear.

For many years the Captain had sailed his vessel with his family on board – two of the children had been born at sea – across the Indian Ocean and the China seas, and the time had come to settle down.

They chose an odd place to do so, eight thousand feet above sea-level and nearly four hundred miles from the sea. It was cold and bleak and truly at the back of beyond, with a few Dorobo hunters in the forest for neighbours, elephants and buffaloes for company, and the nearest settlement two days' march away. They clambered up the scarp, crossed the plateau and, when they reached the forest and could go no farther, said to each other: 'This is where we'll make our home.'[1]

There was a difficulty: the district had not yet been surveyed, and until this had been done no land could be parcelled out for settlement. But the Captain had been told of a loophole in the law. You could take out a temporary prospecting licence, search for minerals and peg out claims, regardless of whether or no the land had been surveyed. Captain Fey was obliged to return to sea, leaving Mary in charge. She was a slight, wiry and energetic New Zealander. Directing a small force of Kikuyu labour they had brought with them, she had holes dug all over the surrounding countryside and pegs stuck in to mark her claims. Then she embarked on a three-day journey to Nairobi, registered the claims, and returned to build a dwelling-place and start to clear bush and forest. When, two years later, the land was surveyed, the Feys got what they wanted for a down payment of one rupee an acre.

The surveyor in question was a young man called Max Nightingale, and he married Nell, the Feys' eldest daughter. I do not know whether Max and Nell's three children were actually born in an ox-wagon, but that is where they spent their early childhood, travelling all over the Protectorate and with no other home. The eldest son, Jim, remembered walking along behind the wagon, at the age of four or five, to escape the jolts and lurches, and weeping in anguish when, unable to keep up, he saw his home disappearing in the distance in a cloud of dust. At seven years old he became the first pupil to arrive, on his Somali pony, at the newly opened Kenton College, a preparatory school housed in an imitation German schloss perched on a mountainside near Kijabe station. The headmaster, Captain Cramb, had been adjutant of the Black Watch. He enforced strict discipline, wielded the cane, lived for his job and kindled in his pupils an abiding interest in the wildlife of a countryside as yet undefiled. 'We small boys had all of Africa at our doorstep,' wrote Venn Fey, one of the sea-captain's grandsons.[2]

It was at Kenton that Jim Nightingale started a lifetime's love affair with bees. He would go off honey-hunting in the cliffs below the forest with other boys, to rob wild bees that bred in crevices among the rocks, taking the dark honey full of grubs. The boys wore no protective clothing and got badly stung, but it was a point of honour not to retreat. At Njabini, the Feys' home, a half-Kikuyu, half-Dorobo man called Gichuhi took Jim on long expeditions into the forest to collect honey from the many hives he owned. Hives were made of hollowed-out logs, which one saw all over the place wedged in the forks of trees, and until I read Jim Nightingale's treatise on the subject, tape-recorded in his old age, I had no idea how complex were Dorobo techniques.[3] Beekeepers like Gichuhi knew just which flowering trees produced the best-flavoured honey, where they grew, and when they were in flower – there was one (*Mimulus solensii*) that bloomed only once every seven years. The commonest bee-tree was the Dombeya, whose clusters of pinkish flowers rather like cherry blossom gave rise to lavish quantities of honey. Every hive was individually owned, and to take another man's honey a heinous crime never, or almost never, committed, for fear of supernatural punishments that would certainly follow.

Nowadays the march of progress, and especially the spread of Christianity, has undermined such sanctions, and hives are often robbed. So now they are generally placed close to peoples' homesteads where an eye can be kept on them, instead of away in the bush and forest; nectar within the bees' reach, therefore, is soon exhausted. The dwindling of the forests has also deprived the bees, who have become more aggressive, because the gentler kinds (there are several sub-species), more easily robbed, have tended to die out, and the fiercer kinds to survive. So bee-keeping has become more painful to humans as well as more difficult for bees. Jim Nightingale won a worldwide reputation among apiculturalists for his studies of wild bees, and for marrying traditional African practices to western skills. He imported modern hives, and taught African bee-keepers to separate grubs, comb, pollen and propolis (a kind of aromatic glue used by the bees in hive construction), formerly all mixed up together, from pure honey. For the first time honey became a marketable product, and a useful addition to African family incomes.

Jim in due course married Barbie Polhill, daughter of a fellow farmer on the Kinangop. Her father, Stanley Polhill, had come to Kenya to take charge of the monster-machines imported by Powys Cobb, including three ponderous combine-harvesters which had no guards to protect people from their moving parts. Stanley Polhill's jacket got caught up in the cogs of one of the machines. He was dragged in and cut open from chest to groin; one lung and several ribs were torn away and his anatomy exposed to the skies. This was at Mau Narok. The nearest hospital was over thirty miles away along the roughest of wagon-tracks, and his ambulance an almost springless early-model Ford. How he survived to reach Nakuru was a miracle. A further miracle was performed by Dr Burkitt. He fitted a football valve to a bicycle pump which he attached to the surviving lung, and organised two-hour shifts of Africans to pump air all round the clock. It was nearly a year before Stanley Polhill was discharged from hospital.

When he settled with his wife and family on the Kinangop in the usual mud-and-bamboo cabin with a cowdung floor, his wounds still needed daily dressing, and he was too weak to drive a tractor. His wife and a young governess took over. They marked out a stretch of grassland, ploughed and drilled it, only to find when they harvested their crop that their wheat was unsaleable – the Depression had started – so it stayed where it was to rot in a shed. His daughter Barbie still remembers the smell of mildew mixed with that of iodoform from her father's dressings.[4]

After she and young Jim Nightingale were married they established what must surely be a record, though it is not in any Guinness book. Since to buy a farm of their own was financially impossible, they moved in with Jim's parents, Max and Nell Nightingale. In twelve years, Barbie bore six children and they all lived together amicably, so Barbie assured me, under one roof. The phrase 'under one roof' is perhaps not strictly accurate, since Kenya houses had a habit of expanding to meet new needs, a rondavel or two being run up now and then, but they did all feed at one table except for children under seven. Jim worked his father's farm and learnt more and more about bees until, after twenty-four years of marriage and living with in-laws, he and Barbie could at last afford to build a house of their own. They called it Sasumua, after the yellow-flowered hypericum so much relished by bees. This was in 1959.

In their mountain fastness they had, like others, failed to read the writing on the wall. In 1962 the Kinangop area was bought up by the Government for division into African small-holdings, and the white farmers had to go. Jim and Barbie took their bees, their cattle, sheep and horses, their turkeys, rabbits and hens and all their possessions as far as Njoro, where a new Sasumua came to birth. Jim's grandparents, the sea-captain and Mary, had died in 1936. Stanley Polhill had lived to breed an improved strain of pyrethrum which he gave away to his neighbours and which is still being grown, and to climb the summit of the Kinangop, at nearly 13,000 feet, with his one lung.

Between the eastern side of the Aberdares and the foothills of Mt Kenya, lie the rich farmlands of the Kikuyu and, north of these, the great open plains of Laikipia. Although I was loyal to my childhood home at Njoro I think this was my favourite region, because of its wildness, its sense of freedom, the feeling that you could see to the ends of the earth and beyond, and the wild animals still there in abundance, whereas in the settled districts round Njoro most of them had gone. Above the plains the great brooding presence of Mt Kenya rose not abruptly but gently, like a swelling breast, to its twin white nipples; even when it was concealed by cloud you always knew that it was there. Something of its spirit seemed to permeate the air, a spirit ancient and impassive, indifferent to all human concerns and yet charged with unvoiced secrets. As I walked in its shadow a few lines from a poem by Walter de la Mare[5] used to come into my mind: although written of the Sphynx that

> Gazes with an unchanging smile
> Man with all mystery to beguile
> And give his thinking grace

they seemed to fit the Mountain.

As a child I stayed in a district north of Nyeri where the shoulders of the mountain began to flatten into the plain. All this land had been surveyed and 'opened up' under the Soldier–Settler scheme launched in 1919, so most of the scattered white community were Captains, Majors, Colonels and even Generals, with an occasional Commander or two, and their wives. My hosts were General Beynon and his wife, who had a permanent, red-bearded guest, with the highest (i.e. best) polo handicap in the country, Colonel Durand. The reason for my intrusion with my pony into this military stronghold was the Beynons' daughter Kate, a few years older than I and assumed to yearn for the company of other children. This was not the case; she was perfectly content with a life centred round the care of a large pack of very large Irish wolfhounds, which constantly barged about with lolling tongues and lashing tails knocking things over, and defeating Mrs Beynon's half-hearted attempts to keep the rondavels which made up the homestead in some sort of order.

However, the wolfhounds turned out to be a blessing, as they needed great quantities of meat supplied by wild animals, anything from zebras to the waggle-tailed tommies of the nearby plain. I was going through a horribly bloodthirsty phase, and was delighted to act as a self-appointed hunter.

I would dress by the light of a hurricane lamp, fill my pockets with cartridges and go forth in the chilly, mysterious dawn, with ribbons of pearly mist lying in the gulleys and the great bulk of the mountain at my back shrouded in cloud which flushed flamingo-pink just before the sun came up behind it to flood the plain. The bush almost came up to the rondavels, and was interspersed with steep little ravines and with tongues of open glade, ideal for stalking; every step you took was an adventure. You picked your way with all your senses tight as a bowstring, your eyes alert for the quiver of a twig or a flash of movement – oryx? impala? eland? – or for a creature frozen into immobility with horns upright for a split second before vanishing like a spirit; and your ears pricked for a rustle in the long grass, the click of hoof on stone, a reedbuck's whistle, the warning call of a bird. For years, in later life, I kept a print made from a watercolour by Bryan Hook: a rhino was emerging from behind a clump of bush to gaze impassively at three oryx with uplifted heads; in the background rose the mountain's peak. This picture trapped a fleeting moment, and encapsulated the loneliness, the wildness, and the spirit of a primeval world that had existed since time began and where man was an intruder. Now the print, the creatures and that world are all gone.

I hoped, when on these sorties, to come upon a lion sloping off, perhaps, to digest his night's kill. A lion was the most sought-after of all the trophies and it could be killed without a licence, which elephants and buffaloes could not. I had a beautiful little Mannlicher-Schonneur

.256, very accurate, which most people said was too light for big game, and that a great big double-barrelled .450, whose kick was liable to knock you down, was the right weapon to use. But I had read that Neumann, perhaps the greatest elephant hunter of all, always used a .256 to bring down his prey. I learnt later that Gilbert Colvile did the same.

One day I saw what I was hoping for – a round, tawny, whiskered face with yellow eyes glaring at me from the long grass about fifty yards away. I fired, the face disappeared. I approached the spot with caution, as I had been taught to do; there was no movement; the tawny body lay stretched out, stone dead. But it was spotted. When half obscured by grass or bush and fleetingly seen, a cheetah's head can be mistaken for that of a lioness. I would never knowingly have killed a cheetah. An African escort always came with me, carrying a knife and a rungu (a kind of club) tucked into his belt. We skinned the cheetah and for years I had its supple, black-and-yellow pelt beside my bed.

To console me for my disappointment, General Beynon undertook to get me my trophy, but in the Indian not the African style. The British in India shot their tigers either from the backs of elephants, or by sitting up all night over a kill in a machan, a platform built in a tree. A suitable tree was selected, a machan constructed, a zebra shot and dragged to a position almost underneath the branches, and at nightfall we ascended by means of a ladder, which was then removed, and settled down for a night's vigil – the General, the Colonel and I. On the first night, nothing came. On the second, we heard crunchings and snufflings and other unsocial noises and saw, by the light of a half-moon, that hyenas had arrived. The zebra had begun to smell. The machan was most uncomfortable. I kept falling asleep and wondered what was to be done if I needed to pee. On the third night, the zebra was stinking to high heaven, the hyenas there in force with a jackal or two, but still no sign of a lion. After that we gave up, and I decided that Indian methods might be all right for tigers but they were uncomfortable, boring and unsporting when applied to African lions.

The Colonel and the General were avid polo players and spent much of their spare time in a wire cage mounted on a wooden horse and bashing polo balls about; the cage was so constructed that the ball always rolled back to the feet of the striker. Fierce weekend battles took place between the Nyeri team and that from Nanyuki, the focus of the soldier-settlers on their scattered, unmade farms. I think the polo ground must have been laid out before almost anything else at Nanyuki except for a few dukas and the rough wooden post-office-cum-store put up by Major Lionel Gascoigne. His wife Renie was a masterful and energetic lady said to be eccentric. This is a quality that can only be defined by giving examples, and actual examples, I have always found, are hard to obtain. 'He did some odd things' is generally about as far as you can get. The only instance of Renie Gascoigne's eccentricity I heard of was related by a friend of hers who met her walking along Nanyuki's single dusty street at ten o'clock in the morning in an elegant blue velvet evening dress. When her startled friend enquired the reason, Mrs Gascoigne replied: 'There's a dance this evening at the club, and it's always such a nuisance changing one's clothes.'

There was no railway to Nanyuki and the railhead was at Thika, about a hundred miles away. Sometimes wagons and the early motor cars could get through and sometimes not, and produce had to get to market as best it could. One of the first settlers in the district, possibly *the* first, was Arnold Paice, who was there before the 1914 war. He sent his pigs to market on foot over the top of the Aberdares. The journey took ten days and the pigs, he claimed, lost no more than twelve pounds each by the time they reached Naivasha station, and fetched £2 a head.[6] Optimism is endemic in the pioneer mentality, and it was carried to extremes by one Paul Chapman who in 1910 started a market garden and poultry farm on the far side of a river that could only be reached, or the produce taken out, by swinging across from the overhanging branches of trees. This must have led to a lot of cracked eggs.

Besides the soldier-settlers, the other main element in the white population was the South Africans. Seagar Bastard was a well-known figure; his wife sent turkeys once a week to Thika in a wagon in two tiers, hens at the bottom and gobblers at the top. The Bastard clan proliferated; it was said that if you walked down the Nanyuki street and called out 'Bastard!' every second European would turn a head. But another South African family, the Randalls, took the palm for fruitfulness with eight boys and six girls. The district's first medico,

Dr Doig, had no car, so he built a hut near his dwelling where wives could come and have their babies, if they got there in time.

Nanyuki was (and is) right on the equator, though you would not think so on a cold August day, and Commander Logan Hook so designed his Silverbeck hotel that the equator ran right through the bar. You could have one drink in the northern and the next in the southern hemisphere, or one drink in both at once, a foot on each side of the line. By the time I re-visited the township in 1934, a second hotel had appeared. It was then about a year old, and could put up eight guests, and the owner and manager was an old friend, Gertrude Hill-Williams, assisted by her daughter Tuppence. Gertrude had sold Marindas at Molo after Hilda, her eldest daughter, married David Furse, and bought the Beynons' farm where they intended to grow wheat. Tuppence had become an expert self-taught mechanic and brought up two tractors, almost the first in these parts – this was in the mid-1920s – cleared some of the bush where I had stalked the wolfhounds' potential dinners, and got in several hundred acres of wheat. Warthog rootled in the wheatfields and then came zebras from the plain. The zebras were having their last fling. They were still out on Laikipia literally in millions, so that 'the very air', wrote Raymond Hook (Logan's brother) 'vibrated with their monotonous call'.[7] The slaughter had already started, carried out mainly by Dutchmen on horseback who could get two or three shillings for each hide. Raymond Hook recorded that a Dutchman he went out with shot forty in a morning, and that this was about an average bag. What finally sealed their fate, so I was told, was a decision by the Bulgarian army to clothe their men in zebra-hide boots.

The Hill-Williams fenced against the zebras, but then locusts came. 'Have you picked your wheat yet?' Tuppence was asked – a sick joke because a few ears on broken stalks was all that was left, together with a nasty smell. Tuppence and her mother tried again. This time they reaped a splendid crop, sent it off, got an advance and reduced their overdraft. Suddenly, prices collapsed. The Hill-Williams had to pay back most of their advance.

That finished them as farmers; and Gertrude decided that she would like to start a hotel. An unusual ambition: she was by then in her sixties, and had no experience whatever of keeping hotels. When I asked her what had appealed to her about it, she replied: 'I wanted to have a swinging sign.' Her son-in-law, farmer-artist David Furze, designed one for her, a splendid sign with a pair of leopards couchants on top, and underneath pictures of heads of buffaloes and several antelopes, and a pair of trout. This was the sign of The Sportsman's Arms. Excellent fishing was to be had in clear, cold streams born in the glaciers and stocked with rainbow trout, and other visitors came to climb the mountain, at least part of the way up. I wondered whether two women on their own in an outback kind of place might have had trouble with roughs and toughs and drunks. 'Not much,' Tuppence said. 'We learned to cope.' I could believe it; Tuppence, tall, deliberate of speech and with a good handicap at polo, would not have been easily ruffled. The landlords' worst troubles, she said, apart from the normal crises of hoteliers, came from certain units of the British army stationed· in Nanyuki. Once a military lorry drove up at dead of night and carried off all the furniture on the veranda.

If you wanted to explore the mountain, the man to guide you was Raymond Hook, brother of the Commander – naturally called Boat Hook – who kept the Silverbeck hotel. Both were sons of the painter Bryan Hook, who in 1912 had travelled in East Africa with his son Raymond and his eldest daughter, and bought some undeveloped land near Nanyuki. Raymond stayed on as a pupil of Delamere's, soldiered through the East African campaign and then settled on his father's land, but never seriously farmed it.

He came to know the mountain like the back of his hand. Tall, heavily built, tough as an old boot and with a voice soft as a dove's, his nature was a curious blend of the gypsy and the don. He lived like a pig, oblivious of squalor and inured to discomfort, yet could quote in the original Greek pages from Homer or Plato, and had made a study of Egyptian hieroglyphics. Off he would go up the mountain with a bag of posho, and another of beans, loaded on a mule, with a groundsheet for shelter and a thumbed copy of a Greek classic in his pocket, to disappear for weeks on end. Nothing escaped his eye. Once, Tuppence told me, as they rode through the bush, a tiny mouse shot across the path, visible only for an instant. Without hesitation, he named its genus and species. Another, and less agreeable, memory was of lunching with him in his dwelling, in which animals were just as welcome as humans. Becoming aware of an unpleasant smell, she enquired as to its origin. Raymond Hook replied: 'Watch where the bluebottles settle.' They settled in a corner on a stinking mess that proved to be a litter of very dead puppies.

He became an expert at catching wild animals to be shipped off to zoos, a cruel and heartless business as it seems to me. He was the first man to trap a bongo, that shy and secret denizen of the forest, and sent it to the London zoo – the poor caged creature gave birth to a calf on shipboard. Raymond crossed zebras with horses to produce zebroids, and tried to do the same with buffaloes and cattle, but without success. 'Although he loved his animals,' I was told, 'he didn't look after them properly but adopted a policy that if you had enough of them, it didn't matter much if half of them died.'[8]

Cheetahs were a speciality. He lassoed them from horseback on the plains and sold them to zoos and to an Indian Maharajah, who used them for hunting gazelle. Since cheetahs have clocked up speeds of sixty-four miles an hour, almost twice that of the fastest horse, he had to tire them out. This involved galloping at full tilt over terrain riddled by invisible pig-holes.

Raymond Hook took twelve cheetahs to London, intending to match them against greyhounds at the White City, but the managers of the track turned down his proposal. A race was organised elsewhere but disappointed; the cheetahs shot away and left the greyhounds standing; the dogs could do no more than forty-two miles an hour. Then he went off into the Aberdare mountains to search for the spotted lion, said by some to belong to a separate species or sub-species. A farmer had shot two specimens and had photographed the skins but not kept them; they were not only spotted but smaller than those of the average lion. With a rich young sportsman, Kenneth Gander Dower, who wrote a book about it called *The Spotted Lion*, Hook searched the chilly bogs and jungles of the mountain in conditions of extreme discomfort, Raymond discoursing on Greek philosophy and comparative religions while soaked through, hungry and benighted in some uncharted ravine. The hunters never caught so much as a glimpse of their quarry.[9]

Surprisingly, perhaps, Raymond Hook married, and Joan, his wife, did her best to civilise him, but with little success. 'He was uncivilisable' was the general verdict. Twin daughters were born. After less than ten years of marriage the parents parted company – Joan Hook couldn't any longer stand chickens nesting under beds, goats bouncing in and out, and snakes under the kitchen stove. Thereafter they lived at different ends of the property, and it fell to Joan to create a farm from the land Raymond had used merely as a perch, and to bring up her daughters. Their father was proud of them in some ways, but ignored them in others – 'he always forgot our birthdays,' one of them said, 'but was most upset if we forgot his'. Yet when they were away at school he wrote them long letters designed to kindle and enlarge their interest in wildlife and their surroundings. When one of them married, he gave her half her mother's cattle as a wedding present.

His story ended sadly. He ran out of money, his health deteriorated and, after several months in hospital, he lost the will to live. Then, in 1968, Joan was found murdered in her house, a mystery that was never solved. The shock worsened his condition, and within a few months he, too, was dead.

In the snapshots of those days, contrasts between black and white were often sharp. A chalky face, a black shadow. So it was with many of the people. In some, like Raymond Hook, the elements were mixed within their natures; with others, the contrast lay between the civility of their backgrounds and the crudeness of their lives. There was, for instance, Taffy, whose sister Lady Bettie, with her husband Eric Sherbroke-Walker, kept the well-known Outspan hotel at Nyeri together with its tourists' magnet, Treetops. This has become a 78-bedroom mansion built theoretically in a tree, actually on a huge platform to which customers are conducted to eat their five-course dinners by characters dressed as big-game hunters in bush-shirts, and carrying rifles. When I knew it first it really was in a tree, and had six camp-beds and little else; we took sandwiches, it cost £5 for Gervas and myself, and your money was returned if you failed to see elephant, buffalo or rhino at the salt-lick below.

The Sherbroke-Walkers opened the Outspan on 1 January 1928, and soon afterwards Lady Bettie's sister, Lady Victoria Feilding, arrived on a visit. The sisters came of a family of ten born to the 9th Earl of Denbigh and his wife. The Earl had been Lord-in-Waiting to Queen Victoria, who had consented to stand as godmother to the Denbighs' newest offspring, but had died before she could fulfil her promise. The child was nevertheless christened Victoria. The Denbighs owned five thousand acres and their residence had one hundred rooms – or so it was thought; no one had actually counted them. In the garden was an elm tree in whose branches the children had built a house from which to watch rabbits. Eric Sherbroke-Walker, when a guest and prospective son-in-law, had observed this tree-house and said to himself: 'If rabbits, why not elephants?' That, so the story goes, was the origin of Treetops.

The resources of the family did not run to supporting their brood, and after she came to Kenya Taffy, who had decided to stay on, rubbed along in a number of jobs, such as delivering milk and helping on a poultry farm, before marrying Miles Fletcher, a brawny and impecunious Tasmanian. Instead of an engagement ring, he gave her a second-hand tyre for her lorry which was so dilapidated, she wrote, that 'it wouldn't pull the skin off a rice pudding'.[10]

After Powys Cobb went bankrupt, Keringet had been sold to a rich Italian, Commandatore Inginero Dario Vincenzini, and it was here that Miles and Taffy Fletcher found a job. Taffy had travelled adventurously, if not actually as a stowaway then not far from it, before her marriage, and had been impressed by the beauty of the flower arrangements in Japan. In the Fletchers' shack set down on what Roy Campbell called 'the bare veld where nothing ever grows save beards and nails and blisters on the nose', elegant arrangements of single thorn twigs and a spray or two of wild jasmine stood in cracked jugs on tables made of packing cases and amerikani. Once a visitor pushed open a bathroom door to find a heap of dirty towels on the floor. 'Which bath towel shall I use?' she asked. 'Oh, take the one that looks the cleanest.'

Taffy could turn her hand to anything – decarbonising engines, plucking fowls, repairing tractors, dosing sheep, icing cakes, rearing lambs – though not so artlessly as a Turkana woman she saw suckling her baby from one breast and a lamb from the other – and she was generous, witty, good fun and rather stout. Eventually her marriage foundered, Miles took another wife (and then another), their two sons sought their fortunes in Australia, and thither, in the evening of her days, Taffy followed them to come to roost in a caravan.

I have sometimes wondered why a privileged background and the habits of a vagabond should have quite often gone together. Indifference to what others think is, of course, the badge of the aristocrat.

Never mind the Jones's, I make my own rules. Also there was reaction against convention, and adoption of a set of priorities in which respectability and tidiness came low on the list. What Karen Blixen (no lover of the British) called 'the fearful living death of English middle-class mediocrity'[11] was, to such people, more to be dreaded than physical death on the horns of a buffalo or in the jaws of a lion.

But it would be wrong to assume that most of the white farmers discarded the standards of their race and class to live like tinkers. It was only a few who did so, and they only did so sometimes. The apparent prevalence of Earls and Old Etonians in Kenya's white society has created an impression that the settler population was drawn mainly from Britain's aristocracy. This was far from the case. Afrikaner transport riders, Scottish cattle traders, Italian mechanics, Irish garage owners, Jewish hoteliers, and farmers drawn from the despised and mediocre middle classes, were all there too, in much greater numbers. They did not make news, whereas errant Earls and dashing barons did. They were in a small minority. We hear a lot about small minorities these days, always making headlines by blowing up, gunning down and outrageously offending the great, virtuous, law-abiding majority. It is naive to dismiss such activists because they are few. The yeast moves the dough. It was, after all, a very small minority of Jews – eleven, to be precise – who started the spread throughout the world of the Christian religion. The errant Earls and dashing barons did set a certain stamp on the colonial society they adorned, and sometimes scandalised.

They came in quest of adventure, stayed to make a colony and, in the process, destroyed what they had come to seek. They brought wives, and wives make homes. An inexorable process began. Patterned chintz replaced the sacking and amerikani spread over packing-cases to be used as tables; curtains went up over unglazed windows; china cups bought at local sales replaced tin mugs. Soon prints of the Midnight Steeplechase hung on mud-block walls, followed by the Laughing Cavalier and Van Gogh's sunflowers on roughly chiselled stone ones; creepers half-concealed corrugated-iron roofs; then came dressed stone bungalows with wide verandas, and tennis courts and stables, herbaceous borders, tea on the lawn. By stealth, civilisation had arrived.

CHAPTER 10

The Powys Saga

I think it was in 1922 that my father decided to inspect some land he had drawn in a lottery under the Soldier Settlement scheme. It lay at an altitude of about 9,000 feet up on Mt Kenya and appeared to be honeycombed with rivers; at any rate, the map Jos got from the Land Office showed a lot of little wiggly lines. The nearest place marked on the map was Nanyuki, so thither we went on our ponies from Thika. We enlisted the help of Major Gascoigne in procuring a few porters, bought provisions from his store, and set forth up a slippery track made by elephants through the forest. Above the cedars came a belt of bamboos whose feathery tops met overhead like Gothic arches, and filtered the sunlight to a lambent green that made me think of crème-de-menthe. Many of the trunks had been knocked over by elephants, and when our ponies trod on them they exploded with loud bangs like crackers. Above the bamboos came the moorland with its strange vegetation, giant groundsel like cabbages on stalks, and giant lobelias like huge phalluses covered with furry scales.

At night we shivered in our tiny tent, and there was ice on the water in our canvas basin. By day, although everything sparkled in the sunlight once the mist had cleared, it did not seem much warmer owing to a chilly wind. The little wiggly lines turned out not to be rivers at all, but gulleys, which may have carried water in the rains but were then bone-dry. Nellie, always optimistic, thought that sheep might do well, but Jos, always fond of weak puns, retorted that the Land Office had fleeced us. Our porters and our ponies were miserable, and I started to develop chilblains. We returned to Nanyuki, and our claim to that bit of Africa lapsed.

Others who drew soldier-settlement 'farms' had the same experience: no water. One man was lucky. He drew a block of one thousand acres in the district of Timau which had on it a spring, Kisima. This was Will Powys, Galbraith Cole's manager. When he had saved enough money he bought twelve hundred Somali sheep and drove them to

Kisima, taking all his belongings, including a wool-press, in an ox-wagon which toppled over the side of a dam, releasing his hens from their crates and cracking the wool-press. At Kisima it was so cold that two hundred of the sheep died during their first night there. He managed to rent land at a lower altitude and moved the sheep in time to save most of the rest.[1] This was in 1925. Then he returned to Galbraith Cole's to complete his contract, leaving the sheep in the care of a young nephew, until he could settle permanently at Kisima and start to breed up his sheep with merino rams as he had learned to do at Kekopey.

Will Powys was one of those men who, like Galbraith Cole, had a natural affinity for sheep and displayed a skill amounting to a form of genius in their management. That half-true definition of genius as an infinite capacity for taking pains applied in his case exactly. He was held in the grip of what is today known as the Protestant work ethic, and lived as austerely as a monk. The white-washed mud-and-timber cottage that he built at Kisima still stands: two rooms, no ceiling, and his bed a bullock-hide stretched between four posts. Four a.m. saw the start of his day. Before dawn, he would be off to some distant dip or shearing station, or perhaps to track down a lion that had seized a steer, or to carry out a post-mortem on a sheep. Much of the land round Kisima had been abandoned, or never taken up, because of lack of water. Bit by bit, Will Powys bought it up and gradually developed it by means of pipelines and dams, and stocked it with sheep which, by judicious breeding, turned in time into almost pure-bred merinos.

Fortune favoured him a second time when he found a mate whose tastes, character and hardihood so closely matched his own. Hers was the comfortable and peaceful background of a country house called High Legh, in Cheshire, where her father, a younger son of a former Secretary of State for India who had been created Viscount Cross, managed the family estates. On the outbreak of war in 1914 Elizabeth Cross, when she was barely eighteen, joined Queen Mary's Auxiliary Army Corps (equivalent to the ATS in the Second World War), hoping to drive ambulances at the front. But only women over twenty-one were sent to France. After a period of frustration, Elizabeth added two years to her age, got away with it and reached Abbeville early in 1917. This was as near to the front line as women were allowed to get.

1. Statue of the 3rd Baron Delamere by Kathleen Hilton-Young, now at Soysambu, Delamere's ranch.

2. Denys Finch-Hatton and Glady Lady Delamere, Northern Frontier District, 1928.

3. Group at Wanjohi, 1924. Left to right: Hon. Josslyn Hay (later Earl of Erroll), Major Roberts, Jos Grant, Lady Idina Hay, Cockie Birkbeck (later Baroness Blixen), Princess Philippe de Bourbon, Nellie Grant.

4. Locust swarm, 1933.

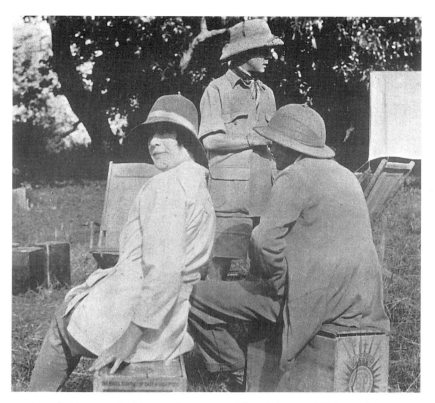

5. On safari in 1930: Cockie von Blixen, HRH Edward Prince of Wales, and Captain Alan Lascelles.

6. Galbraith Cole at Kekopey, Gilgil, 1916.

7. Lady Eleanor Balfour and Galbraith Cole before their marriage in 1917, with dead impala.

8. Llewelyn Powys at Kekopey.

9. Will Powys, the Coles' manager, at Kekopey, 1920.

10. The original Treetops at Nyeri: the modern one has 78 bedrooms.

11. Denys Finch Hatton, Jack Pixley, Tich Miles, with Lady Colvile behind, at Ngara Road House, 1914.

12. Foot Safari on the upper slopes of Mt Kenya, 1936.

13. H. B. Sharpe with elephants at Wamba, 1936.

'*Crossie arrived like a breath of fresh air,*' a fellow officer recalled. '*She had a great gift for leadership. After the retreat of the 5th Army we came in for a lot of trouble. Anyone from anywhere with nursing experience was called for. Crossie volunteered and we two were sent down to the station each time a train came in, where we worked as best we could dressing the wounded, giving morphia and tea to men in cattle trucks till the train left. Then she was sent to Camp I in temporary charge. We were bombed fairly badly and had to get the girls, all over-worked and tired, into trenches when the planes were expected . . . There was a direct hit on the trench and several girls were killed. Crossie was buried in the rubble and her shoes torn off. She organised the girls, then ran half a mile to get help from the nearest camp – her feet were very sore for a long time afterwards.*'[2]

The Military Medal 'for distinguished services in the Field' was her reward. 'She was knocked down', runs the citation, 'but immediately got up and, after obtaining assistance, worked with the doctor amongst the killed and wounded while the raid was still in progress.' The price was shell-shock, for which she was invalided home.

'Oh show me how a rose can shut and be a bud again,' Kipling wrote of a proposal by the Admiralty to turn young men who had gone straight from school into four years of warfare at sea back into naval cadets. To return to the conventional life of a young woman of her class with its round of hunt balls, shooting parties and the London season would have called for a similar metamorphosis in Elizabeth Cross. Most of the ex-WAACs and VADs managed to settle back among the teacups but a few were too restless and emotionally churned up to do so, and sought a more abrasive and demanding scene where qualities of self-reliance and initiative they had discovered in themselves would continue to be tested. Perhaps they also knew instinctively that action was an antidote to bad dreams. Africa offered this scene and this antidote. Elizabeth Cross heard of the Soldier-Settler lottery for which her war service qualified her, entered her name and drew a block of land. It might have been expected that her family would have raised objections, but her father was an understanding man. He gave her a rifle, a shot-gun and his blessing. She sailed in the *Garth Castle* and reached Mombasa on Christmas Eve, 1919.

The land she had drawn lay in the Ithanga hills, not far from where we lived at Thika. I had stayed in these hills with a family called Risley who were trying to grow coffee where coffee did not want to grow – it was too hot and too dry. Buffaloes did much better: there were herds and herds of those. These rocky, bush-clad hills dropped down into the valley of the Tana river, a paradise for wild animals not yet under threat. There were no resident humans. Only foot safaris had gone there, and not many of those, for the valley had a bad reputation for malaria and blackwater fever. Ours was one that did so, a very small safari which my parents gave me in 1923 as a sixteenth-birthday present. Jos had to stay behind to look after the coffee, but Nellie, myself and a young man who was hoping to become a professional white hunter, together with about a dozen porters, trudged over the hills and camped under the shady trees that fringed the river, to watch many kinds of wild animal coming to drink there and, I regret to say, shooting some of them. (I did, that is; Nellie did not care to.) But there were so many; now there is a hydro-electric installation. Our young would-be hunter never achieved his ambition, for he died of black-water fever within the year.

Elizabeth Cross built herself a shack in the Ithanga hills and shared it with a grey pony and a white bull-terrier, and found the attractions of hunting down the Tana irresistible. The manager of a nearby sisal plantation, van Breda, showed her the ropes. To start with, excitement made her hand so unsteady that she missed most of her targets, but as time went on she became more expert, and then reached the stage where, as she wrote to her father, 'I love seeing the game just as much as trying to shoot it, and so does van Breda'.

With the influx of new settlers, a brisk demand arose for the hardy little native sheep and cattle to be crossed with imported rams and bulls. Demand soon outran supply; but in the north, where lack of water was endemic, livestock was easier to obtain. Since the demise of the Boma Trading Company, the Government had discouraged Europeans from going north because of dangers from bandits, and from getting lost and dying of thirst, and it was a no-go area for women; even the wives of district officers were banned. Somehow, Elizabeth managed to get a permit, and van Breda went with her.

She must have been one of the first European women to get as far as

Marsabit, that forested mountain rising so improbably from a parched lava plain. Osa Martin Johnson camped there round about the same time with her husband; they irritated the touchier old hands by naming the lake that lay deep in the mountain's cedar forests Lake Paradise, and implying that they had more or less 'discovered' it. There had been a government post there since 1910. They were American showmen, and pioneers in the business of filming big game. Osa was filmed narrowly escaping furious charges by rhinos, elephants and buffaloes, being stalked by lions and fondling baby antelopes. Raymond Hook had a tame buffalo which was supposed to charge towards a helpless Osa trapped on a river bank, but the animal, overweight from succulent homestead grazing, lumbered along until it spotted an enticing mud-bank by the river and settled down to a good wallow.

At some point in her travels, Elizabeth met and married a young South African called Alec Douglas, who had fought in the King's African Rifles during the war. They settled in the Nanyuki district, and a daughter, Delia, was born. After three years Elizabeth left her husband, and took her daughter first to England, then to Tanganyika, where the movement to 'open up' the southern highlands round Iringa was getting under way. Elizabeth got the lease of about a thousand acres of untouched bush. She located the land, trained oxen to pull a plough, and made a fresh start on her own. Her mother arrived from England, made curtains for the unglazed apertures, and found Elizabeth's mud hut preferable to the grander house built by a couple from Kenya, where rats plopped off the rafters at night.

To tide things over before her first crop was harvested, Elizabeth bought a lorry for £200 and ran transport to Tukuyu on the border of Nyasaland along bone-breaking roads; three trips almost recouped the cost of the lorry. Life became easier when Lord Egerton of Tatton came down from Kenya, obtained the leasehold next to hers, and took her on as manager. For herself she planted onions, carrots, lucerne, potatoes and maize. She never went back to Alec Douglas, who eventually agreed, with reluctance, to give her a divorce.

A romantic and doubtless apocryphal story relates how the romance between Elizabeth Douglas and Will Powys began. One day, while still living near Nanyuki, she was riding across the veld and dropped her revolver. Will Powys came upon it, traced its owner and returned it to her, and in this way they met. Will, a friend recalled, with his tall and fine physique and his tight dark curly hair, 'looked like a young Apollo'. After the failure alike of her marriage and of the prospect of 'opening up' Tanganyika's southern highlands, Elizabeth, together with nearly all her fellow settlers there, returned to Kenya. A lot of hopes were buried on those southern highlands. Elizabeth moved over to Kisima, and in due course she and Will Powys married.

Elizabeth became every bit as hard-working and as sheep-orientated as Will. At shearing times, she would be up before dawn every morning and at the wheel of their lorry taking wool-bales to the station. She bore one more daughter and two sons.

A couple devoted solely to hard work and sheep presents a somewhat drab picture, but their offspring recall a home full of laughter and affection. Their parents shared a rather childish weakness for practical jokes. One concerned a pudding, a round pudding smothered in a white sauce. The principal guest tackled it with a spoon but the spoon bounced off. Puzzled, she tried again with no better success. The spoon gave out a hollow ring, and the hosts could no longer suppress their laughter. Beneath the sauce was a hard, baked-earth termites' nest – fortunately without the termites. April Fools' day was faithfully observed. The family owned one of those silver entrée dishes with a compartment at the base to hold hot water and so keep warm the breakfast dish, covered by a revolving lid. When one of the daughters opened the lid to get at her breakfast, she recoiled before a live chameleon.

Despite lean times and credit freezes, Will Powys gradually added to, developed and consolidated his properties. He ended up with three separate but interdependent units which together totalled about 83,000 acres and supported 29,000 sheep and 7,000 cattle. There was also wheat at Kisima, two crops a year; Galloway cattle imported from Scotland and a property at Malindi on the Coast. This busy, productive, hard-working family life sounded, despite troubles like drought, diseases, thefts and predators, almost idyllic. 'We are all as happy as can be,' Will wrote, 'and deal with all the difficulties that crop up together.'[3]

Throughout his life he took no part in politics, but Elizabeth became a strong supporter of the Capricorn Africa Society. This had been started shortly after the Second World War by Colonel David Stirling, who had won fame and glory as leader of the Long-Range Desert Group that had operated behind enemy lines in North Africa and, in one dramatic foray, nearly captured General Rommel. His Capricorn Society was the first organised attempt to put into practice the ideal of multi-racialism in Africa. Men and women of all races were invited to join. Politically, the aim was a franchise open to all regardless of race, and framed on the principle propounded by Cecil Rhodes of 'equal rights for all civilised men'.[4]

The question, of course, was how to define civilised men. Capricorn's proposal was to winnow from the great black multitude a bushel of people who might be expected to comprehend the issues presented to an electorate, and to cast their votes responsibly. A minimum degree of education or of ownership of property; so many years of public service; these were among the tests proposed. Many 'fancy franchises' were suggested with the aim of creating a balance between the races so that no one race would overwhelm the others. Government by meritocracy was the definition. The vote, attained in stages, would be a prize for achievement, not an automatic right.

David Stirling was a persuasive speaker deeply committed to his cause, and so were his principal colleagues, including the veteran missionary J. H. Oldham, Michael Wood, who was to start and run the Flying Doctor service, and the famous writer Laurens van der Post. Born in Rhodesia, the society had branches in Nairobi, Dar es Salaam and London, and recruited many of the more liberal-minded Europeans, but not many Africans, most of whom were indifferent to its ideals or, in the case of the young nationalists beginning to emerge, looked on it as a trap set by Europeans to thwart their aims. Power is something that few people, if any, want to share. They want to wield it. Capricorn thrived for some years, but in the end succumbed to the slogan-shouts that rolled like drum-beats down through Africa, the cry of 'One man! One vote!'

Will Powys was first and last a farmer, not an intellectual; nevertheless the creativity that ran in his family was in him too. In undeveloped countries, farming is in itself creative; with virgin land as his canvas, the farmer translates his vision into fields and pastures, crops and cattle, as an artist will apply his paint. The artist in Will expressed itself both in husbandry and, like his sister Gertrude, in paint. He painted the landscapes he loved, and used to offer a picture as a birthday present to each of the children. 'Choose any scene you like,' he would say, 'and I'll paint it for you.' The child in question would pick a scene and he would set up his easel. 'Somehow or other,' Delia told me, 'Mt Kenya nearly always seemed to come in.'⁵

In old age Will would sometimes tire before he completed a painting, and call on his servant to finish it off under his direction – in the tradition, perhaps, of those Old Masters whose pupils would fill in the details. All his pleasures centred on his family, his sheep and cattle and his properties: Kisima, Ngare Ndare and Il Pinguan. 'Don't you ever need a holiday?' someone asked him. 'But all my life has been a holiday,' he replied. Also in old age he acquired another skill: the shepherd learned to play the flute.

His life was happy and successful, yet from a self-portrait done in old age a sorrowful, almost tortured face looks out, spectacles on nose, a black skull-cap pushed on to the back of his head. Sorrows did indeed cloud his last years. Elizabeth died in 1963 when she was only sixty-seven. Less than eighteen months later his eldest son Charles, who had inherited the Powys charm and looks as well as the intelligence and energy of both parents, accidentally shot himself on Christmas Eve. He was twenty-five years of age, and left a widow and an infant daughter. One of Will's legs turned gangrenous and had to be amputated, and the stump pained him for the rest of his life. But he drove out daily in a Land-Rover to see to his sheep, and kept his hand on the controls until the end. A friend who stayed with him in his last years, coming in to breakfast to find his place empty, enquired: 'Where's Will?' Hearing that a batch of sheep needed worming, Will had gone out at four thirty a.m. to see that it was properly done.

He died in 1978 in his ninetieth year and was buried beside Elizabeth and Charles in Nanyuki churchyard. The year of his birth was that in which two Austrians, Count von Teleki and Lieutenant von Hohnel, set eyes on Lake Rudolf, the first Europeans to do so. Such has been the speed of change.

It was on the Powys' Laikipia ranch, Il Pinguan, that Theodore, son of Will's brother of the same name, met a tragic end. At the age of twenty-five he had gone out to join his uncle at Kisima. Il Pinguan was not then Powys property, but was Crown land rented from the Government by Nell Cole, Galbraith's widow. It lay in a lonely, sparsely occupied, remote region, then part of the Northern Frontier District, between a settled area to the south and, to the north, the territory of the Samburu.

The Samburu are cousins of the Maasái and share the same social structure. In the recent past their young males formed a warrior caste trained to raid for cattle, and to blood their spears on human victims, before they could marry. The tribe had no chiefs as such: its real rulers were the laibons, who were believed to possess supernatural powers – rudimentary priest-kings. No raid or spear-blooding foray could be undertaken without a laibon's approval, and without the medicines he provided to protect the warriors. District commissioners and other officials found such tribes, which included the Nandi, difficult to deal with because of the undercover influence of the laibons, and the pride and militancy of the young men. For their part, the Samburu no doubt found DCs even more difficult to deal with because of their constant interference with ancient customs such as spear-blooding, which everybody knew to be right.

Nell Cole engaged young Theodore Powys, called Dicky by his family, to look after her sheep at Il Pinguan. One morning in October 1931 he rode out as usual on his white pony to inspect the flocks. In mid-morning the pony returned riderless to camp. It was not until two days later that searchers found his scattered bones, fragments of clothing, and a pool of dried blood. There was no skull. A young policeman from Rumuruti concluded that the pony had shied at a lion and thrown its rider, who had probably broken his neck, and that the lion, together with hyenas and vultures, had done the rest. A thorough search failed to discover the skull. Accidental death was the official conclusion.[6]

Rumours soon began to circulate that Samburu warriors, not a lion, had killed young Powys. It was reported to the authorities that the warriors were openly boasting of having killed a European and were singing a 'song of the vultures' to celebrate their feat. Spear-blooding was common enough, but a European victim would constitute a feather in the killers' caps.

Two months after Powys' death, a man called Kiberenge reported to the police at Rumuruti that he had witnessed the arrival at the local headman's dwelling of six Samburu warriors carrying the head and testicles of a European. The headman had sworn the warriors to secrecy 'over spears', and offered Kiberenge five cows to keep his mouth shut. Finding no proof of this story – not surprisingly, since the headman naturally denied it – the police charged Kiberenge with giving false information to a public servant, and the DC sentenced him to five months' hard labour.

This bizarre procedure angered the scattered ranchers of the region, whose African employees were as convinced as they were that if the Samburu got away with Powys' murder no one's life, white or black, would be safe. After Kiberenge's release from jail he disappeared and, despite exhaustive searches, was never seen or heard of again. Murder was presumed.

The windswept steppes of northern Laikipia might seem, and be, far from Westminster, but it was not long before the death of Theodore Powys, Samburu laibons and 'the song of the vultures' were cropping up at question time in the House of Commons, and forming the subject of despatches between the Secretary of State and Governor Sir Joseph Byrne. The outcome was a much more thorough enquiry which brought to light the implication of the local laibon in the spearing not only of Powys but of twelve Kikuyu men, living on lonely farms, as well. Authority then came up against a brick wall. No one could be found prepared to give evidence against the laibon; so as to remove his influence, he was sent into temporary exile at the Coast. By 1934, the total of spear-blooding murders by Samburu warriors had risen to thirty-two.

It was not until the end of that year that several Dorobo living near Il Pinguan told the police that they had encountered on the plain, at the relevant time, a party of Samburu warriors carrying Powys' head and testicles and boasting of their feat. After the Dorobo had picked them out in an identification parade, seven Samburu warriors were charged with murder. Two turned King's evidence, and in November 1934 the remaining five were brought to trial before a High Court judge in Nakuru.

According to press reports, the trial developed into something of a shambles.[7] The laibon, retrieved from the Coast, gave evidence with 'dark flashing eyes' and 'two mysterious trinkets' fastened to his belt. Four young girls, lovers of the accused, admitted amid bursts of giggles that they had joined in a dance, customarily held to celebrate a spear-blooding, when the 'song of the vultures' had been sung. The two Samburu who had turned King's evidence, together with the headman and two elders, swore to the guilt of the accused, as did three of the Dorobo who had met them on the veld carrying their trophies. The accused themselves displayed rings of the kind traditionally worn by warriors who had speared their victim, and, fortified by the presence of the laibon, were truculent and confident of acquittal.

The prosecution was left in the hands of the most junior and inexperienced of the law officers of the Crown who, in the opinion of many, made a hash of it. All the proceedings had to be translated from the Samburu tongue into Swahili and thence into English, and back again by the same tortuous route. Witnesses grew muddled, contradictory and incoherent. Under the colonial legal system juries were not called in cases in which Africans were accused; instead, two, or sometimes three, assessors drawn from elders of the tribe concerned sat with the presiding British judge. The niceties of English law made little sense to most of such elderly men. At the end of the Powys trial one of the assessors thought the men not guilty, the other two said that they were too confused to make up their minds. The acting judge, a newcomer to the Bench, shared their doubts, and concluded that 'the evidence has fallen just short of that degree of certainty which would warrant a conviction'. So the warriors went free.

I have outlined this case in some detail because it throws into relief two important factors that, time and again, bedevilled relations between rulers and ruled in the colonial period. One was the undercover influence of laibons and witch-doctors, so much more powerful and dangerous to tribesmen than the remote and often nonsensical capers of British law. The other was a fundamental difference between the European and the tribal African concept of justice. In Europe, we believe that the individual, if of sound mind, is responsible for his actions and that, if he breaks the law, he must be punished. Under tribal law the community and not the individual was held responsible for the misdemeanours of any of its members: and recompense to the victim's family, not punishment of the offender, was the usual aim.

Of course there were exceptions and grey areas. The principal exception was in matters of black magic and the activities of witches and wizards, enemies of society, as distinct from witch-doctors who were on the whole beneficial. Practitioners of black magic were like tumours in the body and had to be cut out. They were put to death, often in exceedingly unpleasant ways. Ordinary offenders were fined in cattle, sheep and goats. In cases of murder, manslaughter or serious injury, the object was to compensate the family of the killed or injured person for the loss or impairment of a contributor to the family's welfare. The fine had to be paid not just by the offender, but by members of his extended family; and as a rule it was paid in instalments which might continue for years. It was a highly complicated system, because the livestock's increase was taken into account; but argument, especially about livestock, was a keenly savoured pleasure, and possibly the procedure solved another of society's problems the world over, how to provide interesting and useful occupations for the elderly. Trials were generally conducted by elders sitting beneath a shady tree with a plentiful supply of beer at hand.

The African system of justice no doubt had its shortcomings, but it enabled the people to dispense with police forces, barristers and judges, prisons and the whole paraphernalia of the law as enforced in western nations. I have often thought that compensation rather than punishment is the better principle of the two. Could we adopt it, think what billions we should save, what miseries we should eliminate! It seems a topsy-turvy notion to keep society's least useful members locked up, sometimes for the rest of their lives, at a cost per individual even greater than the sum that would provide a first-rate education for a boy or girl at the most expensive of our boarding schools, or (better still) that would add substantially to the old age pension.

So why not fine offenders, distribute the cash to their victims or victim's families, and let them go free? Alas, it would not work. Substantial fines can be paid only by people with property; few of our criminals are property-owners, whereas almost every African tribesman, through his family, used to be. And in our individualistic society we should be unwilling to contribute to a fine imposed upon, say, a brother's wife's step-son's cousin-in-law, even though it might cost us less to do so than to pay the proportion of our tax spent on getting him convicted and held for years in prison.

The extended family was a powerful influence on the side of good behaviour. Since every member – male member, to be precise – knew that he would probably have to contribute a goat or two, even a heifer in extreme cases, towards the penalty imposed on an offender, it was naturally in his interest to see that even his remotest cousin obeyed the law. We do not have extended families. Also, there is the matter of sanctions. Tribal sanctions were mainly supernatural; an offence was an affront to tribal spirits who would take their revenge against the whole group or family, not just against the individual offender. We, too, used to have our supernatural sanctions in the shape of hellfire and eternal damnation; we have abandoned them, and crime proliferates. Since no one has been able to think of a better alternative we must, no doubt, go on locking up our miscreants and employing people to try to catch them and enforce their punishment, with increasing lack of success. Meanwhile Africans have abandoned their own system in favour of that introduced by the colonialists, and sport the full panoply of bewigged judges, costly law-courts, uniformed policemen, highly paid barristers, and prisons, some of which sound even nastier than our own.

The sequel to the Powys trial was predictable. The 'song of the vultures' was openly sung throughout Samburuland, and spear-blooding murders went from strength to strength. Kikuyu people, male or female, furnished most of the victims. The Government's remedy was 'closer administration', i.e. more district officers and more policemen, combined with heavier collective fines in the shape of livestock. A new station was opened at Maralal in Samburu country, which was transferred from the Northern Frontier District, where colonial officials were few and far between, to the more settled Rift Valley Province administered from Nakuru. A policeman with a 'levy force' was stationed at Maralal to collect fines. PCs and DCs held barazas at which they lectured Samburu elders on the evil of their ways and delivered awful warnings, which the tribesmen ignored. Every

Samburu knew the identity of the various murderers, but despite all the fines and lectures, the elders went on refusing to hand them over to the police.

But 'closer administration' sewed the seeds of social change. A primary school and a dispensary appeared at Maralal; traders were encouraged, dukas opened, and gradually it became less safe to fall upon a solitary herdsman, or group of women carrying loads through the bush. There came a change of age-sets: the wicked warriors had their pigtails shaved, exchanged long-bladed spears for shorter-bladed, ceremonial ones, laid aside their ornaments and turned their minds to marriage. They were replaced by a new age-set of warriors whose spears cried out for blood, but by then the seeds of change were germinating; there were young Samburu who had seen the wonders of Nairobi, some even who had joined the police. Risks were greater, and the elders had had enough of paying fines. The murders did not stop, but they slowed down.

The Samburu bore no grudge against those who had fined and lectured them. When, some years later, the time came for a DC who had won their respect to move on, the elders assembled to bid him farewell and give him a parting present. The present consisted of five good heifers. The DC found himself in an embarrassing position all too familiar to colonial civil servants. The rules forbade, and very strictly forbade, the acceptance of presents of any kind. Yet to give and to receive was a courtesy deeply embedded in African custom. To refuse a token of respect and friendliness – a chicken perhaps, some eggs, milk, tobacco – was considered to be a gross breach of good manners. The white man, in his brash and overriding way, was apparently too ignorant of polite behaviour to give or to receive gracefully.

From the point of view of the Colonial Service, this ban on presents formed the very basis of the rule of incorruptibility. Allow a bottle of whisky or a pound of tea at Christmas, let alone five heifers, and the way lay open to a thousand-pound bribe. This rigid rule underpinned what may well have been the most incorrupt public service the world has yet known. No doubt there were occasional lapses over the years, but the only one I ever personally heard of – and this was not a bribe – concerned, I regret to say, an old friend of ours, a DC called H. B. Sharpe, who was a brilliant and dedicated gardener. After he had quitted one post to take up another, an elderly mowing machine was reported to be missing. Some years afterwards a colleague set eyes upon a machine of the same make and vintage in the garden of a house that Sharpie (as everyone called him) owned at Lamu. By that time he had retired, and the matter was not pursued. In any case, it was a common make of machine.

As to the Samburu: the departing DC, Terence Gavaghan, was obliged to remind the elders of the rule, and to reject their gift of heifers. The elders were deeply offended. Gavaghan hit on what he thought was a solution. 'I'll tell you what,' he said. 'I'll sell the heifers, and put the money towards a new dispensary in the district of which you're in need.' The faces of the elders did not brighten. They conferred. 'We do not give you these heifers,' their spokesman pronounced, 'in order that we should remember you. We give them in order that *you* should remember *us*.' Terence Gavaghan could think of no reply.

CHAPTER 11

Safari with Sharpie

I have already mentioned Sharpie, Major H. B. Sharpe, and his horticultural skills. A common interest in gardening and plant-hunting brought him and Nellie together, and he became my parents' good friend. From 1926 onwards he was stationed in the Northern Frontier District which, with the adjoining district of Turkana, occupied an area about half the size of Kenya and considerably larger than that of the United Kingdom. You couldn't just go to the NFD to look round, it was a 'closed district', as I have explained. So the best way to travel in the North was to join forces with a district officer going on one of his periodic safaris. Such officers normally travelled with a small escort of Kenya police askaris, plus a few men of an irregular force drawn from local tribes and popularly known as dubas, or dingbats. You took your own transport and equipment, but travelled under the aegis of the DC.

So when, early in 1937, Sharpie suggested that Nellie and I should go north with him on such a safari, combining a little plant-hunting on the side, we naturally jumped at the chance. He was a perfect travelling companion. Not plants only, but birds, beasts, the people and every aspect of this vast, hard-hearted, sun-baked country were familiar to him. He had entered the Colonial Service by a back door, having been trained as a botanist at Kew instead of at Oxbridge, and worked for the agricultural department as a plant inspector, a lowly form of life in the colonial hierarchy. In the First World War he rose to the rank of Major and afterwards joined the Brahmins in the administration. The Brahmins never altogether took to him, for various reasons. The man who set his stamp upon the North was Vincent Glenday, who had joined the Colony's service in 1913, spent most of his time in that region and was its Officer-in-Charge from 1934 to 1938. That stamp was one of hard, tough, spartan living, a frontier life whose participants were expected to spurn creature comforts and to march all day on a handful of dates, and a draught of camels' milk if they were lucky.

Sharpie did not subscribe to what some of Glenday's subordinates called the strength-through-misery philosophy. He belonged to the Epicurean, not the Stoic, school. His tastes were sybaritic, his conversation irreverent, sometimes witty and spiced with scandal, and he had no respect whatever for sacred cows. Officers stationed on the lower reaches of the Tana river sometimes safari'd in canoes. Sharpie would take a small kerosene refrigerator and an entourage of ten: two polers, two paddlers, an interpreter, a hospital dresser, a game scout, a corporal of police and two servants. A colleague encountered him proceeding downstream under an awning doing a crossword puzzle while the paddlers kept up a monotonous chant – Sanders of the River come to life.[1]

Another cause of the oblique glances that the Brahmins of the administration cast in Sharpie's direction was the fear that at any moment a major scandal would erupt around his head. Sharpie made no bones, or few bones anyway, about his homosexual tendencies. Bones on this matter were advisable then. The law had not changed since Oscar Wilde's time, nor had social condemnation lifted. Such a scandal, it was felt, would embarrass the whole administration and tarnish the good name of the North. Men serving in the North were very jealous of its good name.

The Brahmins might have been glad to get rid of Sharpie by posting him to the decadent south, but he was too good at his job to be discarded. He seldom talked about his past experiences, but I was told of one that earned him the respect of colleagues not easily impressed. The main concern of colonial administration in the North was, and had been since the start of British rule, to hold back, or at least delay, the unrelenting southward thrust of the Somali into the grazing grounds of the various Galla-speaking tribes. This movement had continued gradually but steadily ever since, about six hundred years ago, the legendary ancestor of the Somalis – a descendant, as they claimed, of the Prophet Mohamed – had first set foot in Africa somewhere on the shores of the Red Sea.

People who know the Somali say that there are no better fighting men in Africa; tough as their sure-footed little ponies and unexcelled in hardihood, audacity, racial pride and courage. To these qualities they add a cunning and skill in intrigue which prompted Richard Turnbull, their historian and reluctant admirer, to describe them as 'the crafty Ulysses of the Horn of Africa'.[2] They achieved their southward advance as much by outwitting the peoples in their path as by military conquest. The key to the situation was always the wells. Get possession of the wells, and you got possession of the grazing grounds they opened up for the nomads' cattle and camels.

The duty of the British, as they saw it, was to prevent, as far as they could, a Somali take-over of the wells and grazing grounds of other peoples under their protection, notably the Boran, but they never had the resources to do so. The first to be confronted by this virtually impossible task was a young Greek, Philip Zaphiro, born in Constantinople, who had reached East Africa in the capacity of taxidermist and interpreter to Northrup McMillan, an American millionaire who led an expedition to southern Abyssinia in 1904. In 1907, Zaphiro was appointed 'British Southern Abyssinia Frontier Inspector' at a salary of £200 a year, plus £900 a year for expenses. A boundary line, of sorts, between Abyssinia and the East Africa Protectorate had been agreed in the same year between the Emperor Menelik II and the British Foreign Office. Zaphiro somehow or other had acquired an Admiral's frock coat and red cummerbund in which he rode about the frontier, persuading the tribesmen to do as he told them. Apparently, quite often they did.

But by this time the Somali had reached the grazing-grounds of the Boran around the wells of Wajir, and nothing but force, and a lot of force at that, could have made them draw back. All Zaphiro could do was to persuade the Boran to give up their wells peaceably in order to avoid their own extermination. This process was completed in 1932 when the last of the Boran retreated, leaving the Somali in undisputed possession of the wells. Meanwhile, Glenday had drawn a 'Somali line' from the Abyssinian frontier to the river Tana, westwards of which the Somalis were not to go, and the administration's efforts were concentrated on trying to hold them back. But the line existed only on a map, and depended on persuasion to enforce its observance.[3]

This is where Sharpie came in. As a junior district officer in the 1920s, he had been posted to Wajir, where he took over from a tall and handsome officer called John Llewellyn. Long Lew, as he was generally known, wore an eyeglass, travelled in some style – clean plates for each course, polished glasses, coffee cups – and had been encountered on the march, so I was told, wearing a hat and eyeglass and a pair of sandals, with nothing in between. The Somali shared with the Maasai a talent for capturing the hearts of their white rulers to such an extent that the rulers almost became the ruled. Long Lew steeped himself so deeply in Somali lore that he could even read their camel brands, a highly complex orthography by which every individual camel could be traced to its owner through his clan, sub-clan and family.

The Somali were, and are, split into a number of clans, or tribes, nearly always at enmity and often at war with each other. One of the most powerful of these clans made Long Lew a blood brother and thereafter could twist him round their little fingers. He allowed them to move with all their livestock and hangers-on as far south as the Tana, where they had no right to be. Sharpie, taking a handful of 'gobbos', was sent to retrieve them. A great deal of nerve and diplomacy, and an extraordinary amount of bluff, were needed to accomplish this without bloodshed, and had blood been shed it would certainly have been Sharpie's. He marched two hundred miles, rounded up about one thousand people and ten thousand head of cattle, marched them back, and reinstated them in their proper ranges. 'A truly Herculean task' was how Turnbull described this achievement. 'It meant a good deal of hard trekking' was Sharpie's own comment.

To get back to our safari: we rendezvous'd at Rumuruti, where Sharpie had created out of nothing one of those superb gardens which became his hallmark at every boma that he occupied. He was middle-aged by then, white-haired, rotund and rubicund, jovial but now and then a little testy. His garden was full of colour, of big shady indigenous trees, and of rivulets rippling about lawns kept green by sprinklers. I remember to this day the melodious fluting of golden orioles in thick-foliaged mununga trees, the glowing colour of scarlet cannas beside a stream adorned with maidenhair ferns and crossed by little rustic bridges, and Sharpie wrestling with a young elephant he had reared almost from birth and who shared his quarters. In his gardening activities it was, of course, a help to have the inmates of the local jail available to do the donkey-work. As a magistrate – DCs were ipso facto magistrates – he was in a position to see that the jail was not empty for long, although I do not for a moment suggest that he took this into consideration when delivering sentences; the supply of offenders was unlikely ever to run dry. The prisoners, for their part, did not look unhappy in the shade of the trees languidly swinging to and fro an implement designed for beheading grasses.

Besides Nellie, myself and Karanja, Rose Cartwright made up the party. Jos was holding the fort at Njoro; this quite often seemed to be his fate, but his breathing already troubled him, he was not a plant-hunter and was happy hatching schemes for making fortunes, writing plays never to be performed, keeping an eye on the farm and gently exercising the dogs. Rose, like Sharpie, could seldom be faulted on the naming of a plant or bird. Beneath a quiet, rather self-effacing manner lay a dry wit, a keen appraising eye, a devotion to wild places and a talent as a raconteur. On a visit to a brother immediately after the First World War she had fallen in love with the country as well as with Algy Cartwright, whom she married; the first love affair lasted, the second did not. Now she had a herd of beautiful Guernsey cows which she dearly loved, as she did her dachshunds, the fire-finches and cordon bleus that hopped about her living room, and sorties into the Aberdare forest with a rifle, a groundsheet, a cooking pot and little else, in search of the elusive bongo, an exercise which seemed to me to plumb the depths of discomfort. There was nothing like that, I am glad to say, about our safari with Sharpie to Wamba and the Mathews range (now called Longeyo) beyond.

Everyone entering the NFD had to go by Isiolo and sign a book proffered by a police askari, who then raised a pole balanced on two posts: such was the Gateway to the North. You approached it through a row of scruffy Indian dukas along a road deep in dust; past the barrier came police and other quarters built of local sunburnt bricks with tin roofs; then a few mud-and-wattle offices and finally bungalows for the handful of white officials, who I think consisted of the DC, a policeman, a doctor and a vet. A rather half-hearted attempt had been made to plant pepper trees and eucalyptus for shade. That was about all there was of Isiolo. The DC was Captain Rimmington, said to have trained a giraffe to be saddled and ridden, and an ostrich to draw a cart. We did not see either of these at Isiolo on our way through.

What we did see, however, surprised us. On the banks of the insignificant and then dried-up Isiolo river was a military encampment accommodating about four hundred Eritreans. They were deserters from the Italian army, which was engaged upon its conquest of Abyssinia, and had sought asylum in Kenya. No one knew what to do with them, so there they were, fed and clothed and looked after by the colonial government. A much larger influx of uninvited guests was to follow. Italian victories released over the Kenya-Abyssinian border a great wave of refugees. Some were demoralised soldiers, some peasants made homeless by the tides of war, and some were the Emperor's Amharic-speaking high officials, together with their wives and children, servants and slaves. Dysentery soon broke out, and the refugees brought smallpox with them; they had no food, no means of shelter, no medicines, nothing but pathetic bundles of possessions carried on backs or heads. Down they came from the mountains and across the border, heading for the great waterless deserts of north-western Kenya. At the north end of Lake Rudolf they had to cross the Omo river which was in flood. The local tribesmen, who detested the Abyssinians with good reason, denied them canoes, and many perished in the flood as they struggled across.

We have all got used to refugees by now; Africa is said to have at least five million of them, and year by year their number grows. These were harbingers. No organised relief agencies existed then, no United Nations, Save the Children, Oxfam, Christian Aid, no teams of rescue workers, airlifts, all the paraphernalia that has since been assembled to cope, however inadequately, with such crises. It was left to half a dozen DCs and junior officers, stationed at three or four scattered outposts, with what help they could summon from Nairobi, to guide these refugees across more than three hundred miles of desert without roads or means of transport, food or shelter. Much of the burden fell on Gerald Reece at Marsabit. The RAF flew in food, medicos and smallpox vaccine, and lorries were brought up to convey the sick, the very old and the infants to Isiolo. Here all the survivors eventually assembled, nearly six thousand of them, including about one thousand children. No one knew how many people had perished on the way, but a general estimate was two thousand.

At Isiolo, a camp was improvised at record speed – by the time it was finished it was said to be the third largest township in Kenya. It had two churches, a hospital and several clinics, a handicraft centre, an irrigated vegetable garden and a court-house, over which Amharic nobles presided, as dignified as acacia branches, thatch and an inscription 'Magna est Veritas' over the porch could make it. The young colonial officials who brought all this into being were particularly proud of the school. The most persistent troublemaker among the refugees had his sting removed by equipping him with a teacher's mortarboard and gown and conferring upon him the title of Dr Smart Aleck. The school was dubbed Narkover. Before long, each child was receiving a daily drink of milk as well as meat, bread and vegetables, and their health took on a spectacular improvement. In due course Kenya's Governor, Air Vice-Marshal Sir Robert Brooke-Popham, paid a formal visit to the camp. He ended his inspection with the usual question: any complaints? Everyone at Isiolo had the same complaint, against an unrelenting, vicious wind that whirled dust around in choking eddies, shrivelled the skin and howled like a thousand lost dogs. The senior notable asked whether the camp could be moved to a more sheltered spot, giving as his unexpected reason: 'The wind aggravates my syphilis.'

The district officer who organised the camp from scratch was a young man just turned thirty, Robert Armitage. He handed over to Richard Turnbull, who was twenty-eight. Gerald Reece I have already mentioned. All three rose in time to become colonial Governors, with appropriate knighthoods. Gerald Reece went on to govern British Somaliland; Robert Armitage to preside over the affairs of Cyprus and then of Nyasaland; and Richard Turnbull to become the first and last Governor-General of Tanganyika, and finally High Commissioner for the Aden Protectorate. The third of this trio has suggested as a suitable comment on the NFD of those times a phrase applied by Horace to North Africa: *Leonum arida nutrix* – a dry-nurse of lions.

When you see a name on a map, you naturally expect something to be there, at least a duka or two, maybe a market and possibly a 'hoteli', a sort of café selling a few basic necessities, Coca-Cola and perhaps portions of dubious-looking stew. This did not seem to be the case at Wamba. There was nothing to be seen except a river that had degenerated into a series of muddy pools, which Samburu cattle shared with elephants on an informal rota system. Generally the elephants waited until the Samburu cattle had finished, but during our first evening, while we were camped nearby, three elephants had got in first, and we saw a Samburu toto driving them off with a stick. They went meekly, and waited about in the bush until the cattle had drunk their fill.

Wamba was a beautiful camp. We had climbed above the parching heat and winds of Isiolo to an altitude of about 4,000 feet, high enough to engender that early morning crispness and purity that lends reality to the fancy of a singing heart. The air of the highlands has often been compared to champagne, but I do not think this apt, for while both are invigorating, champagne prickles, whereas the highland air is smooth and sweet. Weaver-birds chattered, anvil birds (a boubou shrike) sounded their bell-like duet, and multi-coloured starlings, so bold and iridescent, hopped about the camp. The fragrance of acacia blossom, clustered in tight little yellow balls, floated on the air as lightly as thistle-down.

Above our camp, the Mathews range rose almost to 8,000 feet, thickly forested and then only half explored. Here and there families of Dorobo,[4] dwelt in their igloo-like shelters, moving on frequently to make new ones, living by drop-spear traps for elephants, snares for small mammals and by hunting antelopes with bows and poisoned arrows. Their numbers were dwindling, and Sharpie had established a settlement at the foot of the range where several hundred of them were being taught to dig, hoe, plant seeds, harvest crops and turn into farmers, with a Kikuyu agricultural instructor in charge.

Our arrival coincided with a full moon, and moons in Africa seem to get fuller than they do elsewhere. Everything becomes black and white; deep black for rocks and trees and shadows, and all else not chalk-white but a subtle kind of silver, full of mystery. We ate our dinner in the open beside a crackling, pungent-scented camp fire, after a dish of 'first toasties' more imaginative than the roasted peanuts we generally had at home. ('Second toasties' were savouries, more favoured as a rule than puddings.) Sharpie's cook was a Swahili who had been with him for years, and he also had a personal servant – one might say valet – and an odd-job man, plus a driver-mechanic and his mate. The valet had the soft good looks, light-coloured skin and dark, disdainful eyes with a hint in them of wickedness of the young Arab. Some such attractive ganymede was nearly always to be found in Sharpie's entourage.

For some reason, or for no reason, I have never been afraid of elephants. This is not courage, which consists of overcoming fear, but stupidity. Elephants are large, powerful and wild, and have been so harried and tormented by man almost since mankind began that if every elephant charged every human on sight and trampled him to death the score would not be evened. It is fear that stops them from doing this, and fear can lead to desperate frenzy as well as to precipitate flight. Besides, a great many elephants go about with festering wounds, or with memories of man-inflicted pain and terror, and you can never tell whether that creature dozing so peaceably in the shade, and such tempting camera-fodder, bears the scars of bullet-wounds or spear-heads. So it is foolish not to be afraid of elephants. But, if I had harboured such fears, the elephants of Wamba would have dispelled them.

After the meal, I strolled down to the pool below our camp to enjoy the stillness and the silvery light on leaves and grasses and on the sandy verge of the pool. A dark-blue sky was bursting with stars. All was quiet, save for now and again a bark from some distant animal, the hoot of an owl, and once an outburst of frog-croak that started up like an orchestra, swelled to a crescendo and suddenly stopped, as if at the touch of a switch. Turning to wander back to camp, I looked up to see three elephants standing about fifteen yards away, moonlight il-luminating their white tusks, the wrinkles on their foreheads and even a gleam in their eyes. They were altogether tranquil and relaxed, their big ears slowly moving, trunks hanging slackly down. Two or three strides and they could have stretched out a trunk and hurled me out of their path, but I sensed their peaceful intention and felt no inclination to turn and fly.

'The elephant's a gentleman,' Kipling wrote; there is indeed a gentleness about them; they will step aside when a little plover in their path raises her wings to warn them off her nest. There is a legend among both the Kikuyu and the Chagga people of Mount Kilimanjaro that elephants formerly were men and women who, like Adam and

Eve, gave offence to God, not in their case by disobedience but by
vanity and extravagance. To make themselves look beautiful, they
washed in milk. For this, God expelled them from their Eden,
inflicting on them milk-white tusks as a perpetual reminder of their
folly. Sometimes, it was said, when out of sight, a young elephant
would change back into a human. Retreating a few steps, I stood
under a tree and watched them, and they watched me. After about
fifteen minutes they half-turned and moved down to the water's edge
with the dignity of a high priest bearing votive offerings to a shrine.

We set out next morning to climb a part of the mountain, intending to
camp under the crest. This meant enlisting people to carry loads. The
Samburu were too proud to carry anything heavier than a spear, so
some of the Dorobo were recruited. They, too, had seldom carried
anything heavier than a chunk of raw meat, and took it all as a great
joke. They were not over-burdened; one man carried a hurricane
lamp, another a tin basin, another Nellie's sponge-bag, and so on. A
whole army streamed off up the mountain along winding game
tracks, escorted by several police askaris and a squad of tribal
policemen in smart red and blue blankets, armed with rifles. The
theory was that we were sure to encounter a rhino at almost every
step. There were plenty of rhinos about, but as our cavalcade made a
noise like a tank corps going into action, this was unlikely, and did
not occur.

The Dorobo were light-hearted porters and, when we reached the
forest, they vanished among the vegetation to re-emerge wreathed in
smiles and smeared with honey. Here and there treeless patches with
charred stumps told the tale of destruction by fire – deliberate fire
started by the Samburu in order to clear a way for their cattle. They
were doing great damage, Sharpie said, so he had 'closed' the
mountain, and we could see saplings growing up in scorched places,
and vegetation beginning to come back. His action had not been
taken just because he loved trees, or wanted to annoy the Samburu.
Forests are the mother of streams. They nourish and protect the
springs, and if they are destroyed the springs dry up, rivers cease to
flow, people and their cattle have to move elsewhere and another bit
of Africa is turned into desert. This is going on all the time.

We camped that night in a natural forest glade, and all around us Cape chestnuts were smothered in a froth of pale pink blossom smelling rather like jasmine. (They are not chestnuts and had not come from the Cape, being indigenous – *Calodendrum capense*.) Early next morning we scrambled up a rocky shoulder to reach the crest and marvel at the view. It is the immensity of these views that defies description; they seem to have no end. On one hand a lava plain broken by abrupt and jagged mountains stretched away to Lake Rudolf and all Turkanaland and the Sudan beyond; on the other lay another plain dotted with queer little nobbly hills reaching to the sharp and distant lip of the Laikipia plateau. All was flooded with golden effulgence as the sun took possession of the plains.

This was to be plant-hunting day. Sharpie and Rose set out in one direction, Nellie and I in another, escorted by a tall and handsome Samburu tribal policeman with a charming smile who carried a rifle in one hand and a trowel in the other. As the hunt proceeded he laid aside his rifle and dug enthusiastically at any root coveted by Nellie.

Rose was one of those people, like Raymond Hook, Philip Perceval, Denys Finch Hatton and other self-taught naturalists, whose chosen element was the wild places of Africa and who accumulated, bit by bit, an understanding of their plants and creatures. But she was dogged by ill fortune. Birth under an unlucky star seemed the only way to account for the undeserved misfortunes that fell upon her. Dreadful things happened to her prize cows, things that happened to no other people's cattle – unlikely accidents, rare diseases, deformed calves, deliberate sabotage. Once she ran over a favourite dachshund while backing her car. The man she hoped to marry died, after several years of suffering, from wounds inflicted in the war. She trusted her staff, but they frequently betrayed her; others had the same experience, but she seemed to have it more often than most.

On the surface she was gentle, mild and lenitive; underneath, tough. So much was made plain by the story of her daughter's birth. The baby was premature. Rose was alone in a rudimentary shack with no telephone or nearby European neighbours; this was in the days when African employees lived apart in their huts, and none of their women had as yet ventured into European houses or become acclimatised to European ways. She despatched a runner to Naivasha, about twenty miles away, but the term runner was an expression of hope, not of reality; and no one came. The baby arrived, a tiny four-pounder. Rose was uncertain what to do next, and afraid of harming the infant, so it remained attached to the umbilical cord. 'Luckily it suckled madly,' she said. She herself opened a half-bottle of champagne. 'What else could I do?' she remarked. Nearly eighteen hours elapsed before help arrived and the cord was severed. When at last a doctor came, he had to operate, but had brought no anaesthetics. Rose, and the baby, survived.

She was a survivor, despite the blows of fate. She also survived an attack by thieves that left her tied up on the floor, battered and unconscious with broken bones, and permanently semi-crippled – a disaster still to come at the time of our plant-hunt, when she scrambled about the mountains with agility. All this she bore with humour and without despair, continuing her embroideries of flowers and birds in the finest of stitches on the purest of silk woven in China. They are works of art, and a shoal of brilliant tropical fishes, hanging on a wall of my cottage beneath a flight of ducks, never ceases to delight.

Back in camp with our plant loot, Nellie thanked our escort, to be rewarded with a smile more charming than ever, and remarked to Sharpie on his intelligence and courtesy. 'A good fellow,' Sharpie agreed. 'One of the most reliable of our tribal policemen.' He added that our escort had been one of the accused in the Powys murder case.

This case was still having repercussions. Our safari was not just a pleasure jaunt. Its purpose was for Sharpie to hold a baraza in which he was to tick off the Samburu yet again for refusing to give up spear-blooding, and to hand over the murderers to the police. Wherever a DC went, he held a baraza. He took up his position on a camp chair behind a small table, people sat around on their haunches, and an interpreter stood behind the DC's chair. Normally the DC spoke in Swahili, which the interpreter rendered into the local dialect. Anyone could give his views, but generally the local headman was the spokesman, having first consulted with his council of elders – a procedure that might be described as democracy without frills.

The Samburu thrust the hafts of their spears into the ground and gathered round to listen to Sharpie's address. Despite the posting to the district of a 'levy force', and despite heavy fines in livestock, the tally of spear-blooding murders had reached forty-six. Sharpie pointed out that if things went on as they were going, the Samburu would soon have no livestock left at all. They listened impassively; they were not warriors but elders who had to pay the fines. But they still did not reveal the identity of the murderers.

Next day we struck camp and followed what Sharpie called a new road. The road was an idea, not an accomplishment. A guide walked ahead to find a passage between boulders, fallen trees and ant-bear holes, and after a few miles we halted altogether while a path was hacked through the bush. We came at length to a grove of tall acacias beside a stream trickling down a broad bed of pure white sand, and full of tiny fish. A succulent dish of whitebait, we thought, for supper. We trawled with mosquito nets and caught a bucketful, but they were a disappointment – too bitter. So brilliant was the moonlight that we had no lamp upon the table and sat in the open on the white sand with the sound of gurgling water and croaking frogs in our ears, and a little owl sang to us all through supper.

To reach our last camp we wound our way to the top of the Leroghi plateau through some of the worst soil erosion I have ever seen. This plateau, and its steep escarpment, had been unoccupied until a few years before, when Samburu cattle, sheep and goats had started to come in from the north. They had multiplied so quickly that the area was carrying, so said the experts, two or three times as many beasts as it could support without serious damage to the pastures. Who was to blame for this? Not really the Samburu, but the vets. Periodic outbreaks of rinderpest and pleuro-pneumonia had previously held livestock numbers down to a level that the land could support. Now the vets with their vaccines had virtually abolished these checks. The beasts had multiplied, and the pastures had been eaten out and trampled and the soil washed away by storms. An old story. Vets and doctors between them have created the terrifying dilemmas of today's Africa. If ever good intentions paved a way to hell, this is the exemplar.

That night we camped on top of the windswept plateau beside an extraordinary gorge full of deep, dark pools which descended in tiers like steps between steep and rocky walls. Scrambling down, we came suddenly to a sheer drop of at least a thousand feet into an empty valley. All was silent and deserted; of man there was no sign. These black pools, the craggy rocks enfolding them, the brooding silence, the seeming absence of any form of life – all this was chillingly sinister. These pools must surely be haunted; not by ghosts of humans but by monstrous shapes or phantoms rising from the black waters, to sink back into them again. Karanja felt the same. It was cold at nightfall; he had wrapped himself in an old army greatcoat and looked uneasy. His light skin, more coffee-coloured than black, his slender build and something in his posture, a way of speaking with his head half-tilted back, betrayed the Maasai genes carried by so many Kikuyu. In some indefinable way he looked aristocratic. He shivered in his coat and said: 'shetani' – evil spirits. But the topmost pool, near our camp, had hippos splashing in it; elephants came to drink at dusk, and we heard lions grunting round about, which sounded companionable.

So, next day, home to Njoro, limping along at fifteen miles an hour because our car's front springs had snapped in two; three punctures on the way and frequent stops to fill the radiator made our pace even slower. But the old Ford, gallant to the last, made it up the farm track, between the twin umbrella thorns that stood like guardians, and so to the creepered little bungalow, a lamp on the table, a fire crackling in the hearth, and a cacophony of dachshund voices.

CHAPTER 12

Tales of the Northern Frontier

The first pony I ever had – not mine really, but allocated to me – was called Moyale. That was the name of the place he had come from. He was a scraggy little grey, tough as gristle, and covered with scars denoting who knows what adventures and cruelties, for Somalis are not kind and gentle to their animals, nor is life kind and gentle to them. I grew very fond of Moyale, and he kindled in my mind a great desire to see his place of origin, which lay far to the north beyond the desert, on the Abyssinian border.

I never did achieve my aim, but I did get to Wajir, lying on those great dry scorching plains that stretch towards the Juba river. Wajir had an aura of romance about it, created partly by the white crenellated walls of its fort, guarded night and day by smart askaris of the King's African Rifles; by its tall arched doorways; by its slender white minaret; by bugle calls at dawn and sunset; and by tall Somalis in chequered kikois (short wrapover skirts), finely woven shawls, and turbans in bright tomato-red and gentian-blue – lean men with clever boney faces stamped by pride and authority. Lines of camels roped nose to tail converged on the wells outside the fort's perimeter, uttering half-roaring, half-moaning cries as they awaited their turn. The constant clattering of their wooden bells was the signature tune of the North.

These wells seem inexplicable. Suddenly a group of deep caverns, with never-failing water at the bottom, appears in the midst of a desert whose rainfall may be two or three inches in a year, or none at all in some years, and seldom more than ten inches. They are fed by rain falling on the Abyssinian mountains, more than two hundred miles away, that travels underground until arrested by an outcrop of limestone rock. These wells, 126 in number, are said to have been dug by a race of giants called the Madhanleh. Whether these people are mythical or really existed is a matter for argument. A quasi-magical explanation of puzzling objects or events (for instance, eclipses) is common among almost all unsophisticated peoples; on the other hand some evidence in favour of the second hypothesis is suggested by certain burial mounds, not long since discovered, said to contain bones of exceptionally tall men and women. Tall or not, the diggers must have been exceptionally strong.

The drawing of water went on all round the clock, as it still does. A chain of Somali camel-men passed buckets made of calf-hide, or of the hides of giraffes, from hand to hand up the sides of the wells, which are fifty or sixty feet deep, and poured the water into troughs to which the camels came in batches. After each batch had had a turn, the camels were driven some distance away to moan and wait until another turn came round. The men chanted and sang as they passed up the buckets while the women, tall and graceful with eyes ringed by kohl, came with pitchers to draw water like Rebecca of old.

The Somalis, were, and are, Muslims, but among nomads the rigid observances of the faith could not but become attenuated. There was no purdah, nor did women wear the bui-bui, that voluminous black garment with only slits for eyes to peep through, the uniform of Muslim women at the Coast. Even schools had to be nomadic. They consisted of wandering, solitary, bearded teachers, each of whom carried a piece of wood shaped something like a cricket bat on which phrases from the Koran were inscribed. The teacher sat down under a thorn tree near a Somali encampment and the children gathered round to recite after him the holy phrases until they had them by heart. That was all the formal education, if it could be described as formal, that most of these Somali children got. This did not impair their intelligence, and it strengthened their memories. Somali men – I do not think that this applied to women – could recite the names of their ancestors and collaterals back through generation after generation until they reached the founder of their clan, probably a relative of the Prophet Mohamed.

Doves came in great flocks to these wells, flew in, settled near the troughs, sipped and flew off again. At evening sand-grouse came, providing sport for the officers. All night long you could hear the moaning of the camels and the clatter-clatter-clatter of the bells. It was extremely hot at Wajir, and, for Europeans, lonely. Before the Second World War the basic European establishment consisted of a couple of KAR officers, a DC with one or two juniors, a policeman and a doctor, all of whom expected to spend more than half their time away from the station.

'Glenday looks upon the NFD as something he has made and guards it jealously as his own preserve,' wrote a young cadet who kept a diary. 'He is very outspoken – he says, among ourselves in the North we speak freely, but down country we are the silent North.'[1] He was a stimulating talker, wrote this diarist, and immensely knowledgeable – he understood ecology before the word was invented – but by 1937, when the diarist was posted to Wajir, he had had twenty-five years' service on the frontier with many bouts of malaria, and was inclined to mumble and doze off after the evening meal.

Glenday expected his officers, while at their posts, to be celibate. Married men were seldom posted to the NFD, and had to leave their wives behind if they were. One young bride who did manage to wriggle through the anti-feminist net as far as Marsabit wrote that she was more frightened of Glenday than of the buffaloes that browsed around the boma; when she actually encountered him, however, he was mild as milk.[2] Her husband, Gerald Reece, was to succeed him as boss of the NFD.

The district officers were young, fit and virile, and Somali women, in youth so handsome and seductive, offered a temptation one might have thought impossible to resist. But Glenday opposed Somali mistresses as firmly as he forbade wives. For one thing syphilis, he believed, would be the almost certain price of a liaison, and, for another, the young man would find himself drawn into complicated feuds and intrigues that would compromise his impartiality, as had happened in the case of Long Lew. 'In former days,' ran a rather wistful entry in our young cadet's diary, 'most KAR officers had native mistresses. Some were so long-standing that they were almost called on! They knew every secret too.'

Even Glenday could not keep all his officers up to the mark all the time. There was a middle-aged DC called Denis Wickham who was fond of his comforts, inclined to stoutness, widely read, and one of the founders of the Wajir Yacht Club. (Needless to say, the yachts were imaginary.) He took his Somali mistress into retirement at Lamu and left her £30,000 in his will, together with his mother's jewellery. She went through the lot, aided by an Italian lover; married a corporal in the Foreign Legion; and committed suicide in Djibuti by jumping out of a third-floor window.

What of Glenday's own amours, if any? His reputation as a strong, silent man of the North, combined with his bachelor status, naturally fluttered various dovecots when he visited Nairobi. With Loresho as his base on these occasions, it was inevitable that his name should have been linked with Glady Delamere's. These rumours were scotched by one of the country's most incorrigible gossips. 'Just good friends,' he said. 'Glady assures me that V. G. is a bull virgin.' Glenday himself put an end to speculation in 1938 by marrying a young widow, daughter of a former Chief Justice. Then he left his kingdom to govern British Somaliland, and in due course begat three sons, served as British Resident in Zanzibar, and retired first to a small farm in Kenya and finally to Natal, where he died in his eightieth year in 1970.

One of his achievements in the NFD was to build up a powerful esprit de corps which sustained his officers in the loneliness, austerity and dangers of their daily lives. A simple ceremony held every evening at sunset when the Union Jack was hauled down did much to foster this spirit. This ritual has been well described by a young district officer, Robert Tatton-Brown:

The night guard of the police was mounted; they turned out and presented arms as the flag was lowered and the police bugler sounded the Retreat. It was a moving little ceremony which harked back to the honours paid to the Roman eagles. We servants of the Government – administration, police, Goan clerks, syces, agricultural instructors, prison warders, hospital dressers – all were bound to something greater than ourselves symbolised by this flag, with a head in the shape of the King to whom some of us had sworn allegiance. This symbolism inspired not only Europeans but also Goans and Africans who took pride in uniform and medals, and did their duty honourably with a certain panache that gave colour to these out-of-the-way places. It was the rule that everyone within sight of the flagstaff stood rigidly to attention . . .[3]

The official rule book stated that this upright posture was obligatory only within three hundred yards of the flagstaff. A renegade sergeant-major used to pace out the distance and settle himself just beyond the pole to enjoy his beer at ease. After the flag-lowering came another short ceremony, called *timamu*, when the senior policeman presented to the DC a tally of the manpower, arms and ammunition and prisoners, if any; then the head syce enumerated the number of horses, camels and barramils of water;[4] finally the head station hand reported on such matters as the availability of firewood. Then all could adjourn to their evening's relaxation.

'No shadow of coming events,' wrote Tatton-Brown, 'had dimmed the Roman certitude with which we were endowed.'

It was in the NFD that that useful Kenyan institution the goat-bag was born. In the days of its conception, tax was paid in goats instead of money. Most of the goats were fed to KAR askaris. Every one had to be accounted for to the Treasury in Nairobi. But that department's officials overlooked the fact that in any given flock of goats, births as well as deaths will occur. The district officer who started the first goat-bag did not overlook it, and gradually built up a flock that had no official existence, and that could be converted into cash by selling the animals. He also discovered that by drying and marketing the skins, his unofficial fund could be augmented. Every DC in the country was continually being confronted by a need for cash to meet unexpected demands unlikely to be sanctioned by the Treasury. The goat-bag proved to be the answer. It was not long before every DC in the country had latched on to the idea. Each commissioner kept a meticulous account of how the money was spent, which he locked away in his confidential safe, so that when the auditors came round on their annual examination of the station's accounts, the secrets of the goat-bag were concealed from their eyes.

Every DC could give examples of the uses of the goat-bag; here is a single one.[5] On the road between the Tanganyikan border and Nairobi, some unknown person halted his car to fire at a zebra standing on the skyline, missed, and drove on. The bullet proceeded on its way until it dropped through the roof of a hut and into the head of a young Maasai girl, killing her stone-dead. Her family, according to custom, demanded blood-money: but who was to pay? In the Maasai view there was no doubt: the Government. The Treasury disclaimed all responsibility. The elders came angrily to the DC at Kajiado, who feared serious trouble should the claim not be met. The Treasury remained adamant. Luckily, the goat-bag at Kajiado was a fat one. The DC handed over twelve head of cattle and the crisis passed.

At Wajir the north-bound road, such as it was, forked. To the right you could bump across rocky flats and over dry luggas fringed by doum-palms to El Wak, the wells of God, and on to Mandera, where Abyssinia, Italian Somaliland and Kenya met. To the left you could drive almost due north through rough country pale as ashes, swept by fine white dust and peppered with termite mounds, some over twenty feet high, until you reached the foot of the Abyssinian massif and the frontier at Moyale, sited on tumbled hills just above the plain. There were two Moyales, one British, one Abyssinian, a few miles apart. A barbed-wire entanglement protected the British one, which had a fort, large conical huts with thatched roofs steeply pitched, and the usual police lines, dukas and offices. Philip Zaphiro's old house had become a hospital of sorts, rickety, bug-ridden and not very clean. These crude little field hospitals at out-stations had no qualified doctors but were run by sub-assistant-surgeons, almost all Indians, who had received a rudimentary training. Taught to carry out only such routine tasks as inoculations, dressings and the giving out of basic medicines, they had often to cope as best they could with terrible injuries, and did so with considerable resourcefulness and skill. But they could not operate or give anaesthetics. No flying doctors then.

Two names are principally associated in my mind with Moyale: the great Glenday, and the less great in achievement, but scarcely so in character, Tich Miles. They were as different from each other as beefsteak is from a soufflé, but shared a dedication to their task and an ability to deal with such touchy, proud, dangerous and difficult peoples as the Amharic-speaking Abyssinians and the Somalis. Tich, as his name implies, was tiny, and incredibly thin: a medical examination made in 1930 gave his weight at 6 stone 8½ lbs – just 92½ lbs. He was a bundle of energy, of laughter and high spirits when not racked by pain and fits of vomiting that left him limp as a dish-rag. Then he would bounce back and carry on with whatever he was doing as if nothing had happened. Enthusiasm, or sometimes detestation, would bubble up in him like a hot spring. He deeply loved his family, his many friends and those he considered to be the salt of the earth, and despised no less deeply those he believed to be its scum. His was a simple code, black and white, no half measures. He came of a family of soldiers – Miles, Latin for soldier: genes have a long life.[6]

Tich had arrived in East Africa in 1910 at the age of nineteen to seek his fortune, having absolutely none of his own, and had been taken on by a man called Isaacson who was promoting rubber-growing among the Nandi. For a salary of £8 a month he worked in a duka at Kabsabet from six a.m. to six p.m., six days a week, selling trade goods and buying latex. His companions were a dog (taken by a leopard), a mule, a monkey (killed by a Nandi) and a lion cub which, to his grief, he had to shoot after it had sprung upon a goat.

War relieved him of this drudgery. He joined the KAR and fought throughout the East African campaign, winning a DSO and an MC, as well as a Belgian decoration and a mention in despatches. After the war he stayed on for two and a half years in the KAR, mainly in the wilds of Jubaland, where letters posted in Nairobi took two months to reach him. Ever since the Aulihan Somali had sacked a British post at Serenli in 1916, killing the commanding officer, warfare between the Somali tribes and sub-tribes in this region had continued virtually unchecked. In 1920 a small section of the KAR mutinied and killed their officer, and Tich was sent to bring the situation under control. A particularly militant section of the Aulihan Somali raided the local Gurreh tribe, killing eight of them and carrying off two hundred head of cattle. Tich set off in hot pursuit at the head of his detachment of mounted infantry, overtook the raiders, killed seventeen and re-covered all the cattle.[7] During this period of his life he survived not one but two attacks of blackwater fever. Then, in 1923, he success-fully applied for the job of British Consul in Southern Abyssinia. His headquarters were at Mega and his salary £800 a year, plus £50 'horse allowance'.

Mega was three days' march (eighty miles) from Moyale up in the Abyssinian mountains, and here Tich had what he chose to call his palace, with his mules and their syces, his servants, a bodyguard of Abyssinian ruffians armed with antiquated rifles, and no companions save his dachshunds, in particular one called Honey Bees who travelled on his long safaris in a box strapped to a mule's back.

Since time immemorial, tribesmen ruled by the Emperor's Amharic officials had been going down from the mountains and over the Kenya border to raid for cattle, slaughtering in the process a great many tribesmen ruled by the British King's officials. Many of these Abyssinian tribesmen were armed with rifles of a sort, whereas the British forbade the carrying of firearms; it was a case of guns versus spears. The British strove to put an end to these raids, but a company or so of the KAR strung out along a frontier more than four hundred miles long was powerless to bring this about. Part of the task of the British Consul at Mega was to persuade the Amharic provincial governors to control their savage subjects, an underaking for which those governors lacked enthusiasm to say the least.

There was also the matter of the wells, and their failure in the long dry season and in times of drought. Most of the permanent wells lay on the Abyssinian side of the frontier, but custom had long sanctioned their use by Kenya's cattle-men when their own wells dried up. This right had been enshrined in a treaty between the Emperor Menelik II and the British Government signed in 1907, which delineated the boundary between the two countries. Tribesmen on the Abyssinian side often ignored this custom and this treaty, and denied their wells to Kenya's cattle owners. So another part of Tich's job was to persuade the Abyssinian governors to prevent their subjects from closing the wells. These tasks were very far from easy. Tich had no force at his command to back up his words. The Amharic officials, besides being proud and touchy, were suspicious, and in command of retinues of trigger-happy men.

Tich dealt with this situation in the only way, I think, in which he could have brought off any measure of success. If the Amharic governors could be proud and haughty, so could he. If they called their big conical dwellings palaces, so would he. If they could quaff great quantities of tej – and their capacity for downing this fiery barley mead was prodigious – so could he. If they went about with armed bodyguards, so would he. The constant ill-health from which he suffered could only be worsened by the tej, and even his diminutive size was against him. But somehow, by his stylish mode of living and by a great deal of nerve and panache, he conquered these obstacles. Looking back on it, his courage was immense.

It was not as if he liked solitude and rough living. On the contrary, he loved company, and friends, good food and drink, and laughter. It was poverty that bound him to his post. 'I would take anything the powers that be think I can do,' he wrote to a friend, 'to get away from this exile.' And to his sister Dolly: 'It's awful how old we are both getting, but let's pray for a peaceful old age. I believe we both ought to have married and had quantities of young. If I'd had any they would have had to run about naked . . . The bank was rather savage about my overdraft.' He concluded: 'This is a wonderful country but a foul race inhabits it.'

He did escape for two years, when Sir Edward Grigg engineered his posting to Government House in Nairobi as senior aide-de-camp. Here he was the life and soul of many parties. He had a parlour trick he often practised at Muthaiga Club: he went all round the ballroom without touching the floor, swinging by his fingers from the cornice like a monkey. He loved these parties. At an earlier one: 'Berkeley Cole announced that everyone was bathing at Trouville and every few minutes a large wave came and we had to hop over it. I've never laughed so much in my life.'

When his two years were up, it was back to the frontier. This could have been avoided. Through the good offices of friends, he was offered a job on the staff of the Governor-General of Canada. He wanted very much to take it, but the Treasury decreed that if he did, he would lose his pension rights even if he returned to the colonial service. Small though the pension was, it was the only source of income to which he could look forward. Despite Grigg's intervention, the Treasury remained adamant. Tich refused the offer, and thereby signed his own death warrant.

As time went on he grew more sensitive, rather than less so, to the brutalities and disregard of human life he saw all around him. Camped at Moyale was an elderly Afrikaner called Maynier who was engaged in buying Abyssinian horses. Four Somali askaris of the KAR decided to desert and, passing Maynier's tent, wantonly discharged their rifles through the canvas, hitting him in the stomach, chest and limbs. 'The deserters got away into the mountains and a patrol of other KAR Somalis who were sent after them refused to fire on them, so things weren't very nice,' Tich wrote. 'I rode back swiftly fifty miles expecting to find a mutiny but things are quiet now ... It is very sad and depresses me awfully as I had got very fond of the old Dutchman, and why should they want to kill the old man who had nothing to do with them except from fanaticism, and the belief that killing any white man will take them straight to heaven ... I am afraid the poor old man died in awful agony, there was no doctor here and very little anyone could do.'

Despite such tragedies, there were compensations. Tich enjoyed being treated as a minor royalty when he visited Amharic dukes and barons, who measured their own importance by the lavishness of their hospitality. At a town called Gardula, bleakly perched at 9,000 feet up, he found two hundred soldiers paraded to receive him. They bowed to the ground as he advanced to accept a present of two bullocks, five sheep, a hundred flat loaves of barley bread, ten pots of beer, five pots of tej, five pots of chilli sauce and ten bundles of firewood, together with twenty-five bundles of grass and two sacks of barley for the mules. While flattering, this was also embarrassing, as Tich knew that all that bounty had been taken without payment from the peasants. But he could not refuse it.

The Dedjmatch, or duke, of Soddu received him on a throne of Persian carpets, and invited him to enjoy the spectacle of seven robbers who had just been hanged in the market place. They had burned a church, and killed sixteen of the Dedjmatch's soldiers. This was in 1926, when Tich was on his way on mule-back to confer with the British Minister in Addis Ababa.

After the reception came the banquet, when enormous helpings of underdone meat, sometimes scarcely cooked at all, doused in sauces made from chillis and other hot spices, were served with barley loaves, and accompanied by copious draughts of tej. Had he failed to keep up with his hosts in tej consumption, he would have earned their contempt. (A DC at Moyale had got into serious trouble when, feeling that he could stand no more, he observed a dog yawning at his feet, and poured the contents of his drinking-vessel down its throat.) Tich's liver had been permanently damaged by amoebic dysentery, so that alcohol was almost a poison, but he refused to give the Abyssinians best, thereby winning their respect, or rather enhancing it. Their parting present, when he left Mega, was a silver-mounted drinking-horn.

I last saw Tich when he was lying on a sofa on Glady's veranda. He was too weak to rise, but not too weak to kiss my hand and make some joke or other. His face was like a death mask. He was on his way to England for treatment, but died in April 1934 within a month of his arrival. He was forty-four years old.

His sister Dolly – Olive Tremayne Miles – had been his closest companion. Like her brother, Dolly was lightly built, wiry and deceptively strong. She had a nut-brown complexion, dark hair that tumbled about at will, somewhat prominent teeth and large dark-blue eyes, and was impetuous in movement, often funny and quite ruthless in getting her own way. She had followed Tich to Africa in 1910 despite his protests – he wanted her company but dreaded her demands, and felt unable to support her in any style at all on £8 a month. He warned her: 'you will have to live in a mud hut and have only a mule to ride and bad food'. Dolly was not to be put off. Giving in, Tich told her to bring a camp bed and table, a chair, blankets, a saddle, a 'split skirt thing', a sun-helmet and a packed chop-box from Fortnum and Mason to be had for £2, £5, or £7.

He had no need to worry about her response to rough conditions. Four years later she was to be plunged into an existence tougher and more stark than anything East Africa could offer. While Tich was off to 'German East', Dolly set out for Salonika, where French and British forces were assembling to go to the aid of Serbia, whose army was being overwhelmed by Austrian and Bulgarian forces under German command. Dolly had no training in any nursing or military skill, but was not deterred by that. She joined no unit, but with two no less independent and free-lancing friends simply boarded a small, old, dilapidated French vessel bound for the Balkan wars, submarines notwithstanding.

Her companions were Lady Muriel Herbert and Miss Elia Lindon. The appearance of all three khaki-clad lady musketeers struck observers as unusual. A fellow-passenger was a woman doctor travelling to Serbia to join the Scottish Women's Hospital, a unit raised in Edinburgh and staffed, financed and equipped entirely by women. 'All have short hair,' wrote Dr Emslie of the trio – short hair for women was then virtually unknown. 'One is tall, dark and slim, with great tragic eyes and a lovely face [Lady Muriel Herbert]. The second has a great shock of hair and prominent china-blue eyes [Elia Lindon]. The third has a beautiful head and profile but is curiously disconnected in every way, all loose ends, coming undone everywhere.'[8] This was Dolly. All fetched up together at Ghevgeli, where a field hospital was being hastily improvised to receive the wounded of the retreating Serbian army. Dolly and her companions attached themselves to the French Army's Service de Santé. 'They were quite untrained,' Dr Emslie wrote, 'but did excellent work, although their methods would have shocked, indeed did shock, our English sisters. They made up in intelligence and courage what they lacked in training.' They were a curious sight; Dolly with her sweaters 'buttoned up awry and gaping'. Dolly, for her part, was not overly impressed by the correctly uniformed Scottish nurses. 'The Scottish Women's Hospital,' she wrote, 'lost all their tent-poles and kept yelling for men to come and help them.'

For the next three and a half years Dolly worked in French military hospitals, coping in the crudest of conditions with the ghastliest of injuries, and also with epidemics which killed more men than the weapons of the enemy. The bitter cold of the mountains, the biting winter wind, the black mud that blocked the roads, the mosquitoes, lice and flies, the scanty food hastily eaten, the desperate fatigue, the harrowing sights, all these failed to extinguish Dolly's humour and her enjoyment of pleasures snatched whenever she could find them.

One of the leading Parisian surgeons, M. Roux-Berger, taught her to administer chloroform, and thereafter she worked as an anaesthetist, sometimes for so long at a stretch that she 'never knew it was possible to be so tired and be alive'. Skill in giving chloroform, she wrote, was like having good hands with a horse: you were born with the knack, or without it. Dolly was a brilliant horsewoman, and spent much of such leisure time as she was able to enjoy on borrowed mounts, mostly supplied by French generals, from the Commander-in-Chief downwards, with whom she made friends. She described how she would ride a grey horse into the hills and 'Discover all sorts of little plants that smelt good, and all kinds of frog and cigale that were croaking in the pools, with the background of the mountains, and the divine sunsets, and afterglow eternally changing behind the unchanging Olympus.

I would lie down on the down-like turf and sleep, and the grey horse seemed to understand that I was dead-beat, and never ran away but just stayed quite near grazing . . . Sleep overtook one directly one sat down a minute. I slept through all meals, and eventually I took to dozing while standing up, even at operations, only to be woken up by Roux-Berger cursing me.'[9]

When the Balkan war ended, Dolly moved on to the Caucasus to work in an orphanage set up by Americans for Armenian children who were starving to death. 'In its vastness and sadness and aloofness that Caucasian country is like no other,' she wrote. 'Since those days I have wandered much in the far and lonely places of the earth, and yet my mind goes back often to those great plains, and a longing comes over me to see them again.'

I do not know whether she ever did see them again, but certainly she travelled much in the far and lonely places of the earth, and taught herself to speak several of the less familiar languages. She went often to East Africa, and to stay with Tich at Mega. Nellie, an old friend, found her visits a mixed blessing. Dolly talked loudly and persistently in her sleep, the walls were thin and the little house seemed to reverberate with her shouts. As she grew older she became rather deaf, and would turn up her transistor radio to its fullest and keep it blaring away all night. She had a mania for washing her clothes but never pressed them, handing bundles over to poor Mbugwa who had to spend hours at the ironing table. She was mean about tips, and short-tempered when thwarted. Her former companion in the Balkans, Lady Muriel Herbert, was by then married to Dr Jex-Blake, and living on a coffee farm near Nairobi, another of Dolly's pieds à terre. Lady Muriel was still tall, dark and slim though I did not think her bright brown eyes were tragic. She was an expert gardener of the kind who values plants more for their rarity than for their splendour, and might dismiss a bed of dahlias as merely showy while enthusing over some tiny little cactus that bloomed once in seven years. She dressed in bold flowered chintzes except when riding, which she did every afternoon – rather dull rides, I thought, among coffee bushes planted in straight lines. The coffee plantation came almost up to the veranda and was shaded by grevillea trees that made the house dark, as did mosquito netting over every window to keep insects at bay.

Dr Jex-Blake had left Harley Street to practise as a heart specialist in Nairobi. A tall, grave-mannered, precisely-spoken man, like his wife an expert botanist, he had little small talk and so was rather alarming, although at heart good-natured and kind. When out of doors he always wore dark glasses, as he believed that sunstroke came through the eyes, and that hats were therefore unnecessary. His views may have hastened the demise of the sola topee and the double terai, which in the 1930s were beginning to fall into desuetude, although it was not until the Second World War that Europeans altogether abandoned the belief that anyone who ventured hatless out of doors between the hours of ten a.m. and four p.m. would very likely fall down dead.

It was no doubt fortuitous that the phasing out of the sola topee coincided with the decline of the British Empire, but believers in a magical basis of the universe might see the topee as an emblem or totem in which the strength and confidence of the imperial spirit resided. Fell the totem pole, and you strike at the roots of the tribe; discard the topee, and with it goes belief in the virtue of the imperial mission. However, I do not suppose that Jex saw the matter in that light. A governess for their daughter Daphne, and Muriel's former ladies' maid, shared the Jex-Blakes' bungalow, but were seldom seen; each had a bed-sitter at the back where she lived in solitary state, even having meals alone.

Expertise in gardening was the common ground shared between the Jex-Blakes and Dolly Miles, who came and went like a migrating swallow. Dolly had by this time taken to the air. It had been in India, in 1911, that she had made her first flight, sitting on 'what seemed to be a hot boiler, holding tightly on to wires with my feet dangling in the air space.' Her second flight was at Ghevgeli, where a Serbian pilot took her up in an army bomber. From that moment, she wrote, she was determined to learn to fly, and in 1928 she got her pilot's licence. She kept a little aeroplane called Birdie in a field in Gloucestershire, and used it to go out to luncheon, and to visit friends in Scotland. I knew her best when her flying days were over and she had settled – though she never settled for long – at Avebury in Wiltshire, where she lived alone save for a beloved labrador and a ghost. Dolly was ghost-prone and quite often saw them; this was a harmless one who seemed to be a sort of monk. 'He was sitting opposite me last night at dinner,' she would say.

She was a skilful gardener, but her garden, like her person, was often untidy, because she was liable to take off for some distant destination at a few days' notice instead of staying at home to put out the wallflowers or prune the roses. She wore grubby old trousers and shapeless sweaters as a rule, but her wardrobe was packed with well-cut suits and rows of expensive-looking shoes, which looked unworn. She had a number of grand friends, and I suppose wore these garments when she visited their mansions, where she was as much at home as she had been in the Balkans or Caucasian mountains. Once she disappeared for two years in the direction of China, some said on a mission for the Secret Service, a possibility that her closest friends thought most unlikely.

Like Tich, she never married. Before the First World War there had been an 'understanding' with a Gloucestershire neighbour who, in 1914, went off to the wars and did not return. Soon after Tich's death, she started to copy out extracts from poems that had appealed to her into a small red album which she took with her wherever she went. She must have read widely in the poets, and her taste was catholic, ranging from the sonnets of Shakespeare and Sir Walter Raleigh to the moderns of her youth like Yeats, Masefield, Bridges, de Musset, Baudelaire and others less exalted. I found this a sad and touching little volume. The theme of loneliness and loss, reaching sometimes almost to despair, runs through the extracts. A fox-hunting poem by Siegfried Sassoon ends:

> *I shall forget him in the morning light,*
> *And while we gallop on we will not speak:*
> *But at the stable door he'll say goodnight.*

Broken hearts are out of fashion, but I think that the ghost of the young man from Gloucestershire who died in the war rode by her side. Or was it for Tich that she grieved? From Belloc:

> *I said to Heart 'How goes it?' Heart replied:*
> *'Right as a Ribstone Pippin!' But it lied.*

The last entry in the album is the only attempt she made herself to write verse. It is addressed to a horse she loved called Greyman. Scrawled at the bottom is the note: 'I can't bear it here without you.' Beneath her leathery armour lay, bottled up, love that found no outlet save in her dogs and horses. There also lay that fumbling search for certainties to which a dusty answer is so often returned. 'She was a pilgrim', said a nephew, 'in her way.'

Her end, at eighty-one, was mercifully sudden. She fell down stone-dead while answering the door-bell to an electrician.

I have mentioned several of those whom Sir Richard Turnbull has called 'the great men of the North': V. G. Glenday, Gerald Reece, Tich Miles, Sharpie and others. The last name on this roster should be that of Turnbull himself. Unlike the others, he belonged to the post-First World War vintage, having reached Kenya in 1935, but in the NFD he continued the Glenday tradition of toughness, austerity and hard trekking, into the period after the Second World War. Unlike the others, also, he is still alive, and given still to hard trekking, nowadays over moors and sheep-fells instead of deserts and camel-tracks, having exchanged the Ethiopian frontier for the Anglo-Scottish one.

'My poor young man, my poor young man, you have ruined your career! If you had only left it to me I could have arranged your posting. We have our methods.'[10] This was the head Goan clerk at Kisumu addressing the young district officer who, to his unconcealed fury, had been posted to this lakeside station among Bantu and Nilotic peoples when he wanted to be in the North serving under Glenday among the Galla and Somali. (These experienced Goan clerks were the lynch-pin of the administration, and fatherly to young officers – comparable to sergeant-majors in the British army. Their names echoed the great names of Portugal – Albuquerque, da Gama, Almeda, Dias, Pinto, da Costa.) Assisted by the influence of Glenday, he got back to the North, which had already hooked him.

Turnbull made himself an expert on Somali customs and clans, and took pride in his mastery of their complex genealogies. Also he collected, identified and registered in three languages – Boran, Somali and Turkana – pretty well every tree and shrub that grew in the region.

Like Glenday, he was a scientist by training, Turnbull in physics, Glenday in geology and forestry.

After five years as Officer-in-Charge he left the NFD to enter the political world of Nairobi as Chief Secretary, where experience gained by dealing with Somali feuds and intrigues no doubt stood him in good stead in the snake-pit of Legislative Council. The view that the settler-politicians were a bunch of ill-mannered backwoodsmen out only for themselves, unscrupulous and pig-headed, was pretty general in the higher echelons of the colonial service. 'Little, frightened, narrow, heathen men, with nothing to offer but words, tricks, schemes and spite' was how Sir Philip Mitchell, Governor from 1944 to 1952, described them. Turnbull took a much kinder view. 'Don't delude yourself', he advised, 'that the settlers were either silly old Colonel Blimps or rough farmers; there were brilliant educated men amongst them who knew far more about parliamentary procedures and the niceties of government than many of us did. They were at us night and day, and it was an excellent thing. It meant that if I had a letter from a senior settler complaining of x, y, or z, my first reaction was not – here's that wretched man once again; it was – is my conscience quite clear in this matter?'[11] So the emphasis was on efficiency in government, although this was by no means always achieved. Africa's secret weapons, Turnbull has observed, are inertia and apathy.

'A brilliant speaker with a pungent wit' is how one of the unofficial members of the Legislative Council, Sir Charles Markham, has described him. 'His opponents in debate were decisively massacred, yet he was never rude. He gave the impression of a benevolent headmaster having to control firmly and kindly a rather undisciplined bunch of school kids, but had none of the aloofness and pomposity sometimes assumed by big frogs in small colonial ponds.'[12] (When a colonial civil servant reached a certain level in the hierarchy, a KCMG was automatically bestowed; the letters were interpreted by the irreverent to stand for 'kindly call me God'.)

Dick Turnbull did not altogether renounce the austerities of the North, but these became a little softened by Nairobi's sybaritic influence. He became, and has remained, a connoisseur of wine. Charles Markham has related an episode that occurred when Turnbull, as acting Governor during the absence of Sir Evelyn Baring, was presiding over a dinner party at Government House. 'After the ladies had left the room, Turnbull suggested that we might as well broach another bottle of Château Margaux 1947. Having already consumed more than a generous quantity, I suggested that perhaps this was a little excessive, which produced the immediate response: "My dear fellow, if we don't drink it, think of the ghastly chaps who might!" No further argument was needed to convince me that we were doing Sir Evelyn Baring a service.' In his defence Dick Turnbull has pointed out that Sir Evelyn was not really being robbed, for his digestion had been so wrecked by dysentery that he could eat and drink little but rice pudding and soda water.

From Nairobi, Dick Turnbull moved on in 1955 to Dar es Salaam to govern Tanganyika, where Julius Nyerere had emerged as the nationalist leader. A lucky opening gambit got him off to a good start. At their first meeting he said: 'Good morning, Mr Nyerere, you and I have some difficult problems to solve in bringing this country to independence.' Mr Nyerere smiled. If the two were not like kittens in a basket after that they were not like snarling dogs either. This personal liking between the chief of the outgoing colonialists and the incoming African ministers was matched in Kenya by the mutual respect and goodwill that grew up between Jomo Kenyatta and Malcolm MacDonald, Governor-General in the period immediately preceding independence.

As Tanganyika's Governor, Turnbull did not allow the languid airs of Dar es Salaam to erode his dedication to physical fitness. Before dawn broke, mounted on a vintage bicycle that was clumsy and heavy, he would pedal vigorously about the back streets of the capital and among the harbour's sheds and railway sidings. Visiting M Ps from Britain would be provided with bicycles and invited to come too. It was an invitation few had the temerity to refuse. 'It was a useful way', Dick Turnbull said, 'to assess their moral fibre.'

The bicycle went too when he retired at first to Henley, where he could be seen, often in icy winter weather, pedalling along the towpath with a megaphone coaching the crews of colleges and clubs of which he had once been an active member. When he moved to wilder country further north he could be found, by then in his mid-seventies, following beagles in wind and rain over the Northumbrian hills. He was, and is, a perfectionist; I recall at Henley the greenest, smoothest and most disciplined of lawns, a closed district to any vagrant plantain or clover; and, in his hospitable Border home, glasses polished until they shone like crystal and every spoon and saucer precisely in its allotted place. Happily, his wife Beatrice is endowed with humour, good nature, simplicity and a sense of order to match her husband's.

A practical man, down-to-earth, a realist scornful of woolly thinking, rose-tinted outlooks and sentimental judgements – I liked a remark of his concerning 'jam-puff courses such as sociology' – and hardly a romantic, one would say. Yet when I asked him what it was about that other, harsher, crueller border that had so captured his allegiance he replied, pausing only to uncork a bottle of ambrosial German wine, 'The romance'.

Sipping the ambrosial wine from crystal-clear glasses, Dick told me the story of John Ethelstan Cheese. He had first met this strange, itinerant English priest in 1935 in one of the remoter parts of the NFD, trudging along a sandy track carrying a small Gladstone bag, a ground-sheet and nothing else. He wore a crumpled, threadbare suit that hinted at a clerical cut, and a pair of sandals. A trader's lorry had dropped him at a duka where water could be had by digging for it, and the next source of water was fifty miles farther on. He had promised, he explained, to look up the sons of Mohamed Ahamed of the Habier Sulieman clan, and did not like to disappoint the family. In gentle tones he added: 'I hope it will not embarrass you if I tell you that I put my faith in God and that God looks after me. It's a funny business, but I've never queried it, and it has always worked.'

So Dick left him in the desert, but sent out two tribal policemen to follow him at a discreet distance and to go to his aid should aid be needed. That same evening Padre Cheese, as he was known, came up with a Somali 'village' – a family group on the move, with all its possessions, in a never-ending search for camel-browse. The people were on their way to the Lorian swamp and should by then have reached it, but a freak storm had brought up some unexpected browse and so they had delayed their departure. The tribal policemen returned to camp, reporting that this was a very holy man and that it was the will of God that no harm should come to him.

In all Padre Cheese's time in the North he made two Christian converts. But he never despaired, nor did the nomads ever refuse him food and shelter. His grand design was to translate the Gospels into Somali, but as this tongue still lacked a written orthography he was obliged to settle for the use of Arabic characters. He translated the Gospel according to St Luke and the whole of *Pilgrim's Progress*, retreating for the purpose to Lamu, where a hospitable Arab provided him with a room and writing materials.

In appearance he was a pale, thin, ascetic-looking individual with a shy and diffident manner. He had entered Kenya in 1930 from Ethiopia, having been a missionary in Addis Ababa and in Palestine before that. A product of Rugby school and Cambridge University, he had been ordained in 1902, so must have been a man of over fifty when he took to the nomadic life, and nearly sixty when Dick Turnbull came upon him carrying his small Gladstone bag.

Seventeen years later, Dick found him living in Lamu and looking older than his seventy-odd years. On Sundays he would preach to a handful, a very small handful, of Christians, consisting usually of the DC, one or two followers of the Salvation Army, and the DC's staff of Goan clerks, who were Roman Catholics but came to the services to give the old man pleasure. Padre Cheese preached long and rather rambling sermons, and then adjourned to Sunday luncheon with the DC, probably his only square meal of the week. He died in 1959 on his way back to England and was buried at sea. 'He had no aim in life but to serve God' was the Somali verdict.

CHAPTER 13

Among the Kikuyu

After I had finished writing Delamere's biography, Nellie said: 'You've done *White Man's Country*. What about *Black Man's Country* next?' She had been intrigued by the enterprise of Njombo and a few companions who, without saying a word, had turned up at Njoro station to meet her there when she moved from Thika, and by the colonisation of the Njoro district by the Kikuyu. Enterprise always appealed to her, and so did a sense of humour; it was their possession of these two qualities that underlay her liking for the Kikuyu people. Also they were intelligent and good at growing things. So Nellie and the Kikuyu had a lot in common. Some Europeans thought them deceitful, crafty, much given to squabbling and to becoming barrack-room lawyers, and were reluctant to employ them, preferring men and women of more straightforward tribes. There was quite a sharp division among white farmers between the pro- and the anti-Kikuyu.

The Black Man's Country notion developed into a plan to trace through the lives of an imaginary Kikuyu family the coming of the white man into a world of custom and tradition that had remained virtually unchanged for centuries. It was to be in the shape of a novel. No doubt this was a foolhardy idea, since I doubt whether any member of one race and culture can get under the skin of people of a different race and culture. Still, it was worth a try.

The first step was to reconstruct, insofar as one could, the daily life and customs of the people in the days when white men were unheard of. This was not quite as difficult as it sounds because the coming of the white man was so recent. I am writing of 1937. A British Protectorate had been established only forty-two years earlier, and the boma at Nyeri, in the heart of Kikuyuland, had not been opened until 1902. Although trading expeditions and explorers had passed along its margins, they had avoided most of Kikuyuland for fear of poisoned arrows, in whose deployment the young men were highly skilled. The people were still in the process of taking over the forested areas on the foothills of Mt Kenya and of the Aberdare mountains from the Dorobo, or taking them over from no one at all, and cutting down and burning trees to make way for shambas. Men and women still in their fifties and sixties could remember at first hand, not from hearsay, what tribal life was like before white men came along to disturb and then disrupt it.

The Provincial Commissioner at Nyeri arranged for Nellie and me and Karanja, accompanied by several dachshunds, to occupy a government camp about six miles from a market called Karatina. These permanent camps were dotted about the reserve for the use of district officers going on their rounds. Junior officers still made these rounds on foot, the chiefs of each sub-district providing porters and supplying firewood and a few necessities like milk at each camp. Ours consisted of an open-sided mud-and-wattle banda and three rondavels, roofed with banana fronds. The walls were whitewashed and it was all perfectly clean. At an altitude of 6,500 feet the nights were chilly – too chilly until we bought a brazier and warmed ourselves at night by its glowing charcoal – but the mornings sparkled in the sunlight of the clear, fresh mountain air. With a sixty-inch rainfall which seldom failed, with a deep, rich forest soil and a plentitude of crystal-clear streams emerging from the forest, the whole place seemed to be bursting with fertility. Feathery dark green wattle trees were massed on the crests of the ridges; pastures on the slopes were rich with Kikuyu grass and white clover; maize, groundnuts, beans and sweet potatoes shared the shambas; banana fronds stooped over rippling streams; stands of sugar-cane prospered in the valleys. A sharp, aromatic scent from the bush sweetened the air.

All the homesteads, each encircled by a timber palisade, had some shelter round them, banana trees or relics of the forest. Here and there a fig tree stood on its own. Fig trees were favoured by the spirits, so must not be lopped or felled. Peace and fecundity seemed to bathe those ridges in a golden effulgence. I have no doubt that beneath the surface all sorts of wickednesses went on, diseases proliferated, plots thickened, but they stayed beneath the surface and the crust was fair. Certainly there was no hunger or want, and no loneliness; in the fabric of kinship, every thread was woven in.

The location we had come to was called Murigo's after the local chief.

Murigo called on us himself soon after we had settled in to bid us welcome, bringing presents of a chicken and small brown eggs. He was an impressive figure: tall, well built, dignified in gait and courteous in manner. Fortunately he was a great tea-drinker, which solved the problem of our return gifts. Over several mugs of the heavily sweetened beverage I explained my mission as best I could. I had brought with me Routledges' book on the Kikuyu, published in 1910,[1] and showed him its illustrations of tribal accoutrements which younger men no longer used or wore. Customs, I said, were disappearing too, and I hoped that his elders would tell me about them so that I could put their words into a book. Murigo saw the point immediately and promised to help, and proved to be as good as his word.

Next day we returned his call and found him in a sizeable village. He had sixteen wives, each with her separate hut and granary, and one or two extra huts for guests and unmarried sons. Chiefs, as I have said, were appointed by the Government; their salaries were nominal but they had many opportunities to grow rich. Murigo had made the most of these. Every evening, flocks of sheep and goats driven by his smaller sons emerged from the bush, wives arrived with heavy loads of sweet potato tops to feed his cattle, and other wives and daughters came with gourds of water and bundles of firewood. Smoke rising from the thatch of the huts showed that fires were being stoked beneath big, soot-blackened pots to cook the evening meal. It was a busy scene, and orderly, each person going about her task in a leisurely way like easygoing bees in a hive.

Each wife had her own shamba, which was seldom in one piece, but generally fragmented into several little non-adjoining plots. To European eyes, these appeared to have no boundaries, but every inch was known to the owners and elders. Although individual shambas were small, sometimes tiny, they added up to a sizeable area of land. Murigo's children, also, added up to a sizeable family, fifty or sixty, I daresay. I did not ask him how many, and had I done so he would have given an evasive reply, for the Kikuyu, like those of many other tribes, thought it unlucky to enumerate people or cattle or goats; they knew each one as an individual, not by numbers, although in matters of bride-price and of blood-money they would argue for weeks, months and even years as to how many goats and cattle should be paid.

The emblems of Murigo's chieftainship were a heavy brass-topped staff and a wide-brimmed felt hat on which was pinned a brooch in the image of the heraldic prancing lion that was Kenya's crest. Nearly every morning he drove down a red dirt track in a handsome Chevrolet chauffeured by one of his many sons to attend meetings of the Local Native Council or of the Native Tribunal, both of which sat in open-sided bandas beside the crowded market. Murigo presided, but had to heed the opinions of his councillors. These bodies had been set up by the colonial government, but basically they formalised and expanded arrangements that had existed before. There was no question of introducing democracy among the Kikuyu and other Bantu tribes, as there was among peoples with such autocratic traditions as were common in West Africa. The Kikuyu had governed themselves very democratically in the past, but in small units and without a central authority.

Most of Kikuyuland consists of ridges separated by the many rivers running down either from Mt Kenya or from the Aberdares. These ridges form natural units, and, in each unit, law and order and the allocation of land was in the hands of the elders of those families who dwelt on each ridge. All the colonial government had to do was to formalise the system, define the boundaries of each location, and establish Local Native Councils, buds of future district and county councils, and Native Tribunals, buds of future law-courts, and equip them with minor officials and sets of rules.

After making our number with Murigo we went to the Church of Scotland Mission at Tumutumu, near Nyeri, to collect our interpreter. Both the Kikuyu and I got on all right in Kisettla, but when it came to tribal customs recounted by old men, the Kikuyu tongue was obviously needed. I regretted very much that I had not learnt it, but it is a difficult language, and there was no time to remedy the matter. The Kikuyu speak a soft, fluid, honeyed tongue, full of subtle inflections that change the meaning of the words. Robert, the interpreter, was a young teacher with a secondary school education, still a rare distinction. His English was careful rather than fluent, but improved as we went along. He had a pleasant personality and entered into the spirit of my quest; in fact, he knew little more about the history of his people than I did, and was surprised at some of the things he learnt.

The Tumutumu Mission was like a bit of nineteenth-century Scotland transplanted to this smiling but, alas, sinful land. In charge was a young, bony, energetic Scot called Duncan who imposed a strict, fair and healthy regime; cold baths, physical jerks and no nonsense were part of the regime. He and his small European staff spoke fluent Kikuyu, their medical services were good, and they ran efficiently a chain of dispensaries and primary schools throughout the reserve. Mr Duncan spoke of Nairobi with all the fervour of an Old Testament prophet denouncing Sodom and Gomorrah, and a mediaeval hell of fire and brimstone awaited unrepentant sinners. When he felt the need for rest and relaxation he climbed Mt Kenya, and returned refreshed.

There was also a Roman Catholic Mission at Nyeri whose Fathers had quite a different approach, and it must have been confusing for the heathen to find the white man's paths to salvation branching out in so many different directions. In Uganda, matters had reached a pitch where Protestants and Catholics had gone to war, and where several years of fighting had resulted in the creation of a number of martyrs. In the South Nyeri district relations were not so strained, although a pursing of lips might be seen at Tumutumu on mention of Father Cagnolo's neighbouring Mission.

Already there were signs that the Kikuyu were no longer prepared to accept without question the teachings of the various Missions. The two main stumbling blocks were polygamy and female circumcision. They pointed out, rightly I believe, that Christ Himself had nowhere laid down a rule of one man, one wife. Polygamy was their custom, and they did not see why a man with several wives could not claim to be a Christian. Most of the Missions stood firm and expelled from their flock every erring polygamist. As a result, breakaway Churches had begun to appear.

From Murigo's camp I wrote: 'The missionaries are very worked up about a heretic church that has started among the Kikuyu, nominally Christian but supporting polygamy and female circumcision. An "Arch-Bishop" has arrived from South Africa to ordain a "priest-hood" of its own. They say it is very anti-Mission and anti-white generally. The Kikuyu do have a confusing time. The Local Native Council school at Nyeri, non-sectarian, teaches biology, science etc., while five miles away the Italian Catholic Mission adopts an attitude well illustrated by a remark in a book on the Kikuyu published by them which I have just been reading, to the effect that "after the failure of the Darwinian farce and the discrediting of the monkey-makers of Germany, the so-called science of biology . . ."'.

I had expected to be greeted by suspicion and even hostility by the Kikuyu. What were we after? What lay behind all these questions? Most Kikuyu people assumed that, if a white person settled anywhere amongst them, he or she was scheming to get their land. Land to them was the be-all and end-all of everything, and injuries that some of those living near Nairobi had suffered when white farmers had settled on land that had formerly been used by their families were already festering. No one living near Murigo's had been affected in this way, but they would have heard enough about the matter to be on the *qui vive*. They were, indeed, suspicious to begin with, but this soon wore off and, when I turned up at a homestead or gathering, chaperoned by a charming man called Gacheche whom Murigo had detailed to escort me, I was greeted with courtesy, friendliness and feminine giggles. Small children sometimes ran away, but I do not remember one overt rebuff.

To this day I do not know just how the people's suspicions were allayed. I think Karanja had a lot to do with it. He had been with Jos and Nellie since boyhood and, when asked, as I am sure he was, 'are they after our land?' he would have reassured them; Jos and Nellie were too old and had enough already, my bwana was elsewhere, and by that time I think that the sanctity of the reserves was generally recognised. After the report of the Morris Carter Land Commission in 1933, land had in fact been added to the Kikuyu reserve and none had been taken away.[2]

And then, probably the elders came down on our side. If, at this time, you had asked the older members of the Cavalry Club in London to tell you about the battle of Omdurman, the eyes of a dozen elderly gentlemen would have brightened, they would have stirred in their arm-chairs and tales of dashing exploits involving cavalry charges and flashing swords would have been poured into your ears. It was the same with the Kikuyu elders. Had they fought the Maasai, had they defended their fathers' cattle, had they even gone forth to raid themselves? Indeed they had. Not for a long time, in fact probably not ever, had anyone really *wanted* to hear about it all. To the young, old men everywhere are bores. Now the war-horn sounded again in withered ears, painted shields flashed in the sun and ostrich-feather anklets shook as wrinkled elders turned their memories back to a brave, warlike youth. Several of the old men even pulled spears from the thatch of their huts where these had been put by, retrieved their long buffalo-hide shields, and paraded for me outside our banda to demonstrate their battle array. And some of them were not as old as all that. The last Maasai raids had taken place at the turn of the century, or perhaps later still.

It was always fights against the Maasai that were recalled. No mention was ever made of fights against the KAR. I had always assumed, as had many others, that the introduction of British rule into Kikuyuland had been a wholly peaceful process, and it was not until the publication in 1957 of Richard Meinertzhagen's diaries that most people realised how much force had been employed. The Kikuyu in those days were not a peaceful people. Their warriors had attacked and wiped out several trading parties, including one carrying the Royal Mail which was set upon near Thika in 1902, leaving fourteen people dead or severely wounded. A farmer bent on buying sheep had been murdered in an appalling fashion, anticipating the worst atrocities of Mau Mau. To travel without an armed guard was asking for trouble. The KAR had been called in to enforce penalties – the confiscation of livestock – for these murders and attacks, with the young Meinertzhagen in charge. His detachment, which included Maasai levies, captured large quantities of livestock and, when he met with resistance, he burnt villages, razed crops and slaughtered warriors with ruthless efficiency.

The Kikuyu answered back: at Nyeri, in December 1902, they attempted to rush Meinertzhagen's camp and, with their spears and arrows, killed and wounded thirty-two of his men; his guns killed thirty-eight of them. 'I must own,' he wrote, 'that I never expected the Wakikuyu to fight like this.' Early in 1904 an expedition against a section of the tribe called the Irryeni captured 782 cattle and 2150 sheep and goats, and killed a number of 'the enemy'.[3] These were no minor skirmishes, and they had taken place not much above thirty years before Murigo's elders demonstrated to me how they had fought the Maasai. The Kikuyu then were very localised; people who lived on one ridge had litle to do with those living on another; and none of the Meinertzhagen's expeditions had passed through what was to become Murigo's location. Nevertheless it was strange that not a word was said about it all. Ignorance, tact, or just forgetfulness? Perhaps it was because they were recalling only their own personal experiences; they themselves had fought the Maasai but not the KAR, and what others had done was not their business.

Their stories needed to be taken with a sizeable grain of salt. According to them, Kikuyu warriors were every bit as fierce and bold as those of the Maasai, whom they often defeated, while sometimes they themselves carried off Maasai cattle. In actual fact they had been no match for the much more highly trained and organised Maasai battalions, and were a threat only in the forest where they used bows and arrows rather than spears. The Maasai had the upper hand, but the Kikuyu had the forests in which to retreat.

When the people living near Murigo's had got used to my wandering about with Robert and Gacheche asking questions, I told Gacheche of my wish to see a witch-doctor at work. This was a sensitive subject, since witch-doctors had spiritual powers, and spirits must be treated with great respect. Also it was known that white people disapproved of witchcraft, and did not believe in the powers of its practitioners. There was a Witchcraft Ordinance which forbade the more malignant aspects of the practice.

We started with a little harmless fortune-telling, conducted by a witch-doctor who unstoppered a long, thin gourd and scattered the beans it contained on to an ox-hide. From the way they fell he told my fortune, needless to say a propitious one, and refused to accept a fee. The witch-doctor, like his gourds, was tall and thin and had a much more bony face, with a sharper profile, than the average Kikuyu. Maasai blood again. Gacheche told me that this witch-doctor belonged to a section of the Kikuyu, a sub-tribe really, who dwelt somewhat apart on the forest's edge, and were known for their supernatural powers. They were called the Ndia.

This was only a preliminary. I wanted to see, and photograph if possible, a more important ceremony, even though I knew it would involve the evisceration of a goat. This was the removal of a thahu. Everywhere there lurked, as by now I realised, just beneath a peaceful surface, an extraordinary number of ancestral spirits who were extraordinarily prone to take offence. The least little thing offended them – omitting to pour a libation of beer before a feast, forgetting to throw a pebble on a heap, as you passed it, near some sacred spot, inadvertent damage to a fig tree's branches, gazing directly at your mother-in-law instead of turning your head. The spirits were a spiteful lot and, when offended, took their revenge. This might take many forms, the list was endless: your cow might abort, your child break a leg, porcupines might destroy a patch of maize, or, worst of all, your wife might miscarry. Nothing in life was fortuitous. Everything had a cause, and the cause lay either in offence given to a spirit, or in the machinations of an enemy who had laid a spell. In either case, you were afflicted by a thahu, and your only recourse lay in a visit to a witch-doctor who would remove it, or counter-act the spell.

One morning Gacheche, grinning as usual – he wore a little cap at a jaunty angle made from the lining of a sheep's stomach and fringed with beads – appeared at our camp to say that the witch-doctor who had told my fortune was about to cast out a thahu from a client, and was willing to let me see and photograph the process, for a fee of one goat. So we retraced our footsteps to the witch-doctor's abode. Nellie decided not to come. She did not want to witness the cruelty to the goat – nor, indeed, did I – and preferred to pursue her current project of making a collection of plants used in the brewing of local dyes.

The ceremony did, indeed, involve sickening cruelty. All four of the goat's legs were broken, and its stomach was slit open to extract the undigested contents, which were believed to have magical properties. It was essential that the goat should remain alive while all this was done to it, and even then it was not put out of its misery. Horrible as all this was, the cruelty was not deliberate, nor did the witch-doctor and his client derive any sadistic pleasure from it. The object was not to inflict pain on the animal, but to protect the human. Millions of animals suffer in the research laboratories of western nations for the same reason. Pain was endemic in African life, and no ways existed of avoiding it. Pain just had to be endured, and endured it was, with a stoicism that constantly amazed Europeans. Even babies terribly burned by falling into fires were astonishingly apathetic, and recovered from injuries that would have killed any European child.

The contents of the wretched goat's stomach were mixed on a banana leaf with several nameless and unpleasant-looking substances. Then the witch-doctor dipped a goat's horn into the concoction, thrust it into the client's mouth, recited various incantations, marked the man's body all over with chalk mixed with other powders, and eventually assured him that the thahu, like the devils of the Old Testament, had been expelled. I was thankful when it was over – for this goat, but not for many more to come that would be sacrificed, as legions had been in the past, in this distressing way.

Our visit to Murigo's coincided with the time when circumcision ceremonies were held, accompanied by much dancing and singing, and at night we heard the throb of drums and the sound of chanting and stamping. There was no reticence about boys' circumcision, but I was careful to avoid the subject of the operation on girls. Ever since the murder of the elderly American missionary in 1929, everyone had walked warily around the subject of this rite. The Missions had been persuaded, though reluctantly, to damp down their campaign against it, and the Government had continued to sit, uneasily, on the fence. Given time, they argued, education would make the custom obsolete.

I was therefore surprised when Robert informed me that I had been invited to attend the circumcision of young girls from Murigo's location. The only stipulation was that I should leave my camera behind. It was perhaps absurd to feel flattered when invited to witness a clitorodectomy, but I was. It was a gesture of confidence. Evidently Nellie and I were not considered any longer, if at first we had been, to be government or Mission spies. Nellie politely declined the invitation. Robert conducted me to the place where the ceremony was to be held and then retreated; men were banned.

Long before dawn, in the chill of the night, the girls had been taken to the nearest river and had stood for several hours in its cold water to numb their nerves. By the time they had assembled at the appointed place the sun was up, and the numbness must have worn off, but perhaps a psychological effect remained. Scores of married women, heads shaved bare as billiard balls – a sign of matrimonial status –

surrounded the arena, waving banana fronds. The girls were lined up in a rough semi-circle, each sitting on an ox-hide with legs outstretched and with two sponsors whose function was to hold her in position and give moral support. One held her by the shoulders and one sat facing her, grasping her legs.

The operator was an elderly and wizened woman with a little greying hair on her head – hair might again be grown, if it would, when child-bearing was over – clad in the traditional women's garments, a goatskin apron edged with beads and a short cloak of the same material. She was in a sense a professional, being called upon to perform the operation from some distance around. I think her fee was a goat. Her instrument was a rusty razor-blade that looked almost as old as she.

Jomo Kenyatta defended female circumcision, together with all the other customs of his people, and wrote that the operation was performed with the skill of a Harley Street surgeon.[4] Perhaps so, but this toothless old lady with her withered paps and ancient razor-blade was a far cry from the masked consultant in his theatre at a London hospital. But I believe that, despite the absence of anything whatever in the nature of antiseptics and sterilization, both infections and serious after-effects were rare.

Not to flinch or cry out during the operation was an absolute imperative. Any girl who did so would be disgraced, and would never live down her shame. The sponsors who gripped her tightly no doubt controlled the flinching, and the silence that fell as the operator moved from one girl to the next was unbroken even by a whimper. The old woman worked swiftly. There were, and are, two forms of the operation: removal of the clitoris only, and removal of the labia on each side as well, a much more drastic and painful mutilation. So far as I could see, and I did not keep my eyes fixed throughout on the performance, on this occasion clitorodectomy only was performed. When it was over the sponsors staunched the flow of blood with handfuls of leaves, helped the girls to their feet and led them off to huts built for them near their parents' homesteads, where they would spend about a month recovering and enjoying their new status as adults ready for marriage. Most of them were already affianced. As soon as it was all over, a great outburst of lu-lu-lu-lu-lu-ing occurred amongst the spectators, branches were waved about and there was stamping and laughter and rejoicing. The family, the clan and the tribe itself had been strengthened and enriched by the accession of new members; and no initiate had disgraced herself and her family by crying out.

Several theories have been advanced to explain the origin and obstinate persistence of this custom, widespread throughout Africa and parts of Asia, which seems so barbaric to most European minds. Is it a form of male despotism designed to keep women subservient to their husbands? And, by denying them sexual pleasure, to discourage adultery? If so, it did not seem to work very well, and those who have experienced the operation, and are prepared to talk about it, have said that sexual pleasure can still be had despite the absence of a clitoris – other areas take over and develop sensitivity. It is an ordeal, and as such toughens the initiates and teaches them to endure pain with stoicism. Certain it is that circumcision makes childbirth more difficult and dangerous, and it is odd that any human society should cling so stubbornly to a practice that damages a process so vital to its survival. The question of compassion for the girls seems nowhere to enter in.

Everyone enjoys markets, and Karatina's was a splendid one. The coming of the branch line from Thika which linked it with Nairobi had caused it to grow like a bean-sprout, and mouth-watering produce went off every day – citrus fruit, strawberries, asparagus, fresh vegetables, potatoes, pawpaws, eggs and chickens, all sorts of things. Women squatted all day beside their piles of beans, their maize-cobs, stalks of sugar-cane, twists of tobacco, bunches of herbs, and bargained with passion for a few cents. Goats bleated, cattle lowed, sheep baa'd, cocks crowed, women haggled, men strolled about greeting their friends. It was noisy, busy, cheerful, smelly and well conducted without apparent direction from above. Prices were reckoned in cents – one hundred cents, of course, went to one shilling. Here are some examples taken from my notebook of prices that I paid, with their translation into modern British currency in brackets.

5 maize cobs	2 cents ($\frac{1}{10}$ of a penny)
3 lbs sweet potatoes	4 cents ($\frac{1}{5}$ of a penny)
10 bananas	4 cents ($\frac{1}{5}$ of a penny)

eggs	2 cents each ($\frac{1}{10}$ of a penny)
chicken	50 cents (2½ pence)
1 lb maize meal (posho)	3 cents approx. ($\frac{3}{10}$ of a penny)

Everyone living in the reserve had his, or rather her, own shamba, so these were the prices obtained for their surplus produce. Wages paid to Africans were very low, and often quoted in the House of Commons and by such bodies as the Fabian Colonial Bureau as examples of slave labour and exploitation. It is always misleading to say what people receive without also saying what their wages will buy. A shilling went a long way in Karatina's market.

'Yesterday I went out to dinner,' I wrote in a letter. 'Mealies, sweet potatoes and nettle spinach stewed up together in a black pot with salt and something hot, probably chillis, and ladled out in calabashes. Also fat green bananas roasted in the ashes – excellent.' It was an alfresco meal. At this time of year, during the hot weather, families emerged from their huts to eat their supper round a fire built outside the compound. By tradition, any traveller passing by would be invited to join in. I ate my share with pleasure while the conversation of my hosts, mellifluous and lively, flowed around me under the stars.

Memories of smells and sounds can still evoke that camp, whose purpose has long since vanished. There was a bird called in Kikuyu 'thrower of firewood' – heaven knows why – whose monotonous but haunting notes were the first sound I heard when tea came with the dawn, and the sun's precursory beams gilded the trunks of wattle trees on the horizon. Then came the tinkling of goat bells as the sun's strengthening beams fell upon a clump of cassia bushes in full flower, an egg-yolk yellow like the yellowest gorse. A flock of green-winged parrots passed over from the forest to search for breakfast. Human voices called across the valley. An aromatic smell came from a spiky little bush that hugged the ground. Doves dropped their melodious notes like water poured from a bottle. At evening it was the turn of guinea-fowl to call from the shambas as they prepared to take off like overloaded aircraft for their roost in tree tops. And, by the river, as darkness crept up the shadowed valleys, came the rustle of banana leaves beside a whispering river, that most evocative of sounds. So peaceful it all seemed, yet in only fifteen years' time death and terror would be staining these hills.

As a parting present I bought Murigo a large ram. These rams stored fat in their tails, and were fattened on sweet potato tops in the huts until their tails hung to the ground. A fat tail weighed several pounds and was a special delicacy; the whole ram became a feast. We parted with many expressions of goodwill. Murigo was a patriarch, a stallion, a feudal baron on a small scale and an old rogue, but his homestead had an air of contentment as well as prosperity. He saw that all his children went to school. Several of his sons had a secondary education, and one or two, I think, went on to Makerere University. Probably they became politicians.

I left Murigo's camp with a mass of notes and impressions, and the problem of how to turn all this clay, as it were, into a pot. In order to get the background as accurate as possible, an elementary knowledge of social anthropology seemed desirable. Not that I was hoping to trespass on to the territory of anthropologists, but I did hope that, in trying to reconstruct tribal life before it started to crumble, I might avoid some of the more obvious pitfalls. So I enrolled, that autumn, in a seminar held by Professor Malinowski at the London School of Economics. I was doing things, of course, the wrong way round – ground-work should precede field-work. But better late than never.

Professor Malinowski was revered as a pioneer who had more or less founded the modern school of social anthropology based on field-work among primitive tribes, rather than on measurements of skulls and bones and studies of racial characteristics. He himself had published a study of the people of the Trobriand Islands in the Pacific called *The Sexual Life of Savages*. This created a sensation by reason of its detailed and explicit descriptions of sexual behaviour. People were not, as yet, used to such unvarnished treatments of sex as are now to be seen, perhaps too often, on every television screen. He had drawn the conclusion that the Trobriand Islanders were ignorant of the father's part in procreation. This proved hard to credit, and the book aroused a lot of controversy. I remember that I put my copy into brown-paper covers in order to avoid shocking visitors to the flat in London that was then our base.[5]

'Started at the LSE', I recorded in my diary. 'Sat next to Johnston Kenyatta.' This was a shock. Kenyatta – he became Jomo later – was a bogey-man to Kenya's Europeans, an agitator, a revolutionary, a Red, fully equipped with horns and a tail. Now I was not only meeting this wicked man but sitting next to him. Naturally I was intrigued, and also alarmed – not by his evil influence, but by the contempt with which he might well treat my attempts to understand his people. How sinister, if sinister at all, was Johnston Kenyatta? He was courteous, urbane, self-possessed, self confident, and quite different from any Kikuyu I had hitherto met. His most memorable features were his eyes. They had a gleam in them difficult to describe: hard yet subtle, and with a hint – or was this imagination? of the satanic. He dressed flashily, in loud check trousers and a belted jacket, carried a walking-stick with an amber-coloured stone in its top, and wore the ring set with a semi-precious stone, perhaps a cornelian, that was to become, like his fly-whisk, a part of his insignia. In later years, when speaking in public, he would sometimes avoid direct confrontation with the Government by using unprovocative words, which he would contradict by twisting this ring on his finger. His audience always got the point, and roared with laughter.

Kenyatta was a favourite of Malinowski's, who gave him frequent opportunities to express his views. This he did with ease and virtuosity, never at a loss for the correct word. He had mastered the anthropological jargon perfectly. He was forty years of age or thereabouts, and had been living in England for five or six years as representative of the Kikuyu Central Association, the mouthpiece of the political aspirations of the tribe, which were to get back the land they had lost, and eventually to rid the country of white rule altogether and gain possession of the 'white highlands'.

Kenyatta had very quickly realised that it was in London, not in Nairobi, that the groundwork for achieving these aims must be laid. In Parliament he had powerful allies in the shape of Arthur Creech-Jones, who was to become Secretary of State for the Colonies when the Labour Party came to power in 1945, in most of the MPs on the left of that Party, and in the Fabian Colonial Bureau. Another ally was the Pan-African Congress, with headquarters in Manchester, activated by George Padmore, a West Indian with whom Kenyatta was closely in touch.

The theme of Malinowski's seminar was kinship in primitive societies. I found myself struggling in a sea of technical terms and theories which seemed a far cry from Murigo's camp. Each student was required to concentrate on a particular society or tribe and to map out its kinship structure. My choice was, of course, the Kikuyu, and it was disconcerting, to say the least, to find among my class-mates not only a member of that tribe, but its political leader, especially as he was engaged upon the same task as I was, writing a book about his people. His was to be an anthropological study, *Facing Mount Kenya*, and mine a documentary novel, *Red Strangers*. The effrontery of my attempt was so plain that I nearly abandoned it altogether, especially as each student had to read a paper embodying his or her conclusions. This was indeed a terrifying occasion. I had read everything available, and made a complicated chart criss-crossed with arrows pointing in all directions from 'Ego' in the middle, indicating a spider's web of kinship links between, I think, over two hundred persons. When I glanced nervously once or twice at Kenyatta I thought he was listening with a sardonic smile, but when it came to the discussion he let me off lightly with some mild remarks more in the nature of expositions than of criticism. He had chosen one of the Pacific tribes for his own study.

Sometimes I repaired for luncheon, with other students, to a Chinese restaurant in the Strand. Even at a table for four, Kenyatta gave an impression of holding court. The big, dark stone in his ring seemed to reflect the gleam in his eye, not exactly malevolent but not cosy either. The word is overworked, but magnetism is the only one I can think of to describe the sense one felt in his presence. His voice was deep, resonant and compelling. He seemed happy to be treading the conventional path of the revolutionary, consorting with fellow schemers, living in cheap digs, addressing meetings held in cold and dreary halls, corresponding with revolutionary groups abroad, and looked at askance by authority. No one could have predicted in their wildest dreams that twenty-six years later he would be president of the independent Republic of Kenya.

The last occasion when I met Jomo Kenyatta was after he had won his triumph, and become 'First Minister' during a short interim period before complete independence. A party had been laid on for him in London to which I was invited. I arrived rather late, and saw him holding court surrounded by admirers at the other end of the crowded room, dressed in the regalia he had by then adopted: round beaded cap, fly-whisk made of wildebeest tail, and the famous ring. Through a gap in the crowd he saw me, waved his whisk and came charging forward to greet me as an old friend with that African warmth and exuberance that melts the iciest British reserve. It was well over twenty years since we had foregathered at the London School of Economics and our Chinese restaurant, and now the student agitator had become a national hero. Naturally I was touched by his generous recognition.

This was the honeyed side of Kenyatta. There was another side, that of a demagogue who could stir his countrymen to do things, or to leave them undone, which were harmful to their own interests. Soon after the Second World War the colonial government set itself to tackle, belatedly as many thought, a condition that was destroying the country's very basis and threatening its future – the bleeding to death of the land. Rivers were running red with the topsoil of the highlands, and the stain spread fifty miles out to sea. No one could honestly say, certainly not an intelligent man like Kenyatta, that to staunch this blood-flow was not vital to the interests of the African people. Kenyatta did say so. He said that measures to control soil erosion were colonialist tricks designed to steal the land, and succeeded in setting the Kikuyu, though not those of most other tribes, against them.

The terracing of hills and slopes is essential to the control of soil erosion in tropical lands. An agency was set up and equipped with the necessary machinery to carry out this terracing, free of charge to Africans. Kenyatta had meanwhile returned to his native land after fifteen years abroad, having been trapped during the war in England, where he worked in a market garden in Sussex, by then married to an Englishwoman. Back in his own country he organised and united the various nationalist groups, and held meetings to which his fellow-tribesmen were drawn by his charisma, and impassioned by his words. He developed a clever kind of double-talk by which he said one thing and meant another, much to the frustration of the Special Branch, who were unable to nail seditious statements on him. At these meetings he incited the peasant farmers to turn against the conservation measures they had previously supported, and terracing and other measures came to an end. So the fertility of their shambas went on being washed out to sea. It was hard for the British officers, who were doing their level best to get conservation measures carried out, to forgive Kenyatta for deliberately sabotaging them. But I suppose that to win the nationalist battle you must be absolutely ruthless and concede no compromise, no special cases, even if in so doing you harm your own people's interests and employ what your opponents think are dirty tricks.

Then there was Mau Mau. No one doubted that Kenyatta was the real leader of the movement, and used it skilfully to further nationalist ends. He was the puppet-master. It spread underground like a mycelium until it forced the Government to declare a state of emergency in October 1952.

Kenyatta, with a number of others, was immediately arrested, and so could not be held responsible for the increasing obscenity of the oaths which its adherents were obliged to take, and which they forced on others; nor for the increasingly brutal murders committed by Mau Mau gangs and for the mutilation of innumerable farm animals. Kenyatta had started something he was unable to control, because he was in prison. He was unsuccessful in another respect: Mau Mau never spread to other regions and, although the Kikuyu were, and are, Kenya's largest tribe, they were only one of about forty. (The exact number is hard to define, because of sub-tribal divisions.) After being sentenced to seven years for managing a proscribed society, he was jailed at Lokitaung in a remote corner of the north-west, near the junction of Kenya, Ethiopia and Sudan.

The very austerity of prison conditions may have saved his life. Before his arrest, he had been drinking heavily. In prison he was dried out and kept that way. Stories were spread that his jailers were giving him a bottle of brandy a day in the hope of finishing him off. This propaganda, as is so often the case, stood truth on its head.

The prison at Lokitaung came under the supervision of the DC at Lodwar, and the DC at Lodwar was an unusual man. His name was L. E. Whitehouse (known as Wauce), and he had started his African career as a pharmacist in Nairobi. There he had conceived a great interest in the Maasai, and learned their language, which few Europeans spoke in the early 1920s. Then he hired twenty rickshaw-boys in Nairobi as porters and spent a fortnight in the Maasai reserve. More or less by accident he drifted into teaching, and was employed to start a school for Maasai boys on the slopes of Mt Kilimanjaro. To get there, pupils, teachers and Mr Whitehouse walked sixty miles from the nearest station to a spot marked with pegs, and built the school themselves from scratch.

It was then the custom for each Maasai pupil to bring four or five cows with him to provide the needed milk, and a female relative to milk them. So Whitehouse found himself managing a dairy herd as well as a school; also doctoring the Maasai, which included treating warriors for terrible wounds inflicted by lions. In the Second World War he was absorbed into the administration and, when it ended, posted to Lodwar. Here he spent twelve years among the Turkana at his own request, which was granted because he had never encumbered himself with a wife.

Sometime during his imprisonment, and the two-year period of detention that followed, Kenyatta underwent a change almost Pauline in its nature. His devious manipulation of subversive groups, his demagogic fervour, his involvement in the darker side of tribalism, all this seemed to melt away and be replaced by tolerance and generosity of spirit. Or perhaps these qualities had been there all the time beneath a mask of nationalist resolution. Lokitaung was a chrysalis in which the demagogue pupated into a statesman.

How much of a part did Whitehouse play in this transformation? As the DC, he was the head jailer, and he could not, and did not, favour any individual prisoner. But he visited the prison regularly, decided how much latitude to allow in the provision of books, newspapers and correspondence, dealt with complaints, and saw that the prisoners were fairly treated. Special accommodation had been built for the six Mau Mau convicts, who were kept apart from other prisoners and guarded by a corporal warder. When Whitehouse visited the prison it was Kenyatta, not the corporal warder, who showed him round. Inevitably, they got to know each other fairly well.

Whitehouse did no more than his duty but, despite the wall that separated the two men, Kenyatta evidently grew to like and trust his head jailer. The prisoners were not required to work, but had to carry their water for about a mile from the nearest well. They saved every drop they could and made a little shamba where they planted maize, millet and tomatoes. When Whitehouse departed after his inspections, Kenyatta would present him with a small páper bag, saying: 'You haven't any tomatoes at Lodwar, have you? Have a few to take back with you.' So Whitehouse did.

He retired as D C before Kenyatta was transferred to Lodwar, where the only restriction on his movements was to report to Whitehouse's successor once a day. He and Whitehouse met once or twice in the bazaar, and chatted to each other in Maasai. Later they met again on official occasions, when the President greeted his former head jailer with every sign of warmth and affection. Asked, many years later still, for his verdict, Whitehouse said: 'I had a very soft spot for Jomo Kenyatta – I still have. I think in many ways he was a great man. I doubt if Kenya will ever see as great a man again.'[6] At eighty-plus, Whitehouse was still serving as senior resident magistrate, appointed by the African government to dispense justice to the Turkana whom he knew so well.

Kenyatta's period in prison gave him time for reflection away from the turmoil of politics. He could read, rest on his oars and think. Instead of being warped by prison, he seemed to find a new stability. At a press conference just before his final release he said, half jokingly, 'We have been in a university. We learned more about politics there than we learnt outside.'

After Kenyatta became 'First Minister' as a prelude to his presidency, he made two important speeches – more than two, of course, but these were crucial. Most European farmers were frightened, depressed, and could see no hope for the future. For four years many of them had lived under siege, locked in at night with their revolvers for fear of gangs bursting in to hack them to pieces; the personal friends of some had died in this gruesome fashion, and many more had seen their cattle hamstrung or poisoned. The price of land had slumped to next to nothing, and a million acres had already been compulsorily bought to be split up into African shambas. Now the arch-enemy whom they believed to be responsible for all this was to become the ruler of their country.

A meeting of white farmers was called at Nakuru and the arch-enemy invited to address them. By a coincidence of history the son of that Lord Delamere who had virtually started off white settlement was in the chair. It was a glum and hostile audience. This is part of what Kenyatta had to stay.

I am a politician, but I am a farmer like you . . . I think the soil joins us all and therefore we have a kind of mutual understanding. If you want to understand each other, then the best thing is to talk together . . . I believe that the most disturbing point among us is suspicion, fear. These are created by not knowing what the other side is thinking. If we must live together, if we must work together, we must talk together, exchange views. This is my belief. And one thing which I want to make clear is this. It is, that we must also learn to forgive one another. There is no perfect society anywhere. Whether we are white, brown or black, we are not angels. We are human beings, and as such are bound to make mistakes. But there is a great gift that we can exercise, that is to forgive one another. If you have done harm to me, it is for me to forgive you. If I have done harm to you, it is for you to forgive me. All of us, white, brown and black, can work together to make this country great . . . Let us join together and join hands and work together for the benefit of Kenya. This is what I beg you to believe, that this is the policy of your government.

I was not at this meeting, held in mid-1963, but those who were told me that tension and hostility almost tangibly eased, and that Kenyatta's next few sentences drew laughter.

Many of you, I think, are just as good Kenyans as myself. I think some of you may be older than myself a little bit. I am 73 myself and I have my age-group among you. Therefore you are just as good Kenyans as myself. I think some of you may be worried – what will happen if Kenyatta comes to be the head of the government? He has been in prison, maybe he has given trouble. What is he going to do? Let me set you at rest. That Kenyatta has no intention whatever to look backwards. Not at all. I want you to believe what I am saying now, that we are not going to look backwards. We are going to forgive the past and look forward to the future. Because if we start thinking about the past, what time shall we have to build the future?[7]

The M'zee, as he had become, sat down to an enthusiastic clapping of white hands. His words did much to persuade some, at least, of those white farmers who had contemplated leaving to stay on and give the future a chance.

This message of 'forgive and forget' was not addresssed to Europeans only. Kenyatta's own people were deeply divided. Those who had taken an active part in Mau Mau were in a minority; many had joined a Home Guard recruited by the administration, and the chiefs, as well as the numerous Christians, had stayed loyal to the Government. Civil war had left its inevitable bitterness, and many feared that a night of the long knives would follow for those Kikuyu who had fought the freedom-fighters. Kenyatta knew that, unless he could overcome these festering enmities, he could have little hope of leading his nation to a peaceful future. In a speech he made a few months later he told his people that ignorance, sickness and poverty – not, by implication, Europeans – were Kenya's true enemies, and that only hard work and unity could overcome them. Only the burial of hatchets and the dismantling of tribal barriers could create a contented country. We must work together, strive together, join together – harambee! That cry so familiar to drivers stuck in the mud became the rallying call of the nation.

The night of the long knives – or the sharpened pangas – never happened. Wild-eyed 'generals' with matted hair emerged from the forests, and 'rehabilitated' oath-administrators with 'Jomo beards' from the detention camps, to mingle with 'loyalist' home guards and stalwart Christians and all turn back together into ordinary citizens. Harambee worked. How much, so quickly, was really forgotten none but a Kikuyu could say, but forgiveness was apparent, thanks to the wisdom of Jomo Kenyatta, the M'zee.

CHAPTER 14

Lamu to London

All the Europeans resident on Lamu island when I went there with Nellie were bachelors. They numbered six. One of them, our host, was Henri Bournier, a middle-aged Swiss of gentle manners, who lived at Shela, a crumbling village about two miles beyond Lamu town. The waters of the bay lapped at the steps of his terrace; we arrived by boat and paddled on foot the last bit of the way. As in all Arab houses, archways replaced doors to allow the circulation of air, Persian rugs and porcelain vases served for adornment, and white-washed walls with little furniture achieved simplicity.

Behind the village of Shela were sand-dunes overlying bleached bones sometimes exposed when gales swept the island during monsoons. They were the result of a battle fought in 1813 between the people of Lamu and an invading force commanded by the Arab governor of Mombasa, Ahmad ibn Said al-Mazrui, a member of a family renowned even in the blood-stained history of the Coast for violence and brutality. Ahmad had installed one of his lieutenants as governor of the neighbouring island of Pate, and intended to do the same in Lamu. 'Lamu always bowed to the storm and made peace with the victor of the day,' wrote the historian Justus Strandes,[1] but on this occasion the worm turned. Anything was better, the citizens of Lamu evidently thought, than submission to the Mazruis. On the beaches of Shela they won an overwhelming victory.

Lamu seemed like some ancient vessel becalmed in the seas of history, its sails furled, unrocked by tempests, even the barnacles on its keel fast asleep. All sorts and breeds of men had fused to make its Swahili-speaking citizens – Arabs, Bajuns from the many islands of the archipelago, Bantu-speaking tribesmen from the mainland, Gallas and Somalis, Persians (called here Shirazi), Indians, many others who, as in all sea-ports, had come and gone and left their seed. Writing of the island in 1910, C. H. Stigand observed that 'civilised vices' were rife, not to mention uncivilised ones like opium-smoking and, despite the Muslim faith, drunkenness.[2]

According to a document called *The Chronicle of Lamu* the town was founded, together with a number of others, by Abd al-Malik ibn Marwan (AD 685–705) who crossed the ocean with a company of Syrian settlers in the last decade of the seventh century. Thereafter for eight hundred years it remained an outpost of Islam in this land of Zinj, Zinj meaning black. That is, if *The Chronicle of Lamu* is correct, but it is not an ancient document, being a collection of oral traditions assembled early in the twentieth century. The archaeologist Neville Chittock, who has excavated in the nearby islands of Manda and Pate, has suggested that the thirteenth century is a more likely date for the founding of the town of Lamu.[3]

Over the centuries the island prospered modestly, sending its dhows across the Indian Ocean laden with ivory, mangrove poles, ambergris, gums, tortoise-shells, rhino horns and slaves, and welcoming them back with such items as daggers, glass and porcelain vessels, dyed cloth, wheat and ghee. A great Chinese fleet sailed down the coast of Zinj in 1417, following the arrival in Peking of a giraffe from Malindi which was thought to be the incarnation of a mythical creature emblematic of Perfect Virtue, Perfect Government and Perfect Harmony, and which aroused the curiosity of the Chinese court.[4] Malindi followed up this gift with another of a 'celestial horse' and a 'celestial stag', probably a zebra and an oryx. Quantities of Ming and Persian porcelain have been found in various islands of the archipelago.

Then, in 1497, came Vasco da Gama, presaging an end to such scant tranquillity as these settlements had enjoyed. For the next four centuries Arabs and Portuguese contended for mastery, and the story is one of battles at sea, sieges on land, treachery, intrigue, massacre, razings of cities, executions, burnings and flight, punctuated by threats and disasters from other quarters. The worst of these was the descent on the settlements of a tribe of cannibals called the Zimba. They came from the south, according to a Dominican missionary who saw it happen, 'killing and eating every living thing, men, women, children, dogs, cats, snakes, lizards, sparing nothing.' They worked their way up the coast leaving a trail of sacked cities and human bones. If they really ate all their victims they must have gorged themselves on protein to an unimaginable extent – at Kilwa alone, in 1587, they were said by Father Joso dos Santos to have killed about 3,000 of the city's estimated 4,000 inhabitants. Mombasa suffered as badly. The Zimba chief announced his army's intention to 'kill and eat every living thing in the Island.' They very nearly did.[5]

The Zimba met their Waterloo at Malindi. The garrison of thirty Portuguese soldiers plus some local auxiliaries prepared to die fighting, but by a stroke of great good fortune another warlike tribe, though not cannibals, attacked the Zimba in the rear as they besieged the town and wiped out all but one hundred of them – an event which the historian Sir John Gray compared with the repulse of Attila and his Huns at Châlons in 451. So Lamu escaped the holocaust.

Above Henri Bournier's house at Shela, between it and the big Jumaa mosque (there were twenty-eight mosques on the island), rose the ruins of an old Arab mansion which, in its decay, evoked the splendour and sophistication of a prosperous and confident society now altogether gone. The flat façade was scored into squares and rectangles as in a geometrical drawing, punched by slits and arches to form windows, and stamped with abstract designs. No crude or impoverished culture had given rise to this architecture, which combined simplicity with elaboration, stark design with graceful decoration. The building spoke of riches and a certain pomp. In its decay, coconut palms were sprouting from the ruined courtyard's rubble. On Manda island, just across a creek from Lamu, I saw a taller, more imposing mansion buried in the bush and sufficiently intact to invite entry. The whole inner face of the massive stone walls was pitted with innumerable niches, like a giant dovecote. In each niche, in the mansion's heyday, would have stood a porcelain plate, or bowl, or jug, Persian or Chinese, beautifully glazed and painted.

How the great hall must have glowed with colour as sunlight slanted through the slits and arches, or by lamplight with wicks floating in oil! Gowns, jewels, furniture were no less splendid. It was the loss of their commercial supremacy to the Portuguese that reduced most of these Arab nabobs to poverty, and their mansions to neglect and ultimate ruin. Even so, some of the sheikhs kept up their style. A priest who visited Malindi in 1606 wrote that the king 'sat in a skilfully wrought chair of mother-of-pearl and we in chairs of scarlet velvet embroidered with fine gold thread'. When they left, the king 'ordered bugles and trumpets, curved and of ivory, to be sounded, and the mountains and valleys repeated with their echo his pleasure and the affection with which he bid us godspeed'.[6] One of these curved and carved ivory trumpets survives in the DC's office at Lamu, known as the great horn of Siwa.

The DC was another of Lamu's bachelors. Daddy Cornell – I never heard his other name – was more or less a fixture, and knew his district, which included the archipelago and part of the mainland, inside out. He dwelt in an old Arab house and, when on the island, was sprucely clad in a white suit with collar and tie. He was reserved in manner, perhaps shy, a misogynist by reputation and a disgruntled man. His grievance went back to the Powys murder case when he had been DC in charge of the Samburu. The young men were defiant of authority, following their triumph celebrated in 'the song of the vultures.' Half a dozen of these youths, coming before him to answer for some minor offence, displayed an insolence which provoked him into awarding them, on the spot, ten strokes of the cane. The legal code allowed this punishment, but only after a proper trial and confirmation of sentence. Cornell knew that the Samburu were in an explosive frame of mind, and that if they got away with defying administrative officers as well as murdering Europeans, there might be serious trouble. Public opinion had not, at the time, turned against corporal punishment, still practised in almost every British school. But he had sinned. He was reprimanded by the Governor and posted to another district, and knew that his prospects of promotion had been snuffed out for good.

Lamu was a backwater, but a pleasant one. The streets were almost narrow enough for one man to shake hands with another across them from top-storey windows; therefore they were dark, shady and relatively cool. No cars were allowed, but nothing wider than a wheelbarrow could have got along them anyway. They were perfectly clean, and this, it seemed, was due to Daddy Cornell. He was more of a martinet than a lotus-eater.

Another of the bachelors was Coconut Charlie. His real name was Charles Whitton, and he had arrived in the Protectorate in 1912 to manage rubber and coconut plantations on the mainland. Long tufts of hair came out of his ears. He possessed a dignified mien, a white moustache and white hair, and was assembling a collection of artefacts to become the nucleus of a museum. There was a lot of pottery and Chinese porcelain, at that time quite easy to find, and he showed us also Lamu chests, ivory-inlaid chairs and silver-inlaid locks. Eighteen years had passed, he told us, since he had set foot off the island, and here he expected to remain until he died.

His other hobby was to work out how to get from one railway station to another in Britain. There used to be a fat volume called Bradshaw's which gave the times of arrival and departure of every train to and from every station in the United Kingdom. Coconut Charlie spent hours, a Bradshaw at his elbow, planning imaginary railway journeys which, wherever possible, avoided London.

Then there was Percy Petley, who kept the one and only hotel. It was not much of an hotel, and if you wanted to wash, I was told (I never stayed there), an elderly gentleman poured a bucket of water over your head. There is still a Petley's hotel, greatly enlarged and, I feel sure, with better plumbing and without the rats said to haunt the original one. Lamu rats were reputed to be particularly large and aggressive, to come up the sewers at high tide and to defy the cats, which lacked spunk and were, so it was said, sometimes eaten by the rats.

Sharpie had a house on Lamu island, but it was empty when we were there and, when he retired, he decided to live at Ndaragwa, near Thomson's Falls, the better to exercise his gardening skills. He went into the business of designing gardens and advising on what to put in them, sometimes in collaboration with Peter Greensmith, the horticultural genius responsible for the avenues of bougainvillea, jacaranda and other shrubs and flowering trees that are the glory of Nairobi.

When I last saw Sharpie he had grown overweight, he puffed and panted, and his eyesight was failing. He was living alone save for a couple of servants who did not actually neglect him, but furnished no companionship either. His garden had run to seed, except for a bit of lawn and a bed or two within sight of his veranda, and everything out of range was a tangle of weeds.

I had the impression that he was a disappointed man, believing himself to have been misprized. I do not remember his actually saying so; my impression may have been wrong. But it was true that a good many of his colleagues in Kenya's colonial service with his experience had been rewarded with nice fat governorships and 'K's'; I do not think he had even been made a Provincial Commissioner. Perhaps he had not really deserved it. But he had created lovely gardens, and made many friends. He died at Thomson's Falls (Nyahururu) in 1966, aged seventy-seven.

The focus of Lamu town was a square beneath a pock-marked white fort and shaded by a giant African almond tree. The fort, like Mombasa's, was in use as a jail. Piles of sacks lay about, coconuts I think, perhaps simsim, waiting to be loaded into dhows. Under the almond tree little booths offered for sale small sticky cakes and heavily sweetened tea – sweetness was all. The turn of coffee came in the evening, when vendors carried round their swan-necked brass pots kept hot on braziers, and a delicious aroma was wafted on the air. By day men stood about endlessly chatting, clad in kekois or in white kanzus, sometimes with embroidered waistcoats, all spotlessly clean. Scarcely a woman in sight. But on the beach we watched a bevy looking like black beetles in their all-embracing bui-buis climbing awkwardly into a row-boat to take them to the mainland, and then to catch a bus for Mombasa. Richer Arabs and Swahilis often sent their wives there to have their babies. The bus jolted along dreadful roads all through the night, crossing the Tana at Garsen when the river was not in flood. If the driver saw an antelope en route he would stop, get out and shoot it, running at full tilt to cut its throat before it expired. Then he would tie the carcase to the back of the bus and sell the meat in Mombasa.

Most women never did anything so adventurous as go to Mombasa, and I thought their existence must be terribly dull. But, despite purdah, the bui-bui and jealous husbands, intrigues and amours did, I was assured, occur. Visits to female relatives were in order and, while women's lib was unheard of, women's solidarity was strong. A bold young wife on such a visit might slip away from the women's quarters and, concealed in the folds of her bui-bui, keep an assignation; should the husband unexpectedly appear, her relatives would cover up for her until she could be summoned back. Or so I was told; the chances of an outsider breaching the walls of Muslim reticence on such topics were virtually nil.

One day we watched a dhow being put together under a palm-thatched shelter on the beach. Roughly hewn planks were fastened by nails, most of which looked bent and rusty. A few years ago, no nails would have been used. Lamu had been famous for its own special kind of dhow, the m'tepe, whose planks were stitched together by cords made from copra. The masts were mangrove poles, and sails were made of matting woven by women, so everything needed to build a dhow was home-grown. The last of the Lamu m'tepes was built in 1933. Now every dhow has an engine, their numbers have dwindled and most of their voyages are confined to the coastal trade. It is the end of a long and brave tradition.

I have never since been back to Lamu, which has endured some harrowing experiences. In Mau Mau times some of the most unrepentant of the forest gangsters were incarcerated there. Then the tourist industry arrived, at first a trickle, then a flood. The hippies came, expelled from Nepal, bringing their drugs, their ragged clothes, their dirty beards and habits which, however harmless to any but themselves, deeply offended Muslim susceptibilities. One can easily imagine how people in whom modesty was so ingrained would react to the sight of semi-naked women, indeed quite naked ones, on the beach. Some of the hippies stole, and some begged. Esmond Bradley Martin has recorded how, while strolling along the beach, he came upon a naked German girl copulating with a Bajun man who had elephantiasis (then still fairly common, and erroneously believed to come from eating limes).

The hippy tide washed over Lamu, as other tides have done. The tourist tide has not receded, but the Kenyan authorities have wisely refused to allow developers to build hideous high-rise hotels along the waterfront, which they have done elsewhere. The red flag of Oman has been replaced by the green, black and red one of the Republic of Kenya. Coconut Charlie, Percy Petley, Henri Bournier, all are gone where such changes can no longer concern them. Daddy Cornell came to a sad end. He retired to a small farm near Witu on the mainland. Word came to him that a gang of armed raiders was intending to attack Witu during the night. Unarmed, he went out to warn the villagers. The raiders intercepted him, and shot him dead.

On her rare visits to and from the Coast, Nellie generally broke the journey at Kilima Kiu, which belonged to her old friends Frank and Mary-Early Joyce. We spent a couple of nights there on our way back from Lamu.

My earliest memory of the Joyces is of their arrival at our farm at Thika, having ridden across the plains on their ponies because they were too broke to afford the petrol. Frank said that his year's budget had been thrown out of joint by breaking his watch-glass, which cost a shilling to replace. He was tall, good-looking, with crinkly, corn-coloured hair and blue eyes and, as a young man, he brimmed over with gaiety and charm. He was also hard-working and intelligent, not an Irish rattle.

Three young men had arrived in East Africa in 1910 and 1911 to seek their fortunes: Frank Joyce, F.O'B. Wilson and Archie Lambert. They went into partnership in a block of land down the railway line from Nairobi towards Mombasa, lying in another of those buffer zones, this time between the Maasai and the Wakamba, who lived mainly in the hills and were great hunters. They filed their teeth into points, a custom many associate with cannibalism, but they were not cannibals. They hunted elephants for ivory, and they and the Maasai observed an uneasy and sometimes broken truce.

These three partners decided to go in for ostrich feathers, then much in demand for trimming ladies' hats, and bringing fortunes to farmers in South Africa. Two brothers, Harold and Clifford Hill, had already started ostrich farming near Machakos with success. Its great advantage was that very little capital was needed. You simply had to spot newly hatched broods of chicks, catch and put them into sacks, and avoid being savaged by the mother birds. Enough survived into maturity to yield tail feathers, which at one time fetched thirty-five shillings each. Then fashion changed abruptly and feathers became all but unsaleable. By then the partners had turned to other enterprises.

Archie Lambert died during the First World War, a war which left Frank with a stiff leg and an American bride. Small and slender, Mary-Early had all the grace and vivacity, as well as the attractive drawl, one expects from Southern ladies, for whom the War Between The States and Ol' Black Joe never seem far away. They had one daughter, Anne.

I loved Kilima Kiu. You could see for miles and miles across the veld towards the distant Maasai plains in one direction, and towards the red and purple hills of the Wakamba in the other. You could ride or walk for miles and miles in pursuit of Thomson's or Grant's gazelle, zebra or kongoni, across the plains where ostriches still reared their broods; or up into the bushclad hills in pursuit of reedbuck, steinbuck or even the occasional buffalo. During the terrible droughts that periodically afflict eastern Africa, hordes of wildebeest from Maasailand have invaded Kilima Kiu and, despite all efforts to repel them, broken down fences and overrun the dams.

At Kilima Kiu no one seemed to be in a hurry. Breakfast on the sunlit veranda was an especially delicious meal, for Mary-Early had introduced a Southern style of cooking, including muffins and flat maize-meal cakes. Most Europeans stuck firmly to wheat flour; they remarked on African conservatism in regard to food, but were no less conservative themselves. There was thick, dark, local honey – the Kamba were famous honey-hunters. After breakfast, ponies were led to the foot of the steps, and we set forth with Frank to check up on the cattle, the cultivations, dams and boreholes, and on what had gone on during the night. Doves were cooing fit to burst in every tree, and all the sounds of morning rose like bubbles into the air.

Milking into buckets took place in the open with cows tied to posts or trees, and later in a moveable bail; the milkers used one hand to squeeze the teats and the other to hold the bucket. Then the milk was conveyed in ox-carts to the dairy to be cooled. At evening, when the temperature fell, it went off in wagons to the station. There was at first no refrigeration, and it was a wonder that the milk arrived fresh next morning in Nairobi and Mombasa, but it did.

Frank and F.O'B. Wilson ran Kilima Kiu together for some years and then they quarrelled. I was never clear as to just what the quarrel was about, but it was generally believed to have concerned butterfat. One of the partners was said to have accused the other of cheating. The quarrel grew almost to the proportions of pistols for two and coffee for one in the Machakos hills; the two men cut each other in public and so did their families. In 1934, the ranch and herds were divided into two. What was so absurd about the quarrel was that both protagonists were models of rectitude; it was impossible to imagine either of them cheating or doing anything remotely dishonourable. Frank had a quick temper, which may have had something to do with it. Both men were to undertake much voluntary public work and were widely, and deservedly, respected. F.O'B was eventually knighted. At the time of their quarrel, their friends had to split into two camps. Jos and Nellie were in the Joyces' camp and so we never stayed with the Wilsons, or they with us. The feud gradually subsided, and their children finally buried the hatchet.

Apart from this unfortunate rift, the white community of Machakos was a happy one. In numbers it was small and scattered, and the people of the district had the feel of being cut off from the rest of the world and not minding this a bit. Barbecues were popular, and excellent barbecues they were, held under brilliant stars in the soft African night.

Philip Perceval, a famous white hunter, was one of the local stalwarts. His wife ran the farm while he took out safaris. There were many years of stringency. Their daughter remembers a two days' journey in an ox-wagon with her parents to the Athi river, where her father shot a hippo to provide the household's fat, and reims cut from its hide. A shortage of soap during the First World War was overcome by using a root which produced a lather for the wash.[7]

The Wakamba, or A'Kamba, or just Kamba – these prefixes are confusing – were cheerful, friendly people well liked by Europeans, who found them less devious than the Kikuyu, and brighter than lacustrines like the Luo. When Njombo retired as headman, Nellie replaced him with a M'Kamba, called Muchoka.

Intelligent and with a ready, open smile, he had prudently taken as his second wife a Kikuyu girl who was a distant relative of Njombo's; this gave him the entrée, as it were, to Nellie's small Kikuyu community, while his senior wife stayed in Ukambani to till his shamba, and tend his herd of five or six cows. He was reliable except on two counts, periodic drinking sprees – drink was a weakness endemic among the Wakamba – and over-staying his leave. He was supposed to take one month's leave a year, but often disappeared for two or three; as he lacked a postal address, it was impossible to retrieve him. The Kamba people had an affinity for machinery, and were much in demand to operate tinka-tinkas, as all machines were called. Also they liked the police force and the army, and volunteered for these in greater numbers than men of any other tribe.

But one thing they were not good at was conserving their land. Frank used to take us up into the hills to see their homesteads and shambas, where views were marvellous but soil erosion appalling. Their little cattle looked like skeletons with hide stretched over them. Worst of all was the silting up of the rivers that had once run all the year round and now dried up completely every year for six months or more. The hilltops had been stripped of their trees.

In the latter years of the colonial period, much was done to reverse the process of decay in Ukambani. A big drive was launched to persuade the people to terrace their land. It was the women, not men, who made the terraces. They worked, voluntarily, in groups based on clans, reviving an old custom, and singing as they hoed. They also dug dams. A sort of missionary fervour to save not souls, but land fertility, came over those Europeans in charge of the scheme, including Frank Joyce. He set aside one quarter of Kilima Kiu for his employees and their families, each of whom was allotted so much land and allowed to keep so many cattle and no more, and to practice crop rotation. He was very strict about this. The area in question adjoined the Kamba reserve, and the contrast was dramatic: on one side of the fence good pasture, brown and stringy in dry weather but still pasture; on the other, bare red earth and rocks and sand and gulleys. He used to say that to see the Kamba side looking like the Kilima Kiu side was his dream and his ambition, but knew that once he had relaxed his authority, land on the latter side would very soon look like land on the former side of the fence.

Change has hitherto dealt lightly with Kilima Kiu. On my last visit there was honey still for tea, or at any rate for breakfast. A Land-Rover came round to the veranda steps instead of ponies, cows were being milked in modern parlours, machinery hummed in the dairy, but the thorn-tree-speckled land stretched as it always had to distant hills, a dirt track wound away towards the station, an old leather mailbag was brought still from the station, hunting crops hung from pegs on the veranda, the long white house continued to lack a telephone. Bougainvilleas blazed like fires in the garden, their colour almost bruising the eye. An air of calm and leisure concealed, as it did in Frank's day, a lot of work and calculation; and Mui, grey-haired now – he has served the family for nearly sixty years – still greeted every visitor with enthusiasm and never forgot a face.

Since Frank's death in 1959 Anne Joyce has run the 23,000-acre ranch with its 2,000 cattle and 1,000 sheep and goats, its dams and boreholes, tractors and combines and all the rest with the quiet efficiency and firm authority inherited from Frank, perhaps impeded sometimes, though she never said so, by a tendency displayed by her many visitors from overseas to treat Kilima Kiu as a most comfortable hotel.

In the 1970s the Wilsons' half of the original block of land passed into the possession of a company formed by the Wakamba. The Joyces' half will shortly follow. So the two halves are, like a divorced couple who re-marry, once more coming together.

By the mid 1930s Nellie, though active as ever, had turned fifty, and the future of the farm was on her mind. She had always hoped that one day I would take it over, and that perhaps my children, if any, would inherit it in their turn. In fact I think a lot of her endeavour was fuelled by an almost passionate desire to be in a position to hand over a viable concern.

It was clearly impossible for Gervas and myself to contemplate a nest at Njoro while he was constantly on the wing spreading the gospel of tea. So Nellie hatched a plan. On our walks about the farm we had sometimes paused on a certain rise to look down across the river to the forest beyond, a tapestry of different shades of green – very dark for cedars with their grey lichen beards, the lighter, almost brownish-tinted foliage of wild olives, the apple-pale of feathery bamboos – and to remark that this would be a perfect site for a house. You felt as if you might be standing on the bridge of a ship with a green ocean below, rippled by wind into waves of foliage and always changing like the sea. Boughs shook as Colobus monkeys leapt invisibly from tree to tree; a flash of red betrayed a turaco; a distant agitation might mean a herd of buffalo. At night you would hear a leopard's sawing grunt and the cry of the hyrax, concentrating all the wildness of Africa into its harsh note.

Here, suggested Nellie, we might build our house bit by bit, as and when we could afford small dollops of money. Later, under Nellie's supervision, there would come to birth a small farm. She would make over to us one quarter of her land, including the house site and a river frontage, and gradually, bit by bit like the house, we would get it fenced and paddocked, bush cleared away, water pumped from the river and, in time, populated by heifers who would found a dairy herd. Then cheques would start to arrive and, when Gervas was ready to hand over his tea campaign to a successor, there would be a going concern and a home to come to.

This was a neat little plan and, had history taken a different course, it might have been realised. Gervas' feelings were clearly the key factor. It would be no good trying to dig him up if he did not wish to be dug. While he had no experience of farming, a love of the land was in his blood. He was an ardent gardener. On his mother's side he came from a family of Yorkshire landowners, and yeoman farmers before that, and his father was a doctor who, on retirement from a London practice, had started a dairy farm where his pedigree Guernseys became one of the first herds in Britain to produce tuberculin-free milk. (He prescribed for his own bovine patients, and there is a story that the local chemist, having with difficulty deciphered one of his prescriptions, gazed at him in horror and exclaimed: 'Excuse me, sir, but have you gone out of your mind?' The dosage was so massive that no human patient could have survived it.)

We pegged out an outline of the future house, which was soon surrounded by roughly levelled terraces. Then Nellie planted trees, and a mini-forest sprang up around the site. Next came fruit trees in a wire cage, and a road of sorts. Nellie knew a young woman in Nakuru who had just qualified as an architect and was starting her career, Dorothy Hughes. She designed for us a simple, single-storeyed, well-proportioned dwelling with a wide veranda from which we would be able to look out upon the ever-changing cloud patterns that moved across the forest of the Mau.

Before our last pre-war visit to Njoro, a start had been made. The Lindstrom family had a constant flow of visitors of several nationalities, including a young German who had come from Tanganyika with his wife to look for work. We took him on as manager at the going rate, £10 a month. Nellie planned to buy half-a-dozen heifers on our behalf for about £5 each, and Gervas' father ear-marked a bull calf for us from his pedigree herd. When we left Njoro at the end of 1938, the plan was well under way.

This was the year of Munich. 'When elephants fight,' runs an African

proverb, 'it is the grass that is trampled.' Our plan and Nellie's hopes
were blades of grass flattened by the elephants. When, after the war, I
told her that for various reasons the idea must be abandoned, she took
it hard. She had built too much upon sand. Jos had died in 1947 from
emphysema, resulting partly from fragments of a bomb lodged in his
chest during the First World War – 'just like Jos to get blown up on Guy
Fawkes' Day', remarked his brother – compounded by hard living,
dust and malaria in the second war. In 1942 he had somehow got
himself taken back into the army, despite his sixty-eight years. His job
involved taking drafts of raw recruits from Nyasaland (Malawi) and
Northern Rhodesia (Zambia) to Cairo, mainly by rudimentary roads
in overloaded lorries. The journey took at least five or six weeks, and
anything in the way of rest and comfort en route was non-existent.

More than twenty years after his death, I called in at a little pub in the
Welsh mountains, near a cottage I then owned close by. The landlord
greeted me by name. As I turned to go, a man sitting at the bar said: 'I
think you're Major Grant's daughter?' 'Yes', I said. 'Your father stayed
a night with me in Mwanza in the war. I was DC there.' Mwanza is a
port on the southern shore of Lake Victoria. Jos, he said, had been
on his way north with a convoy of recruits, and was suffering from
malaria and difficulty in breathing. 'He wouldn't stop. He was one of
the bravest men I've ever met.' It was heartening to hear this, away in
the Welsh mountains, from one who had known him so briefly and so
long ago. Jos had been invalided out of the army a few months later for
the third and last time – the first time in the Boer War because of
dysentery, the second time because of the bomb fragments in France.
'He was really a soldier at heart,' Nellie wrote after his death. Yet he
was the gentlest of men. Once, half exasperated and half amused by
some display of non-aggression, Nellie had demanded: 'Are you a man
or a mouse?' After a pause for reflection, pulling on one of the small
cheroots he favoured, he replied: 'I'm never quite sure.'

After his death, Nellie knew that she must carry on alone, without
fresh capital and without the prospect of passing on to her offspring
what she had built with so much hope and toil. To have given up and
retreated to England would have been to admit defeat and to
compromise her independence, and independence was in the marrow
of her bones.

Before we left for Britain there was one last safari. Eight of us foregathered at Moshi in Tanganyika: Nellie, Jos, myself and the Lindstroms – Fish was in charge – Gervas together with his 'man in Canada', Ernest Gourlay and his wife Joan. We had our ancient Ford V8, the Lindstroms an even more dilapidated vehicle, and a shaky old lorry had gone on ahead with our camp kit and with Karanja, the Lindstrom's driver and a general factotum. Just where our rendezvous with the lorry was to be on the vast Serengeti plain seemed unclear, but Fish was confident that the driver knew the spot.

The Serengeti was then just a big and tawny slice of Africa with no tourist lodges, zebra-striped buses, roads, rangers and the rest. It was a game reserve, not yet a national park. Both our cars soon boiled away their water. Before nightfall, the Lindstroms' car broke down altogether and had to be abandoned, and all eight of us piled into our over-heated, over-loaded Ford. We stopped every fifty yards or so and turned round to face into the wind, which we hoped would cool the engine, and spent a comfortless and foodless night beside the car. Next day, by one of those little miracles that Africa quite often provides, we came upon the lorry resting happily beneath a tree, with a pool of muddy water at hand – part of the dried-up water-course of the Seronera river, and not far from where the tourist lodge and the research centre were in future to stand.

And here were the lions we had come to see, as tame then as they are now, lolling about under trees in attitudes of sloth and indifference, amber-eyed. Next day Monty Moore, VC, the game warden, appeared, and shot a zebra which we tied to the axle of our car and towed about as bait. Before we had gone two hundred yards, seventeen lions and lionesses emerged from their couches in the shade to pounce upon the zebra's carcase, almost climbing into the lorry over each other's backs. I had screwed my telephoto lens into my Leica, but had to replace the ordinary lens in order to encompass even one lion, let alone seventeen.

The lorry retrieved the Lindstroms' broken-down car and towed it into camp, where Fish took it to bits. After he had re-assembled it, quite a large part was left over. What its function was I did not know, and nor did Fish. After regarding it for a few moments with his head on one side he threw it into the bush, saying in his low-key Swedish voice: 'I think the car will go better without it.' The poor old vehicle did stagger back as far as Parikatabuk, consisting of two Indian dukas on the Kenyan border, where it finally collapsed. Within a week we caught the Uganda mail at Rongai station and next morning were on the first leg of our journey home.

The Nile, wrote Herodotus, 'enters Egypt from parts beyond', and 'parts beyond' just about describes the confusion of lakes, watery cul-de-sacs and swamps whence issues one branch of that river. Elderly paddle-steamers, varied by crowded buses, took us across Lake Kyoga, on to Lake Albert, and to the foot of the Murchison Falls, where, from a few yards away, I photographed a crocodile lying on a sandspit with its jaws wide open. The reptile paid absolutely no attention. Some locking mechanism enables crocodiles to lie for hours with open jaws, which cools them down and allows access to a small plover who cleans their teeth by plucking bits and pieces from their great big molars. Crocodiles were everywhere, lying torpidly in the sun or imitating floating logs, but now are all but extinct in these Nile waters. In fact so rare have crocodiles become that they are being captive-bred in South Africa to save them from extinction.

For two days the *Samuel Baker* took us down the youthful Nile at a leisurely pace, stopping for half a day to allow the crew to cut and load firewood for the ancient engines. We were still passing through Uganda. Four hundred miles of the east bank had been temporarily 'closed' by the Protectorate's government, and the people moved away, as part of a campaign to eliminate sleeping sickness. It succeeded, and the people moved back – only to be slaughtered, some years later, in large numbers, and made into refugees, by the freebooting troops of Idi Amin.

At Nimule we said goodbye to the *Samuel Baker*, and a small fleet of station wagons took us to Juba, and embarkation on another vessel. We were now in the Anglo-Egyptian Sudan. Men with fanciful, elaborate hair-do's strolled hand in hand beside the river, tall and proud and lean as leopards. One coiffure, a thick twist of hair threaded with cowrie shells, looked like an ornamental serpent coiled around the young man's head. The lives of these Dinka people were centred on their cattle, adapted like them to survive the dryness, heat and harshness of their environment. Had the people but known it, they were enjoying a brief and, in retrospect, halcyon respite between two cruel oppressions: that of the slavers whose tentacles, stretching far into the interior, had been scotched by General Gordon and his successors, and that of the rule of Northerners, of Arab blood and Muslim faith like the slavers, who in the not so distant future were to let loose the dogs of war in the southern Sudan.

Soon after leaving Bor, we came to the Sudd. Our vessel butted her way through a green jungle of papyrus which seemed to have no beginning and no end, her bow constantly stuck in mud and roots and reeds. Then members of the crew seized giant punt-poles and pushed her backwards to get her free. She tried another channel that looked clearer, only to meet more floating vegetation and to stick again. It was like some slow, random vegetal pavane, conducted in a moist, oppressive heat amid a smell of rotting reeds and turgid mud. Plops and gurgles disturbed the water – a crocodile, a fish, a hippo? Birds dipped and dived, mosquitoes rose in clouds as evening fell and pinged incessantly all night.

The designers of our vessel, which had been built in Glasgow, had evidently been more concerned to keep her passengers warm than to cool them. The funnel, hot to the touch, rose through the middle of the little dining saloon from the engine room beneath it. The same thought must have occurred to those Glaswegians who had drawn up the menus, probably in mid-winter, since they relied heavily on steak-and-kidney pie and plum duff – all tinned, there was no refrigeration. We almost envied our Sudanese captain, who was observing Ramadan. Every evening a savoury-smelling rice stew in an iron pot was hauled up to the bridge from the deck below. But it is the prohibition against drinking between sunrise and sunset, more than against eating, that tests the willpower of the faithful during the month of Ramadan.

From the air, the Sudd looks like a vast green lawn, level as a plate, threaded with little gunmetal-coloured channels. These offered scant help to navigators of light aircraft following the Nile down from Lake Victoria to Khartoum. They had to decide which *was* the Nile, and which one of the Sudd's shifting waterways. It was the fashion then for owners of little Moths, Cessnas or whatever to fly to England and back for business or holidays. Losing the way was a hazard; pilots had to depend on maps and eyesight, in the absence of radio beacons. We thought, as we chugged along, of two friends of Nellie's, Brigadier Arthur Lewin, who was about the same age as Jos, and his wife Phyl. On a flight back home to Njoro they chose a wrong channel through the Sudd, vainly sought the right one, and started to run out of petrol. There was nothing for it but a forced landing. Their two-seater plane buried its nose in the papyrus and gently overturned. They were unhurt, but stranded.

For provisions all they had was a few sandwiches, a flask of water and another of whisky. All around was mud and water and papyrus. With nightfall came millions of mosquitoes which covered them as with a blanket, and feasted on their blood until their eyes were half buried in swollen flesh. All they could do was to sit there and pray to be spotted by aircraft sent out from Khartoum, but a tiny aeroplane three parts buried in the Sudd was a needle in a haystack indeed.

Then came a haboub. These sudden, violent storms sweep without warning over the desert and were dreaded by pilots, who flew over and above and around them lest their aircraft be torn apart. An approaching haboub roars like a train and scatters before it vegetation, birds and anything else in its path. Suddenly the Lewins found themselves surrounded by birds of every kind: storks, egrets, geese, fish-eagles, and many others. Birds settled on their wrecked aeroplane, at their feet, almost on their heads. The meaning of the phrase 'in the eye of the storm' came home to them. They were in that very eye.

I forget how many days and nights they stayed there, foodless and feverish. Once or twice aircraft flew over, specks in the sky. Then Phyl had an inspiration. She used the mirror in her powder compact as a reflector to beam a ray of sunlight back into the sky. When they saw an aeroplane drop down towards them and circle over, they knew the trick had worked.

To locate a quarry in the Sudd and to effect a rescue were two different things. Next day a plane returned to drop food and medicines, which vanished into the mud. Meanwhile a barge had set forth from Malakal to edge its way towards them. The Lewins reached Khartoum at last more dead than alive. Phyl said that the one thing she would never forget was the company of birds, all fear of man forgotten, sharing their safety in the eye of the storm.

We emerged into a stretch of relatively open water called Lake No, where our branch of the river, the Bahr el Jebel, was joined by the Bahr el Ghazal, the river of gazelles, which winds a tortuous western course to the hills of Darfur. This wild, remote region, little known even today, had been partially explored by the Welsh ivory-trader and prospector John Petherick. Then, in 1863, a Dutch girl called Alexandrine Tinné – only twenty-four years old, beautiful, accomplished and said to be the richest heiress in the Netherlands – set forth from Khartoum with her mother, an aunt, and a retinue which included five scientists. Hers was to be an exploration of the plants, trees, rocks, birds and butterflies of this unmapped region, not only of its geography.

From Khartoum, her barges pushed their way as far as they could get up the Bahr el Ghazal. The party then proceeded on foot into the country of the Niam-Niam, meaning eaters of men, where disaster overtook them. Somewhere near what is now the Sudan-Zaire border, Alexandrine's mother and one of the scientists died of fever, and another scientist was killed by a buffalo. The rest got back to Khartoum, where her aunt also died.

Alexandrine Tinné never went back to Holland. She lived for a while in Cairo, wearing Arab dress, consorting with Arab savants and travelling in Algeria and Tunisia. In 1869 she joined a caravan bound from Tripoli to Lake Chad across the Sahara. She took two Dutch sailors as her escort, and equipped the caravan with two large iron water tanks to be strapped on to camels. The desert Tuaregs had never seen tanks like that before and a rumour spread that they were filled with gold. The Tuaregs killed her two sailors and slashed her so severely that she bled to death on the sand. She was thirty years of age.[8]

At Malakal, swarms of locusts darkened the sky. Men of the Nuer tribe, stork-like and handsome, were casting nets from canoes. They had smeared themselves all over with ash to keep mosquitoes at bay and so looked grey instead of bronze. Flocks of snow-white egrets circled round, alighted in the reeds, took off again into a crimson sunset. We passed Fashoda, consisting of a wharf, a few bedraggled huts, a tea-shop and a half-rotted notice board.

After Kosti, a hot and dirty train took us to Khartoum, another train to Wadi Halfa and the end of the Sudan. From Luxor we drove northwards through clouds of sheep, children, water buffaloes, camels and dust. Women clad from head to foot in black, and carrying dust-pans and brushes, darted from their hovels whenever a passing camel defecated to sweep up the droppings, precious fuel in this treeless land. We observed with interest an Egyptian method of making butter. Beside an unpaved road, where every passing vehicle or creature stirred a dust-cloud, was a goat-skin, fastened by its hollow legs to four posts, and hanging upside down. An old man, one-eyed and toothless, squatted beside the goat-skin and gently rocked it to and fro. Inside a little cream skimmed from the milk of water-buffaloes was thickening slowly into butter. That night, we stopped at a small hotel between Assuit and El Minya and, at breakfast, ignored the pale, watery-looking butter that was put before us.

I have never cared for Cairo, and was thankful when we embarked at Alexandria on a Jugoslavian vessel crammed with three hundred members of the Hitler Jugend whose fares had been bartered for a quantity of Jugoslavian coal. We were the only other passengers on board, and formed a coalition with the captain, who sailed so close to the rocky Adriatic shore in order to wave to his wife that he almost scraped paint from his ship's side. Soon we were in Venice. It was December, raining steadily and icy cold. The chill of the Doges' palace might have been Dante's inspiration for his vision of the inner circle of hell. But dinner on the Simplon-Orient Express restored our spirits, and in London friends were on hand to welcome us back. Over eight years were to pass before I set foot in Africa again.

CHAPTER 15

Fifty Years On

People say that it is a mistake to go back, but I think this is so only if you expect things to be much the same or, if they have changed, to have changed for the worse.

When I went back in December 1983 Nairobi was festooned with banners saluting Twenty Great Glorious Years, and adorned with photographs of the President, Daniel arap Moi, looking stern rather than jubilant. It was the twentieth anniversary of independence. Foreign delegations had arrived from all over the world, the Queen was shortly due. The flag of the Republic flew from standards erected along every street and highway, and arches with excited texts were every-where. To mark the occasion, some 7,000 prisoners were released from jail. To judge from the many stories one heard of muggings and robberies with violence, there were quite enough criminals about already.

One of the people I had hoped to see, and did see, was Major Esther Wambui Njombo. She arrived in time for tea in her civilian clothes, small and trim and neat, driven by a formidable lady twice her size in army uniform. Major Njombo had been born on my parents' farm at Njoro and was the daughter of our headman Njombo, and a much younger wife. Njombo had died in 1952 when she was about three. Her education had begun at the farm school Nellie had started with less than a dozen pupils. I must have seen her when she was a child, but did not remember her, nor she me. She did, of course, remember Nellie. What did people think of her? I asked. 'They did not mind her,' the Major replied – a backhanded compliment, but I think she meant it kindly.

She went on to a secondary school and then became a teacher. One day in 1973 she heard that women were being recruited for the army. This was a revolutionary measure introduced by M'zee Kenyatta, and only ten girls were initially accepted. Esther Wambui got in on the ground floor, and in less than ten years rose to her present rank. After a spell at Sandhurst, she was given command of the women's section of the Kenyan army. When a detachment went to Britain to take part in the Royal Tournament at Earl's Court, she was its commander. Now, at thirty-five, the army provides her with a house, a car and driver, generous pay, and a pension in a few years' time.

Did she ever go back to Njoro? 'Oh, yes, I go back sometimes. I have a shamba there – not on your mother's old farm but close to it, on Major Adams'.' She has two other properties: four valuable acres at Langata, Nairobi's fashionable suburb, and two hundred acres north of Mt Kenya where she grows wheat on contract. She has a son of ten. Wambui, her mother, shares her house in Nairobi. In three days' time the big parade is to take place, and her soldiers will be there – drilled, I am sure, to perfection. Major Njombo has a look of her father, sharpish cheek-bones and prominent teeth, and might be called petite, with a gentle, high-pitched voice; not at all a formidable Major.

It is almost as if a new species has appeared on earth, the young Kenyan woman who has put tribal ways behind her. Self-assured, well-mannered, elegantly clad and with a neat Afro hair-do, these independent young ladies cope competently with word-processors and computers, staff banks, manage shops, work as stylists in hair-dressing salons, as flower-arrangers, as secretaries and drivers. How much initiative and ability must have gone to waste for all those centuries, how much talent lain buried! I know that women had, and have, a respected place in tribal society, that their rights were no less well defined than their duties, and to think that they had been regarded as mere beasts of burden was a superficial view. Nevertheless their place in tribal society was subservient; child bearing and rearing their purpose, and the scope for any form of self-expression small. On any road leading from the capital, within a mile of the Kenyatta Centre, you can see, today, women looking older than their years, toiling along under their loads. The smoke-blackened hut, three cooking stones, the gathering of firewood are far from obsolete. That was Major Esther's background. The image of a butterfly emerging from a chrysalis is compelling.

There are two points of view. I called on Margaret Kenyatta in her office high up in the Kenyatta Conference Centre, Nairobi's tallest and proudest building, all glass and glitter once off the ground but, at the bottom, dark and dim like a cathedral, full of sombre pillars that dwarf the flux of human figures surging to and fro and proceeding, as it seemed, through caverns measureless to man down to a sunless sea. Where were they all going, and what for? Perhaps to the enormous conference chamber, handsomely panelled, dimly lit, designed to hold a thousand delegates from all those international Boards, Organisations, Authorities and quangoes that converge upon Nairobi, bringing prestige, prosperity and that rich prize coveted by all emergent nations, foreign exchange.

On the tenth floor (there are thirty-four, with a jaunty cap on top) Margaret Kenyatta presides over the world headquarters of the United Nations Environmental Programme, on which she is Kenya's permanent representative. A shortish, plumpish, and alert person of late middle age, she reflects the jovial and outgoing side of her father's character, rather than the more devious yet steely aspect called for by the politics of nationalism. She greeted me with a generous warmth. Born in 1926, she is the M'zee's eldest daughter and only surviving child of his first wife Wambui, now in her eightieth year and living in contentment, Margaret said, with her daughter, on the outskirts of Nairobi – still active, still digging in her garden, cooking, bargaining in the market. Margaret has one son practising law in Nairobi, and two cherished grandsons.

Between the ages of three and eighteen Margaret saw nothing of her father, who was in Britain. By the time he returned in 1947 she had left the Alliance High School, the country's co-educational Eton, and had gained some secretarial training which she put at the disposal of her father during those fraught post-war years when he was consolidating freedom movements into the Kenya African National Union, attacking the colonial government, launching the Independent Schools which were the hotbed of Mau Mau, and generally directing the strategy of the nationalist movement.

'I was never a freedom-fighter,' she told me, 'but always involved in the organisation of the movement.' She was on hand to greet her father on his triumphant return to his home at Gatundu, in Kiambu, in August 1961, after nine years in the wilderness.

We turned to another freedom that had been at least partially achieved, that of African women. She did not think much of it. 'I had a very happy childhood,' she said. 'We were happier then than young people are now. I, too, carried heavy loads of firewood on my back; I too, had a leather thong pressing into my forehead. I was strong, I was proud of my strength to carry firewood and water and to hoe in my mother's shamba. I *enjoyed* these tasks. I was making my contribution to the family, playing my part. It was a wonderful life we had then. We were all together. No one was alone or neglected, each person had his place, her place, in the extended family. There was so much love and affection. There was security.'

Her maternal grandmother, Margaret said, had a lot of children, and they had children too, so she must have a great many cousins. 'Now I don't even know of their existence, who they are, what they do. The extended family is breaking down, has broken down already in the towns.' Now there is the nuclear family living in flats and small houses with no room for cousins and aunts. 'Now we have started in Nairobi a branch of Help the Aged. And we are having old people's homes. It is sad, very sad.'

We did not end on a sad note, for Margaret is not a sad person. When she laughs her eyes widen and flash, as African eyes so often do. She enjoys her work with UNEP, which co-ordinates and monitors conservation projects throughout the world. Unlike most officials of the United Nations and other international bodies, she does not relish jetting off to conferences from China to Peru. 'There is no need. This is the headquarters, so all the experts come here.' And she hates flying – London also, cold, grey and overcrowded.

For six years running, Margaret was mayor of Nairobi. Her record of public work reads like that of an English upper-class do-gooder: commissioner of the Girl Guides, on executive committees of the Red Cross, of the National Council of Women, of the Commonwealth Fund for the Blind; social work in Pumwani; and one un-English title, Chief of the Burning Spear. Despite all this she is a down-to-earth person, bestriding two worlds and perhaps, as she grows older and like her father, going back more and more to her roots. In old age the M'zee encouraged tribal dancing, preferred his home at Gatundu and his estate near Nakuru to State House and, despite his perfect English, often talked in Swahili where Kikuyu would not do. In spite of all temptations to belong to other nations, he remained a Kikuyu man.

Nairobi has become, it has been said, the tourist capital of the world. Probably this is too large a claim, but it is undoubtedly a-buzz with tourists. Traffic jams are awful, crowds close-packed like never-ending shoals of mackerel pursued by porpoises, high-rise buildings like rigid glittering flowers sprouting from a concrete earth. Some are imaginative, even fanciful, and make good use of colour, but too much use of glass for the tropics. Older buildings appear to have shrunk. The law courts designed by Sir Herbert Baker have retained their dignity, pressed in on as they are by buildings flaunting their angular modernity; but Torr's hotel, once the last word in progress and importance, has become an insignificant little bank – architecturally speaking, that is. The old New Stanley has vanished beneath enormous accretions, and the Norfolk hotel, once so spacious-seeming and substantial, is now a self-conscious colonial relic trading in atmosphere, and jostled by the fortress-like towers of Nairobi University.

And now there are even Listed Buildings. One is the old DC's office; a squat, single-storey edifice in grey cut stone with the usual veranda. Many is the exasperated settler who has confronted the DC in this office, many more the wrongdoers who have come before him to be sentenced, and quite a few hopeful couples who have come before him to be married. Immediately behind this now historic monument had just arisen another huge tower block honeycombed with air-conditioned offices, a monument to Kenya's major growth industry, bureaucracy – Nairobi's provincial headquarters.

Once you get away from the high-rise glitter, Africa re-asserts itself. Roads develop pot-holes, housing estates tail off into shanty-towns, little plots of maize spring up in every neglected corner. The population of the city now verges on the million mark, and all the time people keep coming. They do not, I am sure, believe the streets to be paved with gold, but when your father's shamba can no more be sub-divided, when your crops have failed and drought has carried off your only cow, what else can you do but seek employment, which you rarely find, in the city? You and your growing family double up with a distant relative, or bivouac on what has been designated as an open space. Somehow or other you scrounge enough to eat. Quite often you take to crime. Scruffy mini-markets appear, illegally: booths roofed with sagging cardboard tucked away in odd corners that offer for sale little piles of beans or spices, sweet potatoes, pawpaws and bananas, snuff, bags of charcoal, plimsoles, T-shirts, all sorts of things – untidy, unhygienic. Come back a week later and it may have been bulldozed away, only to spring up elsewhere. By contrast, on the outskirts of the town Executive Houses are going up, smart two-storey affairs with garages. Opposite is a tumble-down rusty corrugated-iron shed leaning to one side and bearing a placard proclaiming it to be a Video Library.

Nairobi might have been mistaken for an Indian town when I first knew it. Indians and their shops were everywhere. That has changed, but not altogether; there is still the Asian Bazaar, and a top layer of affluent and successful Asians. One, who kindly invited me to cakes and coffee at his home, is a High Court judge. Other morning coffee guests included a consultant dermatologist and a Sikh business tycoon, the latter an elderly gentleman clad all in white and with a fine white beard. He laughed as he said: 'I have lost seventy-three million shillings in Uganda and six million shillings in Tanzania. And I am still a happy man.'

He had started his career as a station-master; done a bit of buying and selling, invested in a posho mill and in a cotton ginnery in Uganda, and gradually built up an empire, mainly in the shape of mills. One day, driving down from Eldoret, he stopped at a saw-mill whose European owner did not shake hands or ask him into the house. The Sikh drove back to Eldoret, arranged matters with the bank, returned and said to its owner: 'I have come to buy your saw-mill. I will pay you £20,000.' This time he *was* invited into the house. 'It was a good investment,' said the Sikh.

Are Asians, I asked, better or worse off now than in colonial times? The High Court judge shrugged his shoulders. 'The upper millstone has become the nether millstone. It does not make much difference to those in between.' He recalled regulations that had formerly prevented him and his kind from buying land in the white highlands, and the exclusion of Asians from the higher ranks of the civil service. 'We had little choice but to become duka-wallahs.' Nevertheless, I suggested, he seemed to have done pretty well. 'I was lucky. The gods watched over me. I used to tell the Europeans with whom I worked that my loyalty was suspect because I was not white, although Kenya did not have a more loyal subject. Still equally loyal, I am not black. I do not know. What I do know is, I do not want any other home than Kenya.' In the past, whites made Asians feel inferior; now, blacks make them feel insecure.

Eboo's filling station in what was then Delamere Avenue used to be a familiar landmark, where one filled one's tank before embarking on the up-country run. It had been swept away but its proprietor, now Sir Pirbhai, is to be found near at hand in a handsome air-conditioned office high up in one of the tower blocks. He came to East Africa from Bombay when he was five years old. Now in his eightieth year, he is president of the Ismaili community, who acknowledge the Aga Khan as their spiritual head, not only in East Africa but in Europe and the USA as well. It used to be a big event when the Aga Khan himself paid a visit to Nairobi and was weighed in gold and diamonds, amid much rejoicing. As he was a portly gentleman the proceeds were considerable, and all were devoted to the welfare of the local Ismaili community, mainly by providing schools and hospitals. The Ismailis looked after their own. The current Aga Khan no longer comes to be weighed in jewels, but Ismaili traditions carry on. Both millstones, it seems, have left a good deal of grist un-ground.

One of the more vociferous settler politicians in pre-uhuru days was an Irish garage-owner in Eldoret, Tommy O'Shea. Sir Pirbhai employed a pleasant and efficient secretary. She is a daughter of Tommy O'Shea.

Until you get out towards the shanty-fringes, prosperity oozes from Nairobi's pores. The ample, well-paid staffs of umpteen embassies and agencies dispensing aid are here established with all their local minions, schools for their children, shiny cars – over one thousand Swedes alone come and go. As for government Ministers, under Ministers, Permanent Secretaries, Assistant Permanent Secretaries, and of course all the members of the National Assembly, their muster runs into many thousands. No wonder Executive Suits are advertised in the newspapers. The current status symbol is a video, or rather several videos. I met an English girl who was here on a visit to a school friend, the daughter of an important Minister, who told me, rather breathlessly, that her Kikuyu host had a video in *every* room. He also breeds orchids, has a herd of pedigree Jerseys and is a connoisseur of wine. Dachas at the Coast or beside Lake Naivasha, shopping at Harrod's, children at British boarding schools and, of course, Swiss bank accounts, are common form among members of this upper crust.

Corruption, I was told by almost every European I met, is rife, from Ministers taking their cut of foreign contracts to post office clerks fiddling stamps. A Provincial Commissioner has built a million-pound hotel at the Coast. Bank managers have acquired large ranches and farms. The President has set his face against all this, so far without noticeable results. 'Here it's called corruption,' said a cynic. 'In Europe, it's called commission.'

For many, hopes that burgeoned with uhuru have gone sour. The bwana has merely changed the colour of his skin, not shared out his possessions. He still drives around in a great big motor car while you trudge or, if you are lucky, pedal on a clapped-out bicycle. Even the ownership of land, the supreme prize of uhuru, has often disappointed, because hopes were built on dreams and not on ecology. Every year the schools release a flood of youths and maidens seeking employment which many cannot find; over half its population is eighteen or under, and no economy could absorb so many newcomers, certainly not this one. Twenty years ago at independence, the population numbered about eight million; in 1985 it topped the twenty million mark. Such an upsurge of people must overwhelm the resources of an ill-endowed country (no oil, no minerals and a lot of desert). One might vary Oliver Goldsmith's couplet to:

> *Ill fares the land, to hast'ning ills a prey,*
> *Where men accumulate and means decay.*

So – will an explosive situation explode? Should the question rather be not will, but when?

There was a badly bungled coup that failed in 1982, but such coups are more in the nature of attempts by one faction to grab power from another faction than peasants' revolts. To succeed, revolts must be planned and organised, and the Government's toleration does not extend to revolutionary groups and plotters. That form of freedom cannot be afforded. Kenya is a one-party state.

And then, African reactions are not always those which Europeans expect. Extremes of wealth and poverty may stoke fires of resentment, but it could be that Africans may tolerate, even admire, the achievements of their fellows whose life-style has come to equal, or even surpass, that of their former rulers. The man whose only wealth consists of half a dozen goats might applaud, and not condemn, the distant cousin with his Volvo, his video and his Swiss bank account. He has made it. Luck is not for everyone. Shauri ya Mungu – God's affair. Inshallah.

I asked an elegant young Englishwoman in jodhpurs who looked in to discuss some matter with my luncheon hostess whether she lived there at Langata, or was out from England on a visit. 'Actually, my husband is a two-year wonder,' she replied. A two-year wonder is a man or woman to whom the Government has granted a permit to work in Kenya because he or she commands some skill not yet possessed by any Kenya citizen. They come on two-year contracts to conduct many projects funded by foreign aid. All over the country you find them: engineers, surveyors, irrigation experts, plant breeders, entomologists, economists, veterinary researchers, experts on every kind of subject, coming from Europe, from America, from Japan. Steam jets erupting from the hill Eburru are being harnessed to generate electricity. Major irrigation schemes are on foot in the Tana valley. Ethologists from a Californian university are studying the social behaviour of a troop of baboons. This project has run into trouble because the habitat of the baboons, part of the Coles' Kekopey ranch, has been divided into ten-acre small-holdings, and small-holdings planted with crops do not go with baboons. One of the team of baboon-watchers, an attractive young lady, is looking for somewhere to translocate (move) the baboons; sad to say, no one wants them. They are a very special troop because they have been so thoroughly studied, and their social relationships worked out. It is said that the local Maasai derive entertainment from watching these daft white people watching the baboons.

I paused by the roadside to look over the haunt of the baboons and the whole Valley and saw a great change. A wide flank of the escarpment, where it slopes to meet the Valley's floor, was speckled no

longer with grey-green leleshwa shrubs and flat-topped thorn trees, but
with tin roofs that winked in the sunshine like spangles spread out on a
pale cloak below. The tin roofs are for catching water, but in times of
drought the tanks run dry and all the sheep and goats and cattle die. This
was to happen soon after my visit, when a stench of rotting flesh hung
over the Valley and vultures were so bloated they could scarcely fly.

In 1965, when she was eighty, Nellie sold what was left of her farm to
eight of what she called her old retainers, men who had worked for her
for some forty years. Her farm had shrunk by then to fifty acres, but she
still had the house, nothing much to look at but comfortable and fairly
sound, with its lovely garden. She had the sheds and stores that go with a
farm, twelve acres of fertile irrigated market garden, some river frontage, and a ram pump with its attendant piping and storage tanks. There
was also an orchard, a cattle dip, an irrigated lucerne paddock and some
pyrethrum (an ingredient of insecticides – harmless except to insects).
She sold it all for £900. She could have got three or four times as much for
her property; several Africans had already come up the hill to make
reasonable offers.

The reason for her decision was that she could not bear to leave the
country knowing that her old retainers, those eight Kikuyu with their
families, would be turned off the farm and have nowhere to go. The
Government was pondering various schemes to re-settle squatters
displaced by the sale of their former employers' farms, but these
foundered on the difficulty of finding alternative land. Nearly all Nellie's
white neighbours had already gone by the time she sold, and in every
instance the new African owners had turned all the former squatters off
the land. They had their own families to consider. The men of Nellie's
group were too old to find employment.

Some of Nellie's friends attempted to persuade her that she was in no
position to sell her only asset for considerably less than a song. But she
was adamant; and so was the bank, which would advance to her old
retainers no more than £900. So Nellie packed up, had a large bonfire,
paid her debts which mopped up most of the £900, packed her possessions into two large wooden boxes to go by sea, said her goodbyes and,
with her last two remaining dachshunds, set out to start a new life on a
quinta – a small-holding – in southern Portugal.

It was with sharp misgivings that I went back to the farm. I had spoken on the telephone – the number was the same – to Benson Karanja, a son of Karanja her former cook. Benson undertook to arrange a meeting with the old retainers, including his father, all of whom were still alive. Pamela Scott, living still at Deloraine, kindly drove me up the track from Njoro to the old farm. The twin thorn trees that had guarded the approach had gone. So had the garden, as was to be expected. You cannot eat roses and delphiniums. All around was maize.

And there they were, all eight of them: Karanja wa Kinoko the cook, Karanja wa Mokorro the herd, Kariuki the fundi, Manvi the gardener, Mbugwa the house-parlourman, and three others, wrapped in ancient overcoats and shapeless sweaters and using the old Kikuyu handshake, each person gripping the other's thumb. We sat on wicker chairs in an open-sided shed which was the first stage of a projected poultry house. Children came to look on, and drifted away again; at intervals a drunken man appeared and shouted incomprehensible remarks which were ignored.

Mbugwa was the spokesman. His face was still bony, his eager manner had not left him, nor his intelligent, rather monkey-like expression, nor his stutter, nor his wide smile. 'There is one important question,' he began, 'that we wish to ask. Where is your mother buried, and when did she die?' After I had answered, he made a little speech. They would like to say that they were grateful for the gift of the land. No other Europeans in the district had arranged for the old people to stay on after the sale of the farms. The squatters on this farm were envied. They had security, and honoured the memory of Mrs Grant. It was a set speech but I think he meant it, and wished that she could have heard.

The old bungalow, naked without its creepers, was unused, and had almost crumbled away. On the site of the garden, a new house had appeared. Built of cedar planks, plaster-board and corrugated iron it was no mansion, but neat and well equipped with electrical appliances: colour television, video and other signs of affluence and modernity. This was Benson's home where he lived with his wife and three small children. His wife brought us tea and a plate of big, juicy tomatoes, while the children sat in semi-darkness glued to the television screen like children the world over. First we were given sports, then a comedy chat show, then a quiz. I wondered what they made of it all. Benson gets the cassettes in Nakuru, paying twenty shillings for a hire of forty-eight hours.

The farm is divided into small plots, each not more than two or three acres, and bursting with the children, grandchildren and other relatives of the old men and their wives. Everyone grows maize, a few pyrethrum; goats and scrawny cattle wander about. The borehole's pump broke down and has not been repaired, so women carry water from the river as they did fifty years ago. The indigenous trees have gone. Had we built our house on the site we had chosen, we should have looked across the river on to regiments of pine trees standing stiffly in rows, planted by the Forest department.

Clearly Benson could not sustain his life-style on a few acres of maize. He runs a pick-up, is elegantly clad, a member of the Rift Valley Sports Club with its tennis and squash courts, swimming pool and excellent food; goes often to Nairobi on business trips, and is about to embark on a tour of Israel organised by the Kenya Farmers' Association. He grows wheat, he told me, on rented land with hired machinery, and has various trading interests; his father was a great trader too.

I asked after the school. It is enormous now, with five or six hundred pupils and an impressive tally of distinguished alumni; also Charles Rubia, a former mayor of Nairobi; Geoffrey Kamau, ex-mayor of Nakuru; and a junior Minister, Kiruiru. Benson, however, does not send his children there. He takes his two eldest in his pick-up to the fee-paying primary school at Egerton College, where they mingle with the offspring of expatriate professors and the like. He himself attended what used to be the Duke of York's, a boarding school run on English public school lines, originally for white boys, in Nairobi. It has been re-named after a famous Maasai laibon, Lenana.

In 1938 Lord Egerton of Tatton, a misogynist and recluse who built himself a castle at Njoro, gave about eight hundred acres of his estate to provide for the training of European lads intending to make their careers in agriculture. Our neighbour Sandy Wright was then his manager. He and Nellie drew up a preliminary scheme to put the idea into practice; after much planning and discussion, the Egerton Farm School came into being. Then, after the Second World War, came a dramatic expansion. Newcomers under the post-war settlement schemes were required to take courses there before acquiring their farms or tenancies, so the institution grew, but it was still a farm school, not a college.

And now . . . The Registrar took me round. We drove for miles and miles, passing building after building, lab after lab, hall after hall of residence, a great new library, a cheese factory, orchards, greenhouses, workshops, playing fields. The gleaming kitchens, full of stainless steel appliances equipped to serve three ample meals a day, would be the envy of many a princely New York or London hotel. The teaching staff is partly Kenyan and partly drawn from many foreign countries, and diplomas can be won in a score of subjects from engineering to food marketing, wildlife management to home economics. Two hundred of the sixteen hundred students are women. That little acorn that we knew of old – Nellie used to supply all the vegetables – has become a great oak indeed.

'My father was a shika kamba on a European farm,' said the Registrar. A shika ngombe was the small boy who walked ahead of a team of oxen to guide them. This shika ngombe (of the Nandi tribe) grew up to start a small primary school, and his son Paul won a bursary to the University of Arizona to study range management. On his return with his degree he was posted to the North, with the task of persuading the nomadic tribes to take part in range management schemes. He found that this was by no means as easy as it was in the United States. 'Our trouble here is people,' he said. 'Instead of cooperating, they quarrel all the time among themselves, especially the Somalis. They will not follow instructions given them for their own good.' It all sounded very familiar. If one closed one's eyes it might have been Glenday, Reece or Turnbull speaking. Same problem, same response.

I thought back to the heady days of freedom-struggling when the world would be the nationalists' oyster once the foreign devils had been expelled. Two quotations from the British poets, I thought then, summed up the two credos. 'Better to reign in hell, than serve in Heav'n', said Milton's Lucifer, a cry echoed by Africans refuting colonialist assertions that they 'weren't ready' to take over, lacking experience and expertise. 'For forms of government let fools contest' retorted Alexander Pope. 'Whate'er is best administered is best.' I could almost see Paul nodding his head.

The arms of Baron Egerton of Tatton are still displayed, and the family motto, Sic Donet, is the motto of the college, soon to become a university.

What becomes of all these students who go forth with their diplomas? Do many, do any, become genuine farmers with mud on their boots and tractor-grease on their hands? Very few, I was told; their sights are set rather on offices and labs; but there are a few, and others may follow.

From the point of view of efficiency it was a backward step, in some cases even a disaster, to split up so many productive farms formerly in white ownership into small-holdings barely able to support a single, if large, family, and in bad years unable even to do that. The banks, hoping to check the process, decreed that the new owners must pay off their loans before the land could be officially sub-divided and title-deeds registered. The unforeseen result was a rush to sell every available asset in order to gain the security of a title-deed. Everything moveable and saleable was moved and sold. So it was something of an agricultural wasteland that I drove through in the Njoro district, formerly the heartland of white farming. Fences, water troughs, corrugated-iron roofing, left-over machinery, all, or nearly all, were gone. Sleek dairy cattle had been replaced by skinny little beasts drinking from muddy pools in a half dried-up river. It was as if the clock had been turned back fifty years.

But there are exceptions, and their number is growing. Men of the new breed of rich Africans, mostly with government connections, who have bought some of the best of the Europeans' farms, now run them efficiently under good managers, some of whom are Egerton-trained. Considerable chunks of the Rift Valley were acquired, and are still owned, by various members of the Kenyatta family; the late President's estate is protected by a high steel fence like that surrounding Whipsnade Zoo, though designed to keep ill-intentioned people out instead of captive animals in. The trend is towards farming cooperatives and companies to keep intact such units under professional management. So perhaps ecology will make a come-back, in time.

Where tea and coffee thrive – Kenya's mainstays – there is a different story. Both have proved, contrary to many expectations, excellent crops for small-holders, given good overall direction and organisation. Prices have soared and production expanded, exports have saved the country from financial undoing, and the small-holders have flourished. They are the lucky ones: both of these crops are particular as to the conditions that suit them, and, if not suited, will not grow.

A little way beyond Njoro township came the unexpected sight of a lot of glossy, handsome horses grazing in a paddock; then a flock of fine-woolled sheep in a green field. This was Sasumua, a word associated in my mind with bees. And here, indeed, were the Nightingales' bees, re-settled after their enforced move from the Kinangop, together with an assemblage of livestock, and joined now by another breed of insect: silk-worms, bred in droves on approved Japanese lines.

The Nightingales' horses are no sideline but a major enterprise. Racing languished after independence, many thought for good, but now it has come back into fashion, bringing a brisk demand for yearlings which the Nightingales breed. That scourge which I so well remember, horse-sickness, had been overcome.

It was at Njoro that the first professional trainer built his stables, and here those stables are today. Instead of a horse, each loose-box is occupied by a heavy, old-fashioned hand-loom. Before it sits a young woman weaving, to her own design, yarn spun from locally shorn wool. In another shed the spinners pedal at their wheels, and outside the dyers thrust skeins of yarn into debbis simmering on a charcoal brazier, together with ingredients of local dyes. Women bring their babies, and come and go to suit themselves. I thought how happy and relaxed it all seemed.

The stables were built by Charles Clutterbuck, who set up as a trainer here in 1904. With him came his daughter, Beryl, four years old. His wife stayed behind. Clutterbuck built a house for Beryl, a squat, three-roomed bungalow, with odd little spikes on its gables that give it a jaunty air. Now it is full of wollen jackets, rugs, shawls and lengths of cloth ready for sale.

It was from here that Beryl used to set out with her spear to chase wart-hogs barefoot with Nandi braves, as related in her autobiography *West with the Night*. She grew up among horses and Nandi stable-boys without benefit of schooling, and it was said that Clutterbuck aged his daughter as he aged his racehorses: that is, the horse became one year older on a certain date, I think 31 August, regardless of when it was born; and that she was therefore only sixteen when she was married to a brawny farmer who had played Rugby football for Scotland and had a posho mill nearby. This is not mentioned in her autobiography.

When she was eighteen her father went bankrupt and left the country, and Beryl rode off with all her possessions in two saddle-bags to start in business as a trainer on her own. All the odds were against her – age, sex, poverty – but she pulled it off. She had a genius for handling horses, and one or two of the leading owners gave her their patronage. She married Mansfield Markham, Glady Delamere's brother-in-law and a rich man, but that marriage, like the first, did not last. Then she turned from horses to flying. One of the early aviators, Tom Campbell Black, taught her to fly and she qualified as a commercial pilot, entitled to fly passengers, mail and anything else to anywhere in the world. This was in 1931 when she was still only thirty-one years old. In little single-engined aeroplanes she flew all over East Africa, where landing strips were few, and three times to England, a flight of about 6,000 miles.

Several white hunters such as von Blixen and Finch Hatton were her friends, and she developed a technique of spotting from the air likely trophies for their clients to approach on foot, such as large tuskers. So intelligent were the elephants, she wrote, that the cows would crowd round the bull, or bulls, so closely as to conceal the big tusks from airborne hunters. This implies a process of reasoning that scientists may not credit, but the intelligence of elephants is well known and no one can be sure of its limits.

The climax of Beryl's career came in 1936 when she set out to fly a Vega Gull from Oxfordshire to New York, and so to become the first woman, and the second person, to fly solo and non-stop across the Atlantic from east to west.[1] The inlet valve of her petrol tank froze up over Nova Scotia and she had to make a forced landing in a swamp, so she did not make it to New York, but she did succeed in flying the Atlantic, solo, in a tiny aeroplane, against prevailing winds. Her time was twenty-one hours and twenty-five minutes.

Beryl's third marriage was to an American, Raoul Schumacher, who helped her to write her book. After that ended, she returned to the land of her childhood to become probably its most successful trainer. The little house her father built for her must be seventy years old, a great age in colonial terms. It ought to be declared a Listed Building with a blue plaque to commemorate East Africa's most famous woman flyer.

From one extreme in the shape of Beryl's cottage I went on to the other, Deloraine, a nine-day wonder when first built by Lord Francis Scott. Trees and shrubs have grown up almost to submerge it in greenery and colour. Sunbirds hover above blue salvias that have invaded a formal brick-pathed garden, and take shelter in mauve-flowering bauhinia trees. The harsh cry of hadada storks as they fly over, and the falling cadences of doves, fill the air.

In my youth I found the Scotts' daughter, Pamela, intimidating, although she was considerably younger than I. Forthright and outspoken, her clear blue eyes held, I thought, a certain coldness, her manner a hint of hauteur. Perhaps I was influenced by the patrician nature of the Montagu-Douglas-Scott connections. Neighbours looking in for a chat about foot-and-mouth disease or army worm might face the hazard of encountering a royal personage – Princess Alice was Lord Francis Scott's niece – or at the very least an earl or viscount. Photographs of a legion of titled relatives lined the staircase, and still do; but the titled relatives, if they came to Deloraine, had to put up with rattle-trap jalopies, brown bath water and jiggas in the toes like everyone else. Eileen Scott – Lady Francis – kept a diary in which she described a visit to Berkeley Cole's farm. Her host was dressed for dinner in a pair of shrunken crêpe drawers that failed to cover his naked legs, and a patched old jacket. 'A huge Russian bear-hound eats off our plates at will. Three sheep came in at luncheon and hens pecked around the table.' Her comment on this experience, an unaccustomed one for a Viceroy's daughter, was: 'Mr Cole was one of the most amusing men I have ever met.'[2]

Time has done its proper job of mellowing. Pam Scott's candid opinions and decisive judgements are still forthrightly delivered, but tempered by a greater tolerance, and her natural generosity remains. For half a century she has farmed this land at Rongai, having been thrown in at the deep end by her father who, on her return from a finishing school at the age of eighteen, told her that he could no longer afford a manager, but felt sure that she could take it on. So instead of Court balls and tea with the Queen she found herself delivering calves, drenching sick cows, setting tasks for labour and dealing with the petty detail punctuated by crises that make up most farmers' lives.

Then came independence, the great divide. You went or you stayed. Pam had no hesitation in making her decision, and little sympathy with those who, as she saw it, ran away. When Daniel arap Moi was a member of the local African District Council he was an occasional visitor to Deloraine, and it was he who signed her application form to become a Kenya citizen.

Deloraine now belongs to a body called the Rift Valley Development Trust, whose chairman is President arap Moi, and which runs the Rift Valley College of Science and Technology situated near Nakuru. Pam Scott rents back for her lifetime the house and sufficient land on which to keep a small dairy herd, assorted poultry and a flock of snow-white goats. The arrangement enables her to experiment with devices to heat the bathwater by fermenting tanksful of manure, with home-made solar heating, with photography and other matters, as well as to entertain innumerable 'winter migrants' who come from Britain to enjoy the sunshine and hospitality which, while no longer colonial, continues in that kindly tradition.

Deloraine as I remember it had no bolts or bars; dogs and people wandered in and out of open doors. Now it has been fortified, and night watchmen (when not asleep) prowl about the grounds. A pump and its engine had just been stolen from a field.

At Olpejeta, one of the country's largest ranches and on the great Laikipia plain, there seemed to be a slip in time. On lawns kept green by sprinklers and under shady trees, a concourse of people strolled about, sipped white wine cup, helped themselves to delicious salads and greeted friends. Nothing unusual in this, a luncheon barbecue: but the faces were white. Olpejeta is a long way from any city and white farmers are supposed to have disappeared. Quite a lot have evidently been left over, and they did not look unhappy or oppressed.

Olpejeta belongs now to Mr Kashoggi, said to be the richest man in the world, but there are a number of claimants to that title. Like his forbears, his life-style is nomadic, but a string of camels has been replaced by a Boeing 727 fitted up as a very superior tent. The bathtub, I was told, really does have gold-plated taps, but I did not see them myself. Mr Kashoggi with his entourage drop down from the sky and take off again without warning as he flits about the world accompanied by a Korean bodyguard, girl-friends and a skilful chef. His American pilots are recruited from the Presidential flight. Whatever he possesses, said his Kenya-born manager, must be of the best, and you couldn't have a better boss. He never interferes.

Many of the white farmers and their wives are Kenya-born. Some have given ground – sold it, to be precise – and stayed on. Robin Davis has sold off most of his grandfather's soldier-settler farm near Nanyuki, and ploughs and cultivates on contract for his African neighbours. 'The days of women hoeing in the shamba,' he said, 'are over.' He has kept back eighty acres and concentrates on highly-priced products, such as apples, turkeys, Jersey cream. Raymond Hook's daughter keeps poultry on a portion of her father's former land. A useful sideline is provided by film companies; Robin has already played the part of a bearded Boer transport-rider and is currently involved in a film about a female Tarzan swinging nakedly about the trees.

Elephants have become a problem, both to the farmers and to themselves. Deprived of their ancient migration routes and harried by poachers, they are forced from their proper habitats to search for food and water. They break fences, and have been known to drink dams completely dry. Farmers and ranchers are putting up electric fences with considerable success; elephants explore unfamiliar objects with the tips of their trunks, which are extremely sensitive. Successful electric fencing still further restricts the elephants' range. 'In the long run it would be kinder,' said a farmer, 'to shoot the lot.'

Not much future for the elephants. How about the humans? The children of the white farmers go to Britain for their secondary schooling and all of them, or nearly all, want to come back. 'Do you think that you'll be here, or your children will be here,' I asked, 'in twenty years' time?' 'If you'd asked that question twenty years ago,' one of them replied, 'the answer would have been an emphatic no. And here we are. Another twenty? Maybe. I wouldn't be surprised.' A lady well up in her eighties gave a forthright reply: 'In twenty years' time we'll be buying back anything we want.' The new settlers, she said, were growing the wrong things in the wrong places and wouldn't survive. Few shared her confidence to that extent. The laws of ecology are one thing and the needs and hopes of people another, and the odds are on the latter to prevail.

Here on the foothills of the Mountain was an object-lesson to show that not all Africans sub-divide the land they buy and then, not always but too often, spoil it. On the road to Timau we passed a paddock fenced and watered with a good grass ley, and on it incongruously grazed some inferior scrub cattle. They were surrogate mothers. The eggs of pedigree Friesians, after being fertilised by champion bulls, are flown from Britain to this farm (which has three European managers) to be inserted into the wombs of these cheap and humble Zebu cows. The ranch belongs to Mr Kenneth Matiba, Minister for Social Services and Culture.

Beyond Timau the A2, tarmac'd now all the way from Nairobi to Isiolo, makes a spectacular dive of about 4,000 feet from the Mountain's foothills to what some people call 'the real Africa', a land of hot, dry savannah bush with rocky gulleys, thorn trees, baobabs, many-fingered euphorbias and, in the river beds, borassus palms. Saucer-eared Grevy's zebra and close-patterned reticulated giraffe are native to this region. You come to Lewa Down, where Delia, Elizabeth Powys' daughter, and her husband David Craig have created an oasis watered by springs.

Like others, the Craigs have discovered that tourists pay better than crops or cattle. Tourists must be fed, so there are vegetables and fruit trees under irrigation, milch cows, steers and almost everything except fish. I remember hearing how Afrikaner women used to bake their bread by scooping out a termite castle to make an oven. The Craigs have built pseudo-termite castles in which to bake for their visitors, who sleep in commodious tents and eat in an open-sided banda which has a hole in the side made by the trunk of an inquisitive elephant.

From the Craigs' house, perched on a rocky hillside, you can see the roofs of Isiolo winking at you from below. The place has grown fantastically, and no one could explain just why. There are no industries, no settled agriculture, no raison d'être at all so far as I could see. It has become a provincial capital, so civil servants have no doubt moved here in droves. The army, too, is here in force with all its sutlers, a comet with a long tail. Mosques have arisen, schools and hotels, a modern hospital; water been piped, electricity generated, an airfield made. The Great North Road, wide and red but not yet tarmac'd, drives northwards to Moyale where it links up with a tarmac'd but sometimes hazardous highway to Addis Ababa. I suppose Isiolo has become an outpost of civilisation. The last time I was here it was to stay with the Adamsons. The lioness Elsa travelled on the roof of George's Land-Rover, Joy sat for hours sketching her loved one, and Patti Patti, her rock hyrax, tried to get at the whisky, stared crossly at all comers from the seat of the loo and, after bed-time, wrapped herself round Nellie's neck and chattered angrily when disturbed.

It is odd how small things stick in the memory while greater ones disappear. Looking down at Isiolo I remembered a queer whirring sound I had heard while sitting beside the Ewaso Ngiro river, like that of a toy clockwork engine being started up a long way off. I couldn't make it out. Then from some crevice in the river bank an enormous ghost-like bird emerged, spread its wings and took off – surely the spirit of some chief or warrior captain soaring away over the trees. An eagle owl.

As we climbed up from plain to highlands the sun was setting in his crimson bed behind the dark rim of Laikipia, and all the hills and valleys far beyond. There is always sadness in a sunset, and I was sad to say goodbye to that great brooding Mountain with its forest girdle, to the wildness of the bushlands at its feet, to the harshness of the rocks and gulleys where the bones of those who once possessed it all, the multitudinous wild animals, have turned to dust.

Michael Blundell first arrived in Africa at the age of eighteen with two tin boxes, a shot-gun, £100 in cash and an agreement with an up-country farmer to work for a year in exchange for his keep. That was in 1925. By the time I first met him in 1936 he had set up on his own, survived the worst of the Depression, and was winning a name as a progressive farmer, with as yet no thought of politics. Like Cincinnatus he was called from the plough, or rather called himself, to the battlefield of politics immediately after the Second World War.[3]

It was the war that brought about this change of direction. Within a few months of volunteering for the KAR on its outbreak, he had become a Lieutenant-Colonel. This rapid promotion was the result of a threatened mutiny by a labour battalion stationed in the NFD, most of whose men belonged to the Luo tribe. Michael had learnt to speak their language fluently, which few Europeans could do at the time, and was sent to quell the mutiny. The trouble was due to a misunderstanding; the men thought that they had joined the army to fight the enemy, but found that they were expected to makes roads and dig latrines. Instead of the slouch hats worn by KAR askaris, their headgear was a pillbox cap with a back flat, like that of French *poilus*. This had become a symbol of their inferior status. Lieutenant-Colonel Blundell managed to get the caps replaced by slouch hats, and the mutiny subsided. The battalion then took part in one of the fastest, if not *the* fastest, advances in military history, from the Juba river to northern Ethiopia, covering 2,800 miles over desert, mountain and gorge in forty-two days. After the campaign's victorious end, Michael and his men were transformed into sappers and went off to fight the Japanese.

They returned, he said, with changed ideas. For four years white officers and black askaris and NCOs had shared dangers and hardships, eaten the same food, slept side by side, lived and sometimes died together, and they had come to gain an understanding of each other's point of view. The officers had formed a new respect for the men under their command, the men had seen that white bwanas were just as fallible as they were, and not entitled to a pedestal because of their race. Also they had rubbed shoulders with people from other parts of Africa and from Asia, to whom the ending of white rule was not a distant dream but an approaching reality.

Whereas many of the white officers could foresee what these experiences would lead to, and sympathise to some extent with the nationalist aims, most of those who had remained at home could not. Thus a generation gap was widened by a further gap in understanding. When, after the war, Michael was elected to the Legislative Council as member for the Rift Valley, and subsequently to the leadership of the European elected members, he found no difficulty in getting his ideas across to those of his constituents who had seen active service, whereas older men and women were inclined to regard him as a dangerous radical. 'Unsound' was a word sometimes used. I remember someone saying, in shocked tones, 'He lets Africans call him by his Christian name!'

Thirty-five years later, after all the ups and downs of politics and government, Michael Blundell lives at ease, though not in idleness, in his home set in a beautiful garden on the outskirts of Nairobi, enjoying the role (as he puts it) of the Grand old Colonial Gentleman receiving television interviewers, journalists, and academics researching into colonial history. The controversies that surrounded him have faded into the past so completely that you wonder what the fuss was all about.

It was, of course, about the end of colonial rule and the coming of African independence: about how this was to be accomplished, quickly or slowly, completely or with reservations, or indeed not at all; and about what was to become of the European and Asian communities when the British Government bowed out. Many opinions, many theories, many hopes and many fears were paraded in these disputes.

After an interlude as Minister of Agriculture, Michael Blundell devoted his energies to attempting to convince his fellow Europeans that it was useless to imitate Canute. The only course open to them, he said, was to bow to the inevitable and make the best terms they could in the light of various pledges given by the British Government over the years, that the 'immigrant communities' would not be abandoned or betrayed. In this task he had wise allies and advisers in the shape of Wilfred Havelock, Humphrey Slade and others.

His political opponents, who substantially outnumbered his supporters, took their stand on these pledges, the last of which was made by Alan Lennox Boyd, Secretary of State for the Colonies, in 1958. Former pledges had been underpinned by actions. The closer settlement scheme of 1948 had offered tenancies to last for forty-four years, and the scheme continued to operate, with an office and director in London, until 1960. Tenants were, presumably, entitled to assume that the landlord would be around in forty-four years' time to fulfil his part of the bargain, which was to hand over the title-deeds of the land. A tenancy entered into in 1959 would have carried through until the year 2003. After the conference held at Lancaster House in London in 1960, the scheme was wound up and the tenancies lapsed. 'No surrender' was the rallying-cry of Michael's opponents, always a more stirring one than 'come to terms'. The Churchillian spirit was invoked – in vain. Between January and March 1960, the Secretary of State for the Colonies, Iain Macleod, wrote 'finis' to the chapters of British rule in Kenya and of white settlement. Both were to be ended as quickly as possible, and in stages; in the event, the process took less than four years.

They were uncomfortable years for Michael. The New Kenya Group that he had formed in 1959, open to all races, cooperated with the British Government in various measures taken to ensure a peaceful transition from colony to independent nation. (By then there were two African parties at loggerheads with each other, which bedevilled the process considerably.) The opponents of the New Kenya Group, led by Group-Captain 'Puck' Briggs, were sincere and honest men and women who kept their heads buried in the sand. In their opinion, Michael and his supporters had sold the pass they had been elected to defend. There was a much-publicised incident at Nairobi airport when, on Michael's return from the conference at Lancaster House, thirty sixpenny pieces were cast at his feet. For two years, he told me, he and Gerry, his wife, avoided Muthaiga Club because so many of its members cut him dead. At a meeting held in Eldoret, a woman speaking in the pinched Afrikaans accent demanded: 'Will Mr Blundell tell us when he is going to have his daughter circumcised?' The names of Judas Iscariot and Quisling were bandied about.

The dogs barked, the caravan passed. The Grand Old Colonial Gentleman sits on his veranda embowered in orchids grown in tubs, looking out on his garden with its flowering creepers, its bougainvillea-smothered trees and its cluster of palms – strange, flamboyant cycads whose feathery foliage reminds me of a Kori bustard giving his display. Fire-finches hop about, and now and then a handsome cock wydah bird, trailing his long black tail, dives from an oleander bush to join in. At breakfast on the veranda come juicy pawpaws and grapefruits, at luncheon soft, ripe avocadoes of enormous size and fat asparagus of delicate flavour. You can hear the milk-provider mooing from a nearby field. Friends and acquaintances, black and white, look in for a chat. Cascades of improvised music flow from a study littered with data on the classification of plants. Michael combines green fingers with botanical erudition: the first volume of an illustrated guide to *The Wildflowers of Kenya* has been published, and a second is on the way.

Botany, ecology, music, politics, cooking (since Gerry's death) and the byways of history are among his many interests, but I think that conversation is his strongest suit. Words flow in sparkling torrents, often witty, unexpected and provocative of thought. As a public speaker he was never a spellbinder. The farmers he addressed in country districts sometimes thought he was speaking above their heads and some of them resented it. His enemies – and he did make enemies – thought him egocentric, conceited, and over-fond of the limelight. He was apt, on occasion, to work himself up into a state where tears came to his eyes, in those days condemned as effeminate. But his friends found him warm-hearted, generous, sensitive, amusing, and refreshingly devoid of that parochialism apt to afflict colonial gentlemen, not to mention ladies, young and old.

Michael was at home with Africans because he spoke his mind and pulled their legs without a trace either of that arrogance they had so often to put up with, as a rule with remarkable tolerance, or with the sycophancy that white people of a later generation sometimes display, and which they despise. It is rare to meet Africans without a sense of humour, and theirs and Michael's strike the same chord.

How much of history is shaped by individuals, and how much by trends of the time, is, I believe, a matter for discussion among historians. There is obviously a balance: the question is, how to apportion the influence of the *Zeitgeist* and that of the leader. A host of men and women have shaped Kenya's recent history, but two have stood out: Jomo Kenyatta and, at least in my opinion, Michael Blundell.

Suppose, in Kenya's case, the leader of the Africans had preached revenge not reconciliation, and the leader of the Europeans a fight to the last ditch instead of coming to terms, the birth of independence would have been bitter and bloody instead of smoother and more amicable than almost everyone had expected it to be. Or suppose, in another context, that Michael Blundell had taken his tin boxes, his shot-gun and his £100 to Rhodesia instead of to Kenya, and that Ian Smith had grown up in Nairobi, the history of those two countries would not have been the same.

The name of Jomo Kenyatta is respected throughout the world as a great African statesman; that of Michael Blundell is little known outside the circle of his friends. Both have done the state some service in their time, and in their way.

So, past all the tributes to Twenty Great Glorious Years and on to the airport, like all airports crowded and chaotic, offering passengers an alternative of rushing for the gate or boring long delays. Everywhere were queues, but nothing to tell you which queue was for where. Looking for Sudan Airways, I found myself swept into a Somali pop group returning festively to their homes, and narrowly escaped getting carried off to Mogadishu. I changed queues just in time, and thought back to earlier flights over Uganda, over Sudan, over the Sudd invisible now more than 30,000 feet below. In three hours' time we halted briefly at Khartoum, with its huge new international airport complex. Then Heathrow.

I shall not be around to see the end of the next twenty years of Kenya's independence but hope they will be Great and Glorious too.

Notes and sources

CHAPTER 1

1 – Dr Burkitt's story has been told in *Under the Sun* by his partner, Dr J. R. Gregory (The English Press, Nairobi, 1951).

2 – This episode is described in full in *East Africa and Its Invaders* by R. Coupland (Oxford, 1938).

3 – *History of East Africa*, Vol. 1, Chapter x, by John Flint (Oxford, 1963).

4 – One such bride was Karen Blixen, née Dinesen; arriving at Mombasa on 13 January 1914, she was married next day to Baron von Blixen-Finecke, but by the District Commissioner, not in the cathedral. Prince Wilhelm of Sweden was a witness; the Protectorate's Governor, Sir Henry Belfield, sent his dining car, and the American millionaire Northrup McMillan his cook, to accompany the pair by rail to Nairobi.

5 – *Africa View* by Julian Huxley (Chatto & Windus, 1931).

6 – *Letters from Africa, 1914–1931*, ed. by Frans Lasson (Weidenfeld & Nicolson and University of Chicago Press, 1981).

7 – Private communication from Mrs Rose Hodson.

8 – See Grogan's own account, with A. H. Sharp, in *From the Cape to Cairo*, 1900, and his biography *The Legendary Grogan* by Leda Farrant (Hamish Hamilton, 1981).

9 – The country was called the East Africa Protectorate from the start of British rule in 1895 until 1920, when it was re-named Kenya Colony. Originally it included part of what is now Uganda.

CHAPTER 2

1 – *Pioneer's Scrapbook*, ed. by E. Huxley and Arnold Curtis (Evans Bros, 1980).

2 – A fuller account of this trek is given in *No Easy Way* by E. Huxley, *East African Standard*, Nairobi, 1957.

3 – The rupee was worth 1s. 4d. until 1920. In the following year the shilling, linked to the British pound sterling, became the Colony's official currency. It is now the Kenya shilling.

4 – *Freedom and After* by Tom Mboya (Deutsch, 1963); and *Tom Mboya: The Man Kenya Wanted to Forget* (Heinemann, 1982).

CHAPTER 3

1 – *White Man's Country: Lord Delamere and the Making of Kenya* by E. Huxley, Vol. 11, Chapter xxi (Macmillan, 1935; Chatto & Windus paperback, 1980).

2 – These and others of Nellie's projects are described in *Nellie: Letters from*

Africa (Weidenfeld & Nicolson, 1981; and paperback, 1984).

3 – *White Mischief* by James Fox (Jonathan Cape, 1982; Penguin, 1984).

4 – *Blackwood's Magazine*, Vol. 253, April 1943: 'The Boma Trading Company' by J. R. Riddell.

CHAPTER 4

1 – These and subsequent comments from the diaries of Lady Moore, 1924–1947, MSS Brit Emp s 466, Rhodes House Library, Oxford.

2 – 'The Night of the Hyena', unpublished autobiography of Eric Dutton, DSO, CBE, lent by his widow Myrtle.

3 – *Kenya's Opportunity* by Lord Altrincham (Faber & Faber, 1955).

4 – *Letters from Africa, 1914–1931*, op. cit.

5 – Sir Edward Grigg, subsequently Lord Altrincham, paid this tribute in the dedication of his book: 'To my wife, whose Welfare League for all races in Kenya opened a new Life to the Womanhood of Dark Africa.'

6 – Lady Moore's diaries, op. cit.

7 – *Kenya Diary, 1902–1906*, by Richard Meinertzhagen (Oliver & Boyd, 1957; reprinted by Eland Books, 1983).

8 – I am indebted to Mrs Kit Taylor for allowing me to quote from her mother's diaries; to her daughter Kathini for help on occasions too many to name; and to her husband Donald Graham for his recollections of the past.

CHAPTER 5

1 – Beryl Markham, née Clutterbuck, describes this incident in *West With the Night* (Houghton Mifflin, Boston, 1942; republished by Virago Press, London, 1984).

2 – From tape recordings made by Mrs Cockie Hoogterp for the author. I wish I could convey in writing even an echo of her wit and talent as a raconteur.

3 – *Indians in Kenya*, Cmd 1922 (1923).

CHAPTER 6

1 – For a full account of Delamere's life and works see *White Man's Country*, op. cit.

2 – Manyatta is the word always used for these Maasai villages, but the correct term is engang. Manyattas were built especially for the warriors with their mothers and girl-friends, while the engang was the family dwelling. See *Maasai* by Tepilit Ole Saitoti & Carol Beckwith (Elm Tree Books, 1980).

3 – Apparent only: a rigid code of conduct governs behaviour in tribal societies. As Clarence Buxton put it: 'An individual Maasai is not free to make a choice contrary to the agreement of the group or groups. He would not dream of doing so.' Buxton papers, MSS BE 390, Rhodes House Library, Oxford.

4 – Ibid.

5 – From diaries kept by Genessie, Lady Claud Hamilton, which she has kindly allowed me to read.

6 – Several tribes have changed their names, because those by which they were formerly known were really nicknames given them either by the Maasai or by Swahili porters of the early safaris. Thus Lumbwa is a corruption of m'bwa, meaning dog, their correct name being Kipsigis. The people formerly known as Suk have become Pokot, Suk being a word for snot.

7 – My thanks are due to Sir Colin Campbell of Finlay Muir's of Glasgow for lending me his company's history of the tea industry in Kenya.

8 – The Nandi bear is discussed in *On the Track of Unknown Animals* by Bernard Heuvelmans (Rupert Hart-Davies, 1959).

9 – Robert Frost's forthcoming biography of Sir Philip Mitchell.

10 – The history of the East African Literature Bureau has been told by Mr Charles Richards, OBE, D. Litt, in *No Carpet on the Floor*, MS in the Rhodes House Library in Oxford.

CHAPTER 7

1 – Grateful thanks to Arthur and Tobina Cole for allowing me to quote from their collection of Galbraith and Lady Eleanor Cole's letters and papers. Also for the loan of photographs.

2 – There is a large literature about the Powys family. I have relied mainly on *The Powys Brothers* by Richard Perceval Graves.

3 – *Pioneers' Scrapbook*, op. cit.

4 – *The Powys Brothers*, op. cit.

5 – *Black Laughter* by Llewelyn Powys (Jonathan Cape, 1925).

6 – *The Letters of Llewelyn Powys*, ed. by Louis Wilkinson (John Lane, 1943).

7 – Cole collection, op. cit.

8 – *Random Recollections of a Pioneer Kenya Settler* by Lady Eleanor Cole (privately printed).

9 – Cole collection, op. cit.

10 – *The Letters of Llewelyn Powys*, op. cit.

11 – Cole collection, op. cit.

12 – I am indebted to Miss Kathleen (Tuppence) Hill-Williams for information about the Moral Rearmament movement in Kenya.

13 – *Random Recollections*, op. cit.

14 – *The Boer War* by Thomas Pakenham (Weidenfeld & Nicolson, 1979).

15 – *White Mischief*, op. cit.

16 – *African Saga* by Mirella Ricciardi (Collins, 1981).

17 – Private communication from Mrs Anne Carnelley.

18 – Several of Gilbert Colvile's former managers have given me their impressions of his character and life-style, including Messrs W. J. Martin, Gerald Romer, David Hazelden, Frank Beletti and Paddy Grattan. Mr Hugh Barclay has been indefatigable in ferreting out information about this enigmatic man, and Mrs Lorna Dempster went to much trouble to put me in touch with people who knew him.

19 – Thanks to Mr David Christie-Miller for these recollections.

20 – *White Mischief*, op. cit.

21 – Mr W. J. Martin, as above.

NOTES AND SOURCES

CHAPTER 8

1 – Mrs Dorothy Vaughan, daughter of the first Mrs Cobb, has generously lent me letters, photographs and the manuscript of her own recollections of her childhood and of her father's career.

2 – Mrs Hilda Furse and her sister Kathleen (Tuppence) Hill-Williams, have helped me greatly over this chapter.

3 – Letter from Mrs Anne Carnelley.

4 – From Delamere to his wife Glady dated 22 April 1930, quoted in *White Man's Country*, Vol II, op. cit.

CHAPTER 9

1 – Mrs Billie Nightingale, Captain and Mary Fey's granddaughter, most kindly helped me with this chapter. There is also a short account of the Feys' arrival on the Kinangop in *Pioneers' Scrapbook*, op. cit.

2 – *Wide Horizon* by Venn Fey (Vantage Press, U.S.A., 1982).

3 – *A Lifetime's Recollections of Kenya Tribal Beekeeping*, by Jim Nightingale interviewed by Dr Eva Crane (International Bee Research Association, London, 1983).

4 – From Mrs Barbie Nightingale, Stanley Polhill's daughter.

5 – 'Ages Ago', by Walter de la Mare.

6 – *Pioneers' Scrapbook*, op. cit.

7 – Ibid.

8 – Raymond Hook's sister Mrs Sylvia Atkinson and his daughter Mrs Hazel Holmes of Nanyuki most kindly helped me with recollections and information about Hook's career.

9 – See *The Spotted Lion* by Kenneth Gandar Dower, and two books about Raymond Hook by John Pollard, *Adventure Begins in Kenya* (Robert Hale, 1957) and *African Zoo Man* (Robert Hale, 1963).

10 – *Castle to Caravan: An Autobiography* by Lady Victoria Fletcher ('Taffy') (Summit Press, Canberra, Australia, 1963).

11 – *Letters from Africa, 1913–1931*, op cit.

CHAPTER 10

1 – *Pioneers' Scrapbook*, op. cit.

2 – From a letter in the possession of Mrs Rose Dyer, who has generously lent me her papers about her mother, Elizabeth Powys.

3 – Letter to Alyse Gregory in the Powys archive in the Harry Ransom Humanities Research Center, The University of Texas at Austin.

4 – From Clarence Buxton's papers in the Rhodes House Library, op. cit.

5 – I am grateful to Mrs Delia Craig and Mrs Rose Dyer for impressions of Will Powys' life and character, and also to his sister Mrs Lucy Penny, and his niece Mrs Isobel Marks, for their help.

6 – Public Record Office, Attorney-General's deposit (Kenya), files 142 and 4/142.

7 – *The East African Standard*, 3 November 1934 and succeeding days.

CHAPTER 11

1 – Grateful thanks to Mr Robert Tatton-Brown for letting me read his diaries, which describe this encounter.

2 – Sir Richard Turnbull, GCMG, probably the greatest living authority on the Somali people of northern Kenya, has been more than generous with his time and advice relating to the old NFD, and I am very grateful.

3 – 'It is worth remembering,' Sir Richard Turnbull has written, 'that but for a handful of District Commissioners and a score of policemen, this Somali wave would have washed over Kenya sixty years ago.' It did, indeed, reach the foothills of Mt Kenya, where a force of Somali invaders was repelled by the Meru tribe in 1892. Its leader, in defeat, ordered his bodyguard to shoot him as he knelt on his prayer-mat. There can be no doubt that the Somalis would have returned to the charge had not the British administration, flimsy as it was, intervened.

4 – Ethnologists say that Dorobo – Il Torobo – is 'a slightly derisive' name given to these forest people by the Maasai, and that they themselves use the term Okiek. Some thirty groups have been identified, living in relative isolation from one another in the forested mountains. Probably their number totals no more than 8,000 or 9,000. Each group speaks the language of the tribe with which it is most closely associated, and many of the groups are in process of assimilation into the major tribes. See *Portraits of Africa*, by Mohamed Amin and Peter Moll (Harvill, 1983).

CHAPTER 12

1 – From the diary of Sir Robert Armitage, KCMG, deposited in the Rhodes House Library, Oxford.

2 – *To My Wife, Fifty Camels* by Alyce Reece (Harvill, 1963).

3 – From Mr Robert Tatton-Brown's diary.

4 – A barramil is a copper vessel, weighing 37½ lbs when empty, holding ten gallons of water. Two barramils make up one camel load.

5 – Related by Mr Robin Wainwright, CMG, whose help and advice, together with that of his wife Bridget, I gratefully acknowledge.

6 – Tich Miles' surviving letters and papers are in the possession of his nephew Canon Robert Miles, who most generously put them at my disposal. The quotations that follow are from this collection.

7 – A somewhat highly coloured account of this action is given by E. A. T. Dutton in *Lillibullero, or The Golden Road* (privately printed in Zanzibar), which also describes in detail Tich Miles' life at Mega.

8 – *With a Women's Unit in Serbia, Salonika and Sebastopol* by Dr I. Emslie Williams (Norgate, 1928).

9 – Dolly Miles wrote an account of her war-time experiences in 1930, from which these extracts have been taken. In Canon Miles' collection.

10 – From Sir Richard Turnbull's papers, most of which are in the Rhodes House Library archives.

11 – Ibid.

12 – From the unpublished memoirs of Sir Charles Markham, Bart. My thanks for letting me read them.

CHAPTER 13

1 – *With a Prehistoric People* by W. S. & K. Routledge (Edward Arnold, 1910).
2 – The Morris Carter Commission was set up by a Joint Select Committee of the House of Commons to survey the land situation, and in particular to assess and report upon the claims of the Kikuyu to land they asserted had been lost by them to white settlement. The chairman was a judge, Sir Morris Carter, the other members F. O'B. Wilson and Rupert Hemsted. The Commission investigated every claim and finally recommended adding land to the reserve, amounting to rather less than three per cent of the total, to compensate for what had been lost. The report was published in 1934, and in due course its recommendations were carried out.
3 – *Kenya Diary, 1902–06*, by Richard Meinertzhagen (first published in 1957 by Oliver & Boyd; republished 1983 by Eland Books, London).
4 – *Facing Mount Kenya* by Jomo Kenyatta (Secker & Warburg, 1969).
5 – The respect in which Malinowski was held in academic circles was not always matched by that of practical administrators in the field. In the journal *Africa*, Philip Mitchell urged that Colonial Service cadets should study 'the modern Africa' rather than 'the eccentricities of remote Papuans, the scars they make on their bottoms and their unsavoury sexual habits scarcely any anthropologist can keep off.'
6 – From a tape-recording made in Kitale, Kenya, in 1984, when Mr Whitehouse was interviewed by Dr David Throup and Miss Pamela Scott.
7 – From a disc recording of several of Kenyatta's major speeches made just before and after independence, issued after his death under the title 'In Memoriam'. This speech was made in May 1963.

CHAPTER 14

1 – *The Portuguese Period in East Africa* by Justus Strandes. Transactions of the Kenya History Society, published by the East African Literature Bureau (Nairobi, 1961).
2 – *The Land of Zinj* by C. H. Stigand (Constable, 1913).
3 – *The History of Malindi* by Esmond Bradley Martin (East African Literature Bureau, Nairobi, 1973).
4 – *Cargoes of the East* by Esmond Bradley and Chryssee Perry Martin (Elm Tree Books, London, 1978).
5 – *History of East Africa*, Vol. 1, ed. by Roland Oliver & Gervase Mathew. Chapter v, by G. S. P. Freeman-Grenville.
6 – *Cargoes of the East*, op. cit. Chapter on Lamu.
7 – *Pioneers' Scrapbook*, op. cit.
8 – A summary of Alexandre Tinné's story is given in *The Challenge of Africa* (Aldus Books, London, 1971) and also in *Africa Explored* by Christopher Hibberd.

CHAPTER 15

1 – Jim Mollison was the first to fly the Atlantic solo from east to west, but he started from Ireland. The next was John Grierson in 1934, who made a prolonged and interrupted flight from Rochester to Hudson's Bay, coming down at Reykjavik and having to return by sea for spare parts. I am indebted to Mr A. Doyle, chief librarian to the Civil Aviation Authority, for this information.

2 – From Lady Francis Scott's diary quoted in Pamela Scott's unpublished autobiography, by kind permission of Miss Scott.

3 – *So Rough a Wind* by Michael Blundell (Weidenfeld & Nicolson, 1964). I am deeply grateful to Sir Michael for his practical help in many ways, and for the privilege of enjoying his stimulating flow of talk on Kenya's past and present and other matters.

As well as those whose help has already been acknowledged, I should like to thank many others who have answered questions, spoken into a tape-recorder and assisted me in other ways; among them Sir John Hewett, whose memories go back to 1912; Mr Mervyn Cowie, father of Kenya's National Parks; Archdeacon Peter Bostock, the missionary pioneer; Mr Hugh Barclay, whose memory is prodigious; Mr Cen Hill, whose name is synonomous with enlightened farming; Mrs Morna Walker-Munro, a friend from the early 1920s; Mrs Cecily Hinde of Timau; Mrs Bey Fletcher, OBE, of Nanyuki; Robin and Biddy Davis, also of Nanyuki; Mrs Molly Hodge; Jimmy and Rose Caldwell; Mr Jim Cooper; Mrs Sylvia Dawson, formerly of Sotik; and others no less helpful, but too numerous to name.

I am grateful to the following friends (in alphabetical order) for lending me the following photographs: to Lady Altrincham for nos 1a and b, 8a, and 14a; to Arthur and Tobina Cole for nos 4a, b and c, 5a and b; to Mrs Lorna Dempster for 1a and 5b; to Mrs Hilda Furze for 6a; to Mrs Hazel Holmes for 3b; to Mrs Cockie Hoogterp for 3d; and to Mrs Dorothy Vaughan for 7a, b and c. The rest are the author's.

Glossary

askari	soldier or policeman
banda	temporary dwelling, often open at one side
baraza	a meeting or gathering
boma	a fort; administrative post; round enclosure for night-time stabling of livestock
bui-bui	black robe covering the whole person, with slits for eyes, worn by Muslim women
bwana	master, sir
debbi	four-gallon paraffin or petrol tin, used as a measure, for carrying water, and, when flattened, for roofing etc.
duka	small shop
fundi	artisan, skilled or semi-skilled workman
harambee	pull together
kanzu	long cotton robe
kekoi	wrap-over skirt, generally brightly printed cotton
khol	powder used to darken the area around the eyes (Arabic)
kiama	council of elders
kikapu	woven two-handled basket
kipande	certificate carried by males outside their tribal areas, with thumb-print for identification if illiterate
laibon	individual believed to have supernatural powers, influential in Maasai and related tribes
machan	platform in a tree for use of big game hunters (Indian)
manyatta	group of Maasai huts occupied by related people
mira'a	twigs of a tree which, when chewed, provide a mild narcotic
m'zee	old
ngoma	dance
panga	double-bladed implement for slashing
posho	maize-meal
shamba	anything from a large farm to a vegetable plot; small-holding; cultivated land
shauri	matter for discussion; dispute; argument; business
siafu	biting ants
sukuma	push
tej	strong barley mead widely drunk in Ethiopia
thahu	a form of spiritual uncleanliness, generally caused by giving offence to ancestral spirits, among the Kikuyu
toto	child
uhuru	freedom
uji	gruel, generally made of maize or millet meal (Kikuyu)

Index

Compiled by Douglas Matthews

Abaluyhia people, 18
Abyssinia, 43–4, 150, 153, 169
Adams, John and Hilda, 44
Adamson, George and Joy, 244
African Highlands tea company, 82
African literature, 87–9
Afrikaners (Boers): trek, 22–6
Aga Khan, 9, 51, 230
Ainsworth, John, 45
Alice, Princess, 240
Amin, Idi, 71, 90, 219
Anderson, Colonel, 18
Archer, Geoffrey, 44
Armitage, Sir Robert, 154
Arusha, 63
Atkinson, Dr A. E., 94

Babati, Tanganyika, 63–5
Baganda people, 71
Baker, Sir Herbert, 47–8, 228
Balfour, Arthur James (1st Earl), 100–1
Barclay, Hugh and Patsy, 40–1
Baring, Sir Evelyn, 178–9
Bastard, Seagar, 126
Beynon, General and Mrs, 123–5
Beynon, Kate, 124
Birkbeck, Ben, 62–3
Black, Tom Campbell, 239
Blixen, Karen (Tania), 15, 51, 62, 132
Blixen-Finecke, Baron Bror von, 62–3, 65,
  239
Blixen, Eva, Baroness (Bror's second wife), 65
Blundell, Gerry, 247–8
Blundell, Michael, 107, 244–9; *The Wild-
  flowers of Kenya*, 248
Boma Trading Company, 42–3, 136
Boran people, 149–50
Bournier, Henri, 204, 206, 210
Boyd, Alan Lennox (*later* Viscount), 246
Breda, brothers van, 24, 136
Briggs, Group Captain 'Puck', 247
British East Africa Disabled Officers Coop-
  erative (BEADOC), 79–81
Brooke Bonds tea company, 81–2
Brooke-Popham, Air Vice-Marshal Sir
  Robert, 154
Broughton, Sir Delves, 108
Broughton, Lady, *see* Colvile, Diana
Buchman, Frank, 103
Bull, Emily, 111
Burkitt, Dr Roland, 3–4, 6, 101, 122
Buxton, Clarence, 75–7
Byng-Hall, John, 73
Byrne, Sir Joseph (Butty), 52–3, 142

Cagnolo, Father, 186
Caledonian Society, 39
Campbell, Roy, 131
Capricorn Africa Society, 138–9
Carnelley, Stephen, 106
Cartwright, Algernon, 152
Cartwright, Rose, 94, 104, 152, 158–9
Chamberlain, Neville, 47
Chapman, Paul, 126
Cheese, John Ethelstan, 180–1
Cherangani hills, 83–4
Chittock, Neville, 205
Church Missionary Society, 89
Church of Goodwill, Kekopey, 104
Church of Scotland Mission, 50, 185
Churchill, Winston, 43
Clutterbuck, Beryl, *see* Markham, Beryl
Clutterbuck, Charles, 238–9
Cobb, Dorothy, 112
Cobb, Edward Powys: life, 110–15, 131; EH
  visits, 116–17; retirement and death, 117–
  18; and Polhill's accident, 122
Cobb, Mrs Edward Powys, 110, 112
Cobb, Ethel (*née* Dicksee; EPC's second
  wife), 114–15, 117–18
Cockie, *see* Hoogterp, Jacqueline
Coffee Board of Kenya, 57
Cohen, Andrew, 71
Cole, Arthur and Tobina, 104
Cole, Berkeley, 93, 96, 103, 170, 240
Cole, Lady Eleanor (Nell; *née* Balfour), 100–
  4; builds church, 104, 118; on Cobb, 115;
  rents Il Pinguan, 141
Cole, Galbraith: land and farming, 92–5, 99,
  101–2, 134; deported, 96; health, 96, 101–
  3; character, 99; marriage to Lady Elea-
  nor, 100, 104; children, 102; death, 103
Colonial Office, 68–70
Colvile, Diana (*formerly* Broughton *later* Del-
  amere), 108–9
Colvile, Gilbert, 92, 104–9, 125
Colvile, Sir Henry, 104–5
Colvile, Lady (Gilbert's mother), 101, 105
Cook, Albert, 51
Cornell, 'Daddy', 207, 210
Corrigan, Laura, 61, 66
Coryndon, Sir Robert, 25
Cotter, Captain J. L., 68
Craig, David and Delia (*née* Powys), 140, 243
Cramb, Captain, 120
Creech-Jones, Arthur, 71, 196
Crespigny, Sir Claud de, 60

Davis, Robin, 242

Dawson, William and Sylvia, 81
de Ganahl (American gold miner), 20–1
de Janzé, Alice, 39
de la Mare, Walter, 123
Delamere, Hugh Cholmondeley, 3rd Baron:
    death, 2, 66; EH's biography of, 2, 44,
    53–4, 182; and Grogan, 17; and develop-
    ment of Tanganyika, 29; farming, 30,
    73–4, 77–8, 92–3; and Maasai, 75, 94,
    105; land ownership, 92, 95; character,
    92–4; and bush fire, 101; and Cobb, 115
Delamere, Lady Florence (née Cole; Lord D's
    first wife), 92–4; death, 103
Delamere, Lady Gwladys, (Glady; Lord D's
    second wife): agrees to EH's biography of
    Lord D, 2; meets EH in Nairobi, 15, 17;
    appearance and character, 15, 46, 57; and
    Byrnes, 52; home in Loresho, 54; social life
    and good works, 55–6; death, 57; relations
    with Delamere, 94; and Glenday, 165
Delamere, Tom Cholmondeley, 4th Baron,
    109
Deloraine (house, Rongai), 67, 240–1
Dempster family, 73
Denbigh, Rudolph Feilding, 9th Earl of, 130–
    1
Devonshire, V. C. W. Cavendish, 9th Duke
    of, 68
Dinka people, 219
Doig, Dr, 127
Dorobo people, 121, 142–3, 155, 157
Douglas, Alec, 137
Douglas, Delia, 137
Dower, Kenneth Gander, 129
Duncan (Scots missionary), 186
Durand, Colonel, 123, 125
Dutton, Eric, 46–8

East Africa High Commission (later Com-
    munity), 89–90
East African Literature Bureau, 89–90
East African Standard, 53, 55, 83
East African Syndicate, 97, 99
East, Rupert, 88
Eboo, Sir Pirbhai, 230
Eddy, Mr and Mrs (of Eldoret), 25
Edward VII, King, 64
Edward, Prince of Wales (later King Edward
    VIII), 46, 48–9, 52, 63–5
Egerton College, 235–6
Egerton of Tatton, Maurice, 4th Baron, 137,
    235, 237
Eldoret, 20–2, 24–5, 229
Elgeyo people, 84
Elgon, Mount, 85
Elkington, Mr and Mrs Jim, 59–60
Elkington, Margaret, 61–3
Elmenteita, Lake, 73, 100
Emslie, Dr, 172–3
Enniskillen, David Cole, 6th Earl of, 104
Erroll, Idina Hay, Countess of, 39, 52
Erroll, Josslyn Hay, 22nd Earl of, 39, 56, 108
Erroll, Molly, Countess of, 108
European Agricultural Settlement Board, 117

Fabian Colonial Bureau, 144, 196

Farah, Jama, 102–3
Fey, Captain Ernest and Mary, 119–20, 123
Fey, Jim and Nora, 119
Finch Hatton, Denys, 62–3, 158, 239
Finlay, James, and Co., 81
Fletcher, Miles, 131
Fletcher, Lady Victoria (Taffy; née Fielding),
    130–1
Forbes, Rosita, 78
Fort Jesus, 7–9
Fox, James, 105–6
Freddie Mutesa, Kabaka of Buganda, 71
Furse, David, 127–8

Gacheche (Kikuyu), 187, 189–90
Gascoigne, Major Lionel and Renie, 126, 133
Gavaghan, Terence, 147
George V, King, 49, 64, 88
Gichuhi (Dorobo beekeeper), 121
Gikammeh (farm), 28–9
Girouard, Sir Percy, 23, 44
Glenday, Vincent G., 148–50, 164–5, 167,
    177–8, 236
goat-bags, 166–7
gold fields, 17–22
Goldsmith, Oliver, 231
Gourlay, Ernest and Joan, 218
Grant, Hugh, 75
Grant, Major Josceline (Jos; EH's father): at
    EH's homecoming, 27–8; early farming,
    28–30; business enterprises, 31; servants,
    34–5; and Kikuyu parties, 36; and Erroll,
    39; visits Fey, 119; rejects soldier-
    settlement land, 133; and EH's safaris,
    136, 152, 218; and Kikuyu, 187; in world
    wars, 217; death, 217
Grant, Nellie (EH's mother): at EH's home-
    coming, 27–8, 31; early farming, 28–32;
    servants, 34–6, 213; and Kikuyu parties,
    36–7; social life and neighbours, 38–41,
    44; and Charles Taylor, 57; and Genessie
    Long, 79; visits Cobbs, 115–16; visits Fey,
    119; and soldier-settlement land, 136; on
    safari with EH, 136, 152, 157–8; and H. B.
    Sharpe, 148, 152, 157–8; and Dolly Miles,
    174; and Kikuyu, 182–3, 187, 190–1;
    visits coast, 204, 210–11; plans inheritance
    for EH, 215–17; and Jos's death, 217; and
    EH's final safari, 218; sells farm, 233;
    retirement and death, 233–4; and Egerton
    School, 235–6
Gray, Sir John, 206
Grigg, Sir Edward, 46–9, 52, 68
Grigg, Joan, Lady, 49–52, 55, 170
Grogan, Ewart, 16–17, 66

Haldeman family, 52
Hamilton, Lord Claud, 79
Happy Valley, see Wanjohi Valley
Harcourt, Lewis, 1st Viscount, 96
Harries, Mr and Mrs 'Black', 40
Hasan, Sheikh of Malindi, 8
Havelock, Wilfred, 246
Hayes-Sadler, Sir James, 23
Herbert, Lady Muriel, see Jex-Blake, Lady
    Muriel

Herodotus, 219
Hickey, John, 55
Hill, Harold and Clifford, 211
Hill-Williams, Gertrude, 111, 113–14, 127
Hill-Williams, Hilda (*later* Furze), 111, 113–14
Hill-Williams, John, 110–11, 113
Hill-Williams, 'Tuppence', 111, 113, 127–8
Hoey, Cecil, 22–6
Hohnel, Lieut. von, 140
Hollis, A. C., 83
Hoogterp, Jacqueline ('Cockie'; *formerly*: 1, Birkbeck; 2, Blixen), 61–6, 116
Hoogterp, Jan, 42, 47–8, 65–6
Hook, Bryan, 124, 128
Hook, Joan, 129–30
Hook, Raymond, 127–30, 137, 158
Hook, Commander Logan, 127
Howden, Frank, 73
Hughes, Dorothy, 216
Huxley, Elspeth: return to Africa (1933), 1; goes hatless in sun, 4–5; photography, 14; lunches with Mboya, 26; flies back to England, 85–6, 90–1; reports on African literature, 87–9; hunting and shooting, 124, 136; on crime and justice, 143–5; on safaris, 148, 152, 155–61, 218; journey down Nile and return to England, 219–23; *Red Strangers*, 197; *White Man's Country*, 54, 182
Huxley, Gervas (EH's husband): goes to Ceylon, 1–2; buys gold shares, 21; bell trick, 35; rejoins EH, 79, 82; and tea production, 82; and Nellie's inheritance plans, 215–16; on safari, 218
Huxley, Julian, 11

Imperial British East Africa Company, 10
Isiolo, 152–5, 243–4
Ismailis, 230

Jacobs (of The Dustpan), 62
Jex-Blake, Dr, 174–5
Jex-Blake, Lady Muriel (*née* Herbert), 172, 175
Johnson, L. A., 20–1
Johnson, Osa Martin, 137
Joyce, Anne, 211, 214
Joyce, Frank and Mary-Early, 211–15

Kakamega, 17–18, 20–2
Kamau, Geoffrey, 235
Kamba people, 15
Kapila (lawyer), 108
Kapsiliat (farm), 83–5
Karanja wa Kinoko (cook), 27, 34–6, 152, 161, 183, 187, 218, 234
Karanja wa Mokorro (herdsman), 36–7, 234
Karanja, Benson, 234–5
Karatina, 193–4
Kariuki the fundi, 234
Kashoggi, Adnan, 242
Kekopey (ranch), 93, 95–6, 99–100, 102–4, 134, 232
Kenton College, 120

Kenya: depression in, 10–11, 55; gold, 17–22; birthrate, 52; and health of whites, 54; government and administration, 67–70; Africans' rights, 68; composition of settlers, 132; women in, 224–5; since Independence, 224–49; population, 231; European contracts in, 232; education in, 235–7; economy, 237–8; tourism, 243; achieves independence, 246–7
Kenya and Uganda Railways and Harbours (*formerly* Uganda Railway), 10–12, 25
Kenya Meat Commission, 107
Kenya, Mount, 47, 123, 186
Kenyatta, Jomo, 179, 192, 196–8; imprisonment, 199–201; political aims, 201–3; recruits women's army, 224; family, 226–7; achievements, 248–9; *Facing Mount Kenya*, 202
Kenyatta, Margaret (JK's daughter), 225–7
Kenyatta, Wambui (JK's first wife), 226
Kericho, 79–82
Keringet (farm), 110, 112–14, 131
Kiberenge, 141–2
Kigoma, 29
Kikuyu people: work for EH's parents, 28–9, 32; social system, 33, 185; parties and dancing, 36–8; and Lindstroms, 39; female circumcision, 50, 191–3; body-smell, 72; Maasai attack, 79, 188–9; killed by Samburu, 142, 145; EH studies, 182–95, 197; tribal life, 182–3; fighting, 188–9; and spirits, 190–1; influenced by Kenyatta, 198; and Mau Mau, 203; handshake, 234
Kikuyu Central Association, 196
Kilima Kiu, 211–12, 214
Kilimanjaro, Mount, 12
Kilindini harbour, 6
Kinangop district, 122–3
Kipling, Rudyard, 135, 156
Kipsigis (Lumbwa) people, 79, 81–2
Kisii people, 79
Kisima (farm), 133–4, 138
Kisumu, 20

Laikipia plains, 123, 127
Lambert, Archie, 211
Lamu island and town, 204–10; *Chronicle*, 205
Lancaster House conference, 1960, 246–7
Lascelles, Alan, 64
Lee, William, 81–2
Legh, Hon. Piers, 63
Legislative Council, 66, 68–9, 178
Lettow Vorbeck, General Paul von, 57
Lewin, Brigadier Arthur and Phyllis, 221
Lindon, Elia, 172–3
Lindstrom, Gillis ('Fish') and Ingrid, 39–40, 216, 218
Lipscomb, Jack, 115
Llewellyn, John (Long Lew), 150–1, 164
Loder (Scotts' maid), 67
Lokitaung prison, 199–200
Long, Caswell (Boy) and Genessie (*later* Hamilton), 77–9
Loresho (farm), 17, 44, 54, 59

Luo people, 33, 79, 245
Lusaka, 48

Maasai people: and animals, 13; and Sirikwa, 23; wealth, 56; livestock and herding, 73–4, 77, 95, 105; and Delamere, 75, 94, 105; character, 75–7; fights against Kikuyu, 79, 188–9; Colvile and, 105–9; raid Cobb's cattle, 112; Whitehouse and, 199–201; and Wakamba, 211
MacDonald, Malcolm, 179
Mackinder, Sir Halford, 47
Mackinnon, Sir William, 10
Macleod, Iain, 247
Macmillan, Harold, 3
McMillan, Sir Northrup, 150
Makerere University College, Kampala, 87–8
Malindi, 205-6
Malinowski, B., 195–7
Mannin, Ethel, 98
Manvi (gardener), 234
Maralal, 145–6
Marindas (farm), 111, 113–14
Markham, Beryl (née Clutterbuck; later Schumacher), 62, 238–40; West with the Night, 238
Markham, Sir Charles, 17, 178
Markham, Mansfield, 239
Marsabit mountain, 137, 153
Martin, Esmond Bradley, 210
Martin, Hugh, 46
Mary, Queen, 49
Masara (farm), 59–60
Matiba, Kenneth, 243
Mau hills, 27, 30
Mau Mau crisis, 88, 103–4, 107, 199, 202, 210
Mau Narok, 114–16, 118, 122
Maynier (Afrikaner), 170
Mboya, Tom, 26
Mbugwa (servant), 27, 34–6, 82, 116, 174, 234
Meinertzhagen, Richard, 60, 188–9
Menelik II, Emperor of Abyssinia, 150, 169
Menengai mountain, 27, 40
Miles, A. T. ('Tich'), 47, 167–72, 174, 176–7
Miles, Olive Tremayne ('Dolly'), 170, 172–6; death, 177
Milne, Dr and Alison (née Balfour), 100
Milner, Alfred, 1st Viscount, 48
Mitchell, Sir Philip and Lady, 86–8, 178
Moi, Daniel arap, 224, 241
Mombasa, 6, 8–10, 51–2
Moore, Daphne, 46–7, 52
Moore, Henry Monck-Mason, 53
Moore, Monty, VC, 218
Moral Rearmament (MRA), 103–4
Morris Carter Land Commission, 187
Muchoka (headman), 213
Mui (servant), 214
Munster, Count and Countess Paul, 61
Murigo (Kikuyu chief), 183–7, 189, 191, 195
Muthaiga Club, Nairobi, 56, 67, 94, 108, 170, 247

Nairobi: EH arrives in, 15–16; described,

45–6; social life, 60; modern, 225–31
Nakuru, 22–3, 32, 39–40
Nakuru, Lake, 27
Nandi hills, 23; bear, 82–3
Nandi people, 141, 238
Nanyuki, 126–8, 133
Native Lands Trust Ordinance, 1930, 19
Ndabibi (ranch), 106, 109
Nderit (ranch), 78–9
Ndia people, 189
Neumann, Arthur, 125
New Kenya Group, 247
Ngong (farm), 62
Nightingale, Barbie (née Polhill), 121–3
Nightingale, Jim, 120–3, 238
Nightingale, Max, 120, 122
Nightingale, Nell (née Fey), 120, 122
Nile, river, 219–21
Njabini (house), 121
Njombo (headman), 32–4, 36, 182, 213, 224
Njombo, Major Esther Wambui, 224–5
Njoro, 27–9, 32, 42, 73, 85, 93, 115, 123, 161, 216, 237–8
Noor Mohamed, 25
Northern Frontier District, 145, 148, 152, 154, 164–6, 177–8
Northey, Sir Edward, 83
Nyerere, Julius, 179
Nyeri, 130, 182, 185–6
Nzoia river, 25

Obote, Milton, 71
Oldham, J. H., 139
Olivier, Piet, 26
Olpejeta (ranch), 241–2
Oserian (house), 108
O'Shea, Tommy, 68, 230
Outspan hotel, Nyeri, 130

Padmore, George, 196
Paice, Arnold, 126
Pelham-Burn, Reggie, 41
Perceval, Philip, 158, 213
Petley, Percy, 208, 210
Petrie, Tom and Kate, 41
Pinguan, Il (ranch), 140
Polhill, Stanley, 121–3
Pope, Alexander, 237
Popp, Dr, 63
Powys, Alyse (née Gregory), 98
Powys, Rev. Charles and Mary, 96–7
Powys, Charles (William's son), 140
Powys, Elizabeth (née Cross; later Douglas), 134–8, 140
Powys, Gertrude, 97, 139
Powys, John Cowper, 97
Powys, Llewelyn, 96–102; Black Laughter, 100
Powys, Marian, 97
Powys, Theodore, 97
Powys, Theodore (Dicky; son of above): murder, 140–3, 145, 207
Powys, William: settles, 96–7, 102; farming, 133–4, 138–9; marriage, 134, 137–8; painting, 139–40

Rainey, Paul, 78
Ramsay-Hill, Major Cyril, 108
Randall family, 126
Reece, Sir Gerald, 153–4, 164, 177, 236
Rensburg, Jansen van, 23
Rhodes House Library, Oxford, 53
Rhodes, Cecil, 139
Ricciardi, Mirella, 106
Richards, Charles Granston, 89
Riddell, Jack, 43–4
Ridley, Mervyn, Sybil and Susan, 83–4
Rift Valley College of Science and Technology, 241
Rimmington, Captain, 152
Risley family, 136
Robert (Kikuyu interpreter), 185, 189, 191
Rocco family, 106
Rochefoucauld, Viscomte de la, 61
Roux-Berger (surgeon), 173–4
Rubia, Charles, 235
Rudolf, Lake, 140

Salim, Liwali Sir Ali bin, 9
Samburu people: spear-blooding, 141–3, 145–6, 159–60, 207; and Sharpe's safari, 155, 157, 159
Sanderson, Ted and Helen, 58
Sandford, Sir George, 53
Sasumua (farm), 122–3, 238
Schindler, Fritz, 78
Schumacher, Raoul, 240
Scott, Lord Francis and Lady Eileen, 66–8, 240
Scott, Pamela, 234, 240–1
Serbian campaign (1914–18), 172–3
Serengeti plain, 218
Sewell, Billy, 42–3
Sharpe, Major H. B. (Sharpie): gardening, 146–7, 151, 208; character, 148–9, 177; safari, 148, 151, 155–60; and Somalis, 150–1; and Dorobo, 155; and Samburu, 159–60; on Lamu island, 208; death, 209
Shaw, J. C., 25
Sheen, Trevor, 41–2
Shela, 206; battle of (1813), 204
Sherbrooke-Walker, Eric and Lady Bettie, 130–1
Silverbeck Hotel, Nanyuki, 127
Simpson, Mrs Wallis, 65
Sirikwa people, 23
Slade, Humphrey, 246
Smith, Ian, 248
Soddu, Dedjmatch of, 171
Soldier-Settlement scheme, 123, 133, 135
Somali people, 149–51, 163, 167–8, 177, 236
Soysambu (ranch), 73–4, 77, 93, 109
Spiers, Len and Kay, 44
Sportsman's Arms, Nanyuki, 128

Steenkamp, Martha, 26
Stigand, C. H., 204
Still, John, 1
Stirling, Colonel David, 138–9
Stumpf, Miss, 50
Swahili language, 34, 87, 89–90

Tanganyika: gold in, 17–18, 21; railway link, 29; early farming in, 29–30
Taru desert, 12
Tatton-Brown, Robert, 165–6
Taylor, Charles, Kit and Kathini, 57
Teleki, Count von, 140
Thika, 29, 57, 126, 193
Thiong'o, Ngugi wa, 90
Times, The (newspaper), 17
Tinné, Alexandrine, 222
Torr's hotel, Nairobi, 16, 94, 228
Trans Nzoia district, 24–5, 85
Treetops, 130–1
Trotter, G., 65
Tumutumu Mission, 185–6
Turnbull, Beatrice, Lady, 180
Turnbull, Sir Richard, 149, 151, 154, 177–81, 236
Turner, George, 88

Uasin Gishu plateau, 22–3, 85
Uganda, 71, 86
Ukambani, 15, 214
United Nations Environmental Programme, 226–7

van der Post, Sir Laurens, 139
Vincenzini, Commendatore Inginero Dario, 131
Voi, 11

Wajir, 162–4, 167
Wakamba (Kamba) people, 211, 213, 215
Wamba, 154–6
Wanjohi Valley (Happy Valley), 38–9, 49, 56
Wanjui (wife of Njombo), 33–4
Ward, Freddie, 43
Whitehouse, L. E., 199–201
Whitman, Walt, 12
Whitton, Charles (Coconut Charlie), 207–8, 210
Wickham, Denis, 164
Wilson, Captain Sir Frank O'Brien, 211–13, 215
Wood, Michael, 139
Wright, Sandy, 41, 235

Yala river, 21
Yusuf (Dom Geronimo Chingulia), 8–9

Zanzibar, 7, 9
Zaphiro, Philip, 150, 167
Zimba (cannibals), 205–6